Visual Impairments and Learning

Visual Impairments and Learning

FOURTH EDITION

Natalie C. Barraga
Jane N. Erin

8700 Shoal Creek Boulevard
Austin, Texas 78757-6897
800/897-3202 Fax 800/397-7633
www.proedinc.com

8700 Shoal Creek Boulevard
Austin, Texas 78757-6897
800/897-3202 Fax 800/397-7633
www.proedinc.com

Library of Congress Cataloging-in-Publication Data

Barraga, Natalie.
Visual impairments and learning / Natalie C. Barraga, Jane N. Erin.—4th ed.
p. cm.
Rev. ed. of: Visual handicaps and learning. 3rd ed. 1992.
Includes bibliographical references and index.
ISBN 0-89079-868-0 (alk. paper)
1. Visually handicapped children—Education. I. Erin, Jane N. II. Title: Visual handicaps and learning. III. Title.
HV1626.B37 2001
362.4'1—dc21
00-045802
CIP

This book is designed in Goudy.

Printed in the United States of America

1 2 3 4 5 6 7 8 9 10 05 04 03 02 01

Contents

Foreword

During the time I have known Dr. Natalie Barraga, a generation of children with visual disabilities has been born, educated, and reached adulthood. Dr. Erin and I have known each other for nearly that long; children born in 1984 when we met are fully entrenched in secondary school programs, the time when transition planning is an essential part of their education. Just as our friendships and professional relationships have been witness to positive changes in educational services for children and youth with visual disabilities, we have been witness also to the continuing need for information to be available to new and practicing teachers, parents, and youngsters with visual impairments. We have seen challenges and successes both in the lives of children we have known and in the delivery of educational services to them.

Prior editions of *Visual Handicaps and Learning* were available in 1976, 1983, and 1992. These books reached people who needed the scope of their content, from how a person who is blind learns about his or her environment through nonvisual senses to how a child with low vision learns strategies to access his or her visual environment. These are the basics, the information that has been passed on through the generations. New information comes as we learn to refine this knowledge, as assessment instruments are developed and updated, as new understandings come from studies of how children incorporate new tools and technology into changing education programs, and how we learn of the emotional and social experiences of children who continue to benefit from adult and peer support and encouragement.

With this fourth edition, the authors not only include the basic information, but they also have added new understandings of how children with visual and additional disabilities learn, new ways of looking at curricula for children with visual disabilities, and new legislative requirements in such areas as literacy instruction and orientation and mobility. They discuss the changing roles of special schools for children with visual impairments, and they bring the reader up to date on such national efforts as the Expanded Core Curriculum for Students with Visual Impairments, interest in career education and employment, and current research on topics ranging from education placement decisions to new optical devices. The past 8 years have seen many changes, and the authors bring the readers into the new millennium by highlighting those changes.

Drs. Barraga and Erin also have chosen to give readers new insights into the lives of the children who were introduced in previous editions and who are reintroduced in the first chapter and revisited throughout the text. The fictional case studies of Carlos, Lucy, Sharon, Michael, and Ching Lan are the foundation of the text. In this edition, their lives continue to link the reader to the content. When Lucy is becoming an active member of her school community, when Sharon is benefiting from a day program, and when Michael is receiving help from additional specialists, we are reminded of the varying needs of children who share the experience of visual disability. When one learns of Carlos's progress and the services he receives, or how Ching Lan and her family and teachers are addressing changing visual needs, one is reminded of why every parent and professional is compelled to seek out all the knowledge and skills needed for these children to have every opportunity to grow and develop. Changes in educational procedures and offerings have been added to the richly developed children's stories. Once again, I found myself looking for these children throughout the book.

This book is truly a blend of a classic text and a new and exciting addition to professional literature. This contribution of Drs. Barraga and Erin will surely prepare a new generation of teachers, parents, and children for a journey that will lead to quality education services and equal opportunities.

Anne L. Corn
Vanderbilt University

Preface

Historical documents and literature throughout the ages have shown that philosophers and others have expressed a fascination about impairments in sensory organs, and have speculated endlessly about the phenomenon of blindness and its impact on learning and functioning. Denis Diderot (1916) is one philosopher whose theories have been translated and published. He spent much time with blind men and studied their learning techniques extensively, especially their perceptions and interpretations of information acquired solely through the tactile sense. Others in the 1500s thought the eyes were mystical organs related to the soul. Some people supported legal sanctions for the destruction of those without sight, while others advocated veneration and worship of blind people. A few people actually suggested isolated care as a benevolent societal attitude.

Not until the seventeenth century was consideration given to the idea of educating people with severe visual impairments. Even then, the major concern for hundreds of years was to train these people for service to society in asylums and residential schools or workshops. In 1949, the ideas that some sight might be present in blind people and that vision could be a learned process were introduced; these ideas were not confirmed by experiments until the middle 1900s when teaching students to use impaired vision efficiently was incorporated into educational methodology. Concentration on public education during the twentieth century has helped to change some societal attitudes around the world. Nevertheless, superstitions and emotionally laden thoughts regarding visual impairment or blindness still can be found in many parts of the world, even in the more advanced countries.

The passage of Public Law 94-142, The Education for All Handicapped Children Act, in the United States (retitled Individuals with Disabilities Education Act [IDEA] in 1990) has facilitated progress in public attitudes beyond expectations. IDEA was reauthorized with amendments for additions and clarifications of the act in 1997. Three very important changes improve the regulations regarding students with visual impairments. First, orientation and mobility services are now considered related services and may be provided during the school day. Second, assessment for and consideration of braille as a reading medium for students with visual impairments is required. Third, grants are provided to states for early intervention services for children 3 to 5 years of age, and as early as 2 years of age, when there are no state laws for provision of preschool services. Unfortunately, all preschool services are not mandated by federal law; discretion is left to the states in this matter.

The trend toward national legislation relating to special education has spread throughout the world, especially in developed countries. The influence of international organizations working with governments and providing educational seminars may have stimulated this progress.

Medical technology has saved many lives, but in the case of premature infants, the vulnerability of damage to body parts, including the sensory organs and particularly the brain, has increased. Premature birth often results in children having severe multiple disasbilities, including visual impairments, whose futures may not be optimistic. The advent of infant and early childhood programs makes intervention at a much earlier age possible; thus, children and parents receive assistance that may minimize the severity of some developmental delays.

To understand the areas of development most vulnerable to visual impairment, one must think objectively about the role of vision in incidental learning and plan interventions appropriate to the nature and degree of limitations. Preventing lags in any area of development is possible when substitutions and adaptations are made to foster learning and development to the child's maximum capacity. The organs that are intact and functioning are far more important than the impairments to other organs. To redirect thinking toward this goal, attention should be shifted from the causes or medical diagnoses of visual impairments and other conditions that stress visual damage and incapacity, to healthy organs and the potential for development and learning through alternative senses and processes.

The discussions in this text are addressed to students studying education and teachers, generic special education teachers, clinical and educational vision specialists, parents, and support personnel, such as orientation and mobility specialists, psychologists, occupational and physical therapists, and social workers. One major objective of this book is to present a new way of thinking about individuals with visual impairments that allows them to be viewed as participating members of a seeing world despite their reduction in visual functioning.

Developmental and learning processes are presented from a descriptive and functional frame of reference rather than as generalized characteristics, factual data, or statistical information that relies heavily on measurement criteria. Some ideas discussed in the text are based on the personal experiences of the authors; others have emerged through study, observation, and research. As teacher educators (the first author is also the mother of a person who had low vision but is now totally blind), we have tried to translate theory into practice. Our philosophy includes a firm belief that measurements, labels, materials, equipment, and legislation are less important than the personal factors in human beings—both teachers and students—as they relate to or influence development and learning. Regardless of impairments or labels, educators' major concern must be to develop to the fullest each student's potential for learning.

The vignettes presented in Chapter 1 are purely fictional and do not describe any real people known to the authors through personal experience or from reading actual case histories. The children depicted represent the variability in severity of visual impairments and the range and diversity of the influence that these conditions have on development and learning. Children similar to those portrayed are likely to be found in almost any community or school setting in any part of the world. Frequent reference to the children described in the vignettes is for the sole purpose of illustrating ideas and should not be associated with any real person.

Chapter 2 examines some of the consistent terminology used in describing visual and other impairments, service providers, and placement options. The terms presented represent stability of present thought and rejection of obsolete words reflective of stereotypic notions. Because environmentally influenced development and learning in all children begins at birth, Chapters 3 and 4 identify the concerns of the earliest years of life and present both a theoretical basis and empirical evidence for evaluating developmental patterns reflected in learning behavior. Chapter 5 addresses an ever-increasing percentage of the population of visually impaired children—those with multiple disabilities. The interaction of a visual impairment with other medical and developmental problems is sometimes greater than the sum of the discrete conditions; there are likely to be interruptions in emotional and physical development, as well as a marked limitation in the potential for mental development.

Chapter 6 focuses on the sensory aspects of learning and the sequences and processes through which children develop the highest level of efficiency possible. Chapter 7 examines the range of present educational settings and the variety of services provided in each. The issue of assessment and other evaluative approaches to intellectual and personal functioning is explored in Chapter 8.

Chapter 9 provides a comprehensive discussion of the core curriculum with appropriate adaptations. Chapter 10 identifies the specialized educational materials appropriate for students with visual impairments. The culmination of school learning is applied to achieving the goals of independent living and vocational success as described in Chapter 11, and a look to the future is offered in Chapter 12. Some of the major issues and challenges facing the field conclude the discussion.

Because these ideas have been fostered by many people and have evolved out of a wide variety of literary sources, documentation of references is more often general than specific. When appropriate, the reader is directed to specific literature for in-depth study. It is notable that many of the references on specific topics are from many years ago; the paucity of literature in this field during some periods of time may leave gaps in certain areas. Even so, this does not negate the relevance and quality of the research and literature of previous years, on which much of the basic knowledge in the field is dependent. Undoubtedly, the field of visual impairment is in need of more personnel who are willing and able to use the tools of the new century in exploring the impact of blindness and low vision on learning.

The authors assume full responsibility for inaccuracies, provocative controversies, and limitations in discussions. Grateful appreciation is expressed to all the children, teachers, students, and colleagues who have had a part in generating and shaping these thoughts through the years. We are deeply indebted to Dr. Anne Corn, coordinator of the program to prepare teachers of the visually impaired at Peabody College of Vanderbilt University. She has taken time to read the entire manuscript and offer helpful suggestions, as well as to write the foreword.

Challenges for Students with Visual Impairments

Most of the things we learn when we are children come to us through vision. Life is full of incidental visual learning experiences. Billboards and street signs, adults working or going to work, photographs, paintings, television shows, and the faces of friends are so common that children learn to take them for granted by the time they are aware of the world around them.

The idea that a child may not have access to all this visual information may seem unjust or tragic. Those people who have never met a child with a visual disability may imagine the child in one dimension, as a person who is responding only to a loss and not as someone who is learning about a world full of sounds, tastes, textures, or visual forms that are perceived through different means. While reading this book, you will learn about a world you may not have experienced, but it is one that excites the child with visual impairments just as keenly as a world full of visual detail excites a child with sight. As you read this book, keep in mind that children with visual impairments have only their visual characteristics in common. They have individual interests, motivations, and experiences. They are more like their brothers and sisters, and as much like their playmates next door, as they are like any other child who has a visual impairment.

The similarities among children with visual impairments are few, and the differences are many. Some are totally blind from birth or become blind shortly thereafter. Many have serious structural or pathological conditions of the eye or visual system at birth but are still able to learn to function visually throughout their lives. A few have medical conditions that become progressively serious until total blindness occurs at some time during their school years. In other cases, an accident may be responsible for sudden blindness. Still other children have serious visual and other impairments at birth because of unknown factors, such as possible intrauterine viruses, interruptions in embryonic development, underdevelopment of visual and related systems because of premature birth or the ingestion of drugs by the mother during pregnancy, or all of these factors. To emphasize the differences among children identified as visually impaired, the following vignettes depict several typical children who have visual and other impairments.

CARLOS

As the counselor for children with visual impairments and the young college student who was accompanying him approached the home, they could hear a little boy say, "Car stop. Somebody coming." His mother responded with, "Thank you. I'll be there." The student looked at the counselor with a puzzled expression. She had understood that they were going to see a child who was totally blind and who would soon have his third birthday. She wondered how he knew they were coming to his house.

They rang the doorbell, and when the mother opened the door, the counselor spoke. Immediately Carlos squealed the counselor's name and rushed to grab him in a big hug before the mother could invite the visitors to enter. The student was introduced as the counselor's friend and, by the time they sat down, Carlos was asking the young girl one question after another, as if she were already his friend, too.

Events during the past few moments had shattered the student's preconceived notions of blindness. She became so enchanted with Carlos that all anxieties seemed to flow away as she sat quietly, watching and listening. She began to realize how much there was to learn by observing Carlos as he moved about, played with his toys, and interacted with the adults. He was totally blind, but this fact was forgotten as soon as the mother and the counselor began a conversation. They responded to Carlos's questions or addressed him occasionally, when he was not completely absorbed in his own play. At times, he would seek contact by approaching one of them or calling their names to determine whether they were still nearby.

In many ways, Carlos seemed much like any other child of almost 3 years, as he talked to himself, then to his toys, and at times to one of the adults. Other children might look for a smile or a wave of the hand for assurance or to maintain contact, but Carlos frequently asked a question or made a comment to reassure himself that an adult was present.

Although the student had not expected to see a child moving from place to place so freely, she noted that when Carlos moved, he often seemed to move toward a voice. Also, as he moved away from the voice, he was able to avoid chairs and other objects in the room as if he could see them. When he was near another person, Carlos would usually touch the person or the person's chair to maintain close contact as he talked or questioned. He sometimes asked for help in playing or in finding a particular toy. Frequently, Carlos's mother described verbally where he would find the toy or instructed him that he could look in a particular place in his room for what he wanted. Encouraged and reassured by his mother, Carlos searched with his hands until he found things and continued with his play, or went to another room and came back with the object he wanted. If he left the room, he put out his hands to verify the locations of doorways. He used his feet to find toys that he thought were located in his general vicinity.

The student was somewhat surprised to hear the mother ask Carlos to bring things to her, to take objects to the counselor, or to tell the visitor something about what he was doing. She even let him go outside by himself to ride his tricycle, after reminding him to ride only to the end of the sidewalk and then back to the front steps.

By the time she found herself outside with the counselor after cheerful goodbyes, the student's thoughts were going in all directions. She had so many questions: Are all 3-year-old children who are totally blind like Carlos? Do all parents relate to their blind children as Carlos's mother did? How did he know to avoid a chair or to stop before he bumped into the door? Did he listen for cues as to his location?

Continuing to reflect on the visit, she began to recall ways in which Carlos differed from sighted 3-year-old children whom she had known. As he played or moved around, he seemed to hold his head down rather than up unless reminded, and he made more than the usual amount of noise as he handled his toys and played with them, sometimes using them simply for the purpose of making a sound. Were all blind children so noisy in their play? She recalled also that if the conversation stopped and the room was very quiet, Carlos would usually be the first one to say something, to ask a question, or to find some way to interact with an adult. Did she imagine this or was it really so? Other things appeared to be unusual—Carlos frequently used his toys differently from the way most children would and not always for the purposes they were intended, and he seemed to change often from one toy to another and to misplace them, at which time he would return to the adults to be a part of the group. What were the reasons for these seemingly discrepant behaviors?

Looking back over the total experience, the student had a good feeling, although she still felt confused and was unable to resolve all her questions. Nevertheless, she recognized some of her misconceptions and expected she would be quite comfortable with other children with blindness that she might encounter.

Not all young children who are blind are like Carlos, nor are all parents like his mother in their attitudes and interactions with their children. Carlos's mother had the benefit of continuous support and assistance from specially trained educational personnel since shortly after Carlos's birth. This was possible because shortly before Carlos was born, services to children with visual impairments were extended to infants and young children and their parents through legislation in the state where they lived. Now, legislation in the United States titled the Handicapped Infants and Toddlers Act of 1986 (retitled in 1990 as Disabled Infants and Toddlers Act), P. L. 99-457, makes it possible for services to be provided to infants and young children in all states with assistance from grants provided by the federal government.

By the time Carlos and his mother arrived home from the hospital after his birth, a counselor and a specially trained teacher of children with visual impairments had contacted them. Despite this support, both Carlos's parents experienced mixed feelings of sorrow, insecurity, guilt, and even resentment that their baby was blind. The counselor tried to discuss with them that feelings of shock, denial, and resentment could be therapeutic and that they should not resist these feelings (Gardner, 1982). Dealing with and acknowledging these feelings could lead to a rapid, stable adjustment. Even then, Carlos's mother sometimes doubted her own ability to do all that was expected of her. As she began working with Carlos and trying to look carefully for his responses, she felt more comfortable and gradually gained confidence in her ability to interpret his movements and other behaviors. A child without vision, she realized, has more subtle and quite different communicative responses than those of a child with vision. She learned how to help Carlos use his other senses and began to think of him as a baby who was cuddly and interesting to play with. She spent much time teaching him to use his hands and his ears, and she noticed very early how quickly he learned to discriminate sounds. Every time she had a question, teachers helped find an answer, and she enjoyed her relationships with other parents of children who had visual impairments. All these resources, as well as his mother's attitude, may have made a real difference in Carlos's behavior at 3 years of age. She also learned that not all children with visual impairments are totally blind, as can be seen from the following description of Lucy, who was born with a severe visual impairment but showed evidence of developing some usable vision.

LUCY

At the age of 2 Lucy was still a puzzle to her parents; they had many conflicting thoughts about her development and behavior. At the most unexpected moments she appeared to reach out toward things as if she could see them, and at other times she seemed unable to see at all. Because of her prematurity and the many medical procedures necessary, she seemed to exhibit little visual behavior in the early weeks. The doctor had told her parents to observe her visual development carefully because some damage to the eyes might have occurred. The doctor also had said, "There is nothing medically that we can do now, and I don't know anything to tell you to do." Fortunately for Lucy, her parents wanted a baby very much, and although they were confused and upset, she was so lovable and responsive that they found it possible much of the time to think of her as they would have thought of any other baby.

Much to their surprise, a few weeks after they took her home from the hospital, they received a call from a teacher of children with visual impairments who offered to help them learn how to observe and work with Lucy. During the teacher's first visit, she told them to give Lucy lots of love and attention and to keep a record of anything she did that suggested she might be responding visually. When Lucy was a few weeks old, they noticed that she turned her head repeatedly to the light in the room or to the window when near it. Was it possible that she could see the light? When the teacher returned, she told them to dim the light in a room and hold a penlight at different distances and angles from her face to get Lucy to try to look for the light. As soon as she was attending to the light each time, they used mobiles and small multicolored objects with a light shining on them to which she also began to respond. Several months later, when Lucy was playing with her mother, she tried to reach out toward her mother's face; but she never followed her mother around the room with her eyes, and often her eyes seemed to move as if she had little control of them. At age

6 months, when Lucy could sit up alone, she would often reach toward the soap in the bath water or extend an arm in the direction of her feet when being dressed. Surely these actions were indications that she was visually aware of certain objects. At the age of 1 year, Lucy picked up objects or toys and moved them back and forth in front of her eyes, holding them very close to her face. However, if she dropped or lost something with which she was playing, she never seemed to be able to find it easily, and would either cry or feel around as if she could not see at all. Crawling, standing, and walking posed no unusual problems, although she was a bit hesitant to move very far and seldom directed her body purposefully, except within a very limited area.

Despite a few lingering doubts and many questions, Lucy's parents knew that she was beginning to learn to see quite a few things, but just how much was still not clear. They played games with her, to try to get her to focus on objects and to encourage her to find things. They showed her every possible object in the house and outside. Soon they developed the habit of calling her attention to interesting things by saying, "Look Lucy," and helping her direct her gaze toward the object. When she was only 18 months old, Lucy looked up at the moon one night and said, "Light." This was a remarkable behavior for a child who could hardly see the food on her plate and who always seemed to be reaching for things by grasping too far to the right or left, or not reaching far enough, and frequently knocking the object to the floor in her efforts.

When Lucy was 2 years old she was able to attend a morning class with other children 2 days a week. The teachers could evaluate the developmental progress of the children, as well as their visual and orientation behaviors. During the classes, parents could observe the children and teachers through a two-way mirror and listen to the interaction. Some mornings there were discussion groups for parents; other times, speakers or consultants with whom the parents could discuss problems or ask questions were present. At first, the school team planned the activities, but soon parents were taking the leadership in deciding what they needed and wanted during the 3-hour period, which became a real learning experience for them. As mentioned previously, such educational services had been available in their state for several years, but with the passage of federal legislation, children with impairments in all states in the United States could now receive educational services from birth.

At the age of 3, Lucy began to look voluntarily through magazines she found in the house, and she also showed much more interest in exploring. She began to attend a daily morning class for preschoolers with visual impairments. In a matter of a few months, she was so active and independent in her movements and exploration abilities that she was invited to spend a small part of each morning in the regular early childhood preschool class with children who did not have visual impairments. It was quite a challenge for her to keep up with children who could see much better and at greater distances. Lucy learned to listen to them and move to the sound of their voices. In classroom activities, she asked many questions, and the other children were eager to help her and to respond to her need to move closer to the teacher or to find toys on the shelves. She learned to make marks with crayons, although she used them a bit differently than the other children. Her pictures were not so much imitations of people or things as they were marks with many colors. She seemed to enjoy the experience of drawing and painting, just as the other children did.

On the playground, where all the preschool classes were together, Lucy could move from one piece of equipment to another and take turns with other children who were eager to give her assistance even when she did not really need it. The teachers encouraged them to let Lucy find her own way and to get in line by herself. There were some things she could not do as readily as the children who could see well. For example, she was inclined to approach the swing without listening or looking carefully to see if someone was swinging toward her, and she often tripped over things directly in front of her in her eagerness to keep up with the others. However, she could move several feet directly ahead to an object that was dominantly visible. She made great progress in the early childhood programs, and she became a curious, busy little girl who wanted to be a part of every activity at home and to help her mother and father with whatever they were doing. Their joy increased daily when they saw her doing so many things and gaining self-confidence. She even began to play outside with other children in the neighborhood and to move around the block with caution.

The teachers gradually increased her time in the preschool class with normally seeing children until she spent as much as 2 hours each day with them. Her time in the special class was spent in developing greater visual efficiency and in refining orientation and movement skills, as well as in making discriminations at greater and greater distances.

When it was time for her eyes to be checked, her parents took her to a low vision specialist to be sure she had the best possible evaluation. Her distance vision was a concern and they knew she would soon be in kindergarten where more close work would be required. They were quite relieved when the doctor showed great delight with Lucy's evident looking and seeing behavior. She told them Lucy could see at about 10 inches what a child with normal vision could see at 20 feet. That meant that she could function visually quite well at a very close range but would continue to have difficulty seeing at greater distances, especially in large spatial areas such as the playground. To assist her in distance viewing, she prescribed a monocular for distance viewing. Even that news was very encouraging. The doctor told them to continue what they were doing with her, always encouraging her to look closely and carefully. They could help her by moving her closer to objects or people, or by bringing them closer to her, when possible. When this was not possible, she could use the monocular to orient herself and locate playground equipment or buildings in the distance. The doctor also suggested that Lucy have a stand magnifier at home, such as the one they had in the classroom at school, to allow her to examine details of household objects and designs on her clothing and to begin to make pictures of objects and designs she had seen.

As the time for kindergarten approached, the teacher recommended that Lucy be enrolled in the class with normally seeing children. With only minor attention from the teacher, and occasional assistance from her vision-specialist teacher in learning new skills, such as using the monocular for seeing the chalkboard, she was soon participating in most activities. While the other children were working with letters and flash cards, Lucy's vision-specialist teacher sat with her and helped her to hold them close enough to see easily. It took her longer to do things that required vision, but she was persistent and her teachers were patient.

For the most part, Lucy usually used the regular materials, and if she had difficulty seeing them, she would take them to the stand magnifier to verify the details. She also learned to make her letters by placing her paper under the magnifier and copying those her vision-specialist teacher had provided as models. She could match pictures, letters, and numbers with little difficulty when she could bring them as close to her eyes as needed. Her progress was rapid, and she was able to keep pace with the other children with a minimum of special help.

As the time neared for Lucy to begin first grade, her parents still had many questions about how well she was able to see. Would she be able to see all her schoolwork and to learn to read visually? Would she learn to use braille? These were questions that indicated that a learning media assessment might be appropriate to determine whether print, braille, or both would be the most efficient approach at this time in her school career. Because of Lucy's love of learning, her vibrancy with other children, and her winning ways with the teachers, her parents would agree to whatever was best for her school progress. Lucy might read some print materials but also learn to read braille, enabling her to use all her senses and have more materials available to her. By learning braille, she could rest her eyes if they became tired, or she could use braille when the light was insufficient for her to see the print easily.

Many children with severe visual impairments are similar to Lucy. The prospects for such a child's future remain somewhat unclear; the child may behave sometimes as a seeing child and at other times as a child who cannot see at all. Parents, educators, and vision specialists can make few conclusive statements or predictions. One medium or the other, or a combination of both print and braille, might be useful for several years until the child has more close work to do, at which time the child might decide what is most effective for his or her progress.

Nevertheless, one possibility is evident—a child who demonstrates an ability to see may be able to learn more efficient visual functioning. Certainly, no child who can see to do the things that Lucy has been described as doing could be considered a blind child, even though this term would once have been used to describe such a child. As Lucy develops, there will continue to be many unanswered questions. For the moment, Lucy is a child who sees and is learning to explore her world visually and to find her place among her friends who have much better vision. With continued improvement and her evident speed in learning, Lucy might complete high school and go on to college. This is in contrast to another child in Lucy's neighborhood, Sharon, who will always need a specialized program to enhance her learning.

SHARON

When Sharon's mother entered Sharon's room to get her up each morning, she always went to the window and opened the curtains before going to Sharon's bedside. Just a few months earlier, Sharon had begun to notice the patch of light that widened when the curtains opened. Each morning, she turned her head toward the window, waved her arms with their tiny fists, and called out loud, excitable sounds. To her mother, those sounds meant, "Good morning, Mother. I love you! I can't wait to get up!"

At 4 years old, Sharon was beginning to do many new things. There was a time when Sharon's mother had not believed that the child could learn at all. Soon after Sharon's birth, one doctor had indicated alternative plans for Sharon's care when her parents had wondered how they would be able to care for her at home. She would require a great deal of special care, the doctor said, and she might never even recognize her family. During Sharon's delivery, her brain was deprived of oxygen for several minutes; this resulted in severe cerebral palsy, profound mental retardation, and a loss of vision, which the ophthalmologist called *cortical visual impairment*. Sharon had remained in the hospital for several months. Her parents decided to take her home even though she required almost constant care. She was often ill, and for the first 18 months, all her nutrition was provided through a tube that was placed into an opening in her stomach. Sharon's parents often wondered whether they had done the right thing by bringing her home to live, with two active older brothers who also needed their parents' attention.

But now, at 4 years of age, Sharon was an important member of the family; her mother could not imagine life without her. Almost weekly, Sharon learned or tried something new. She smiled when her brothers or parents spoke to her; she reached with her right hand for brightly colored toys like her clown doll; and she eagerly ate soft or chopped foods that were fed to her, often just what the rest of the family was eating. She was usually a healthy little girl, although her mother was careful not to expose her to others with colds or flu because Sharon's lack of muscle control made it difficult for her to cough or reposition herself for sinus drainage.

Perhaps the most exciting change over the last year had been the development of Sharon's vision. Sharon's doctor had said she had no vision as an infant, so her family had tried to communicate with her through sound and touch. However, when a teacher for infants with special needs began coming to the house when Sharon was less than 1 year old, the teacher pointed out that Sharon sometimes seemed to look at bright lights and shiny toys. Although Sharon's mother had noticed this before, it was so slight that she thought that it might be her imagination. A teacher of children with visual impairments came to the house with the infant teacher on several occasions. She did a functional vision assessment, which was helpful in suggesting to Sharon's mother ways to help Sharon understand that she could reach out for the forms and colors that she perceived in order to provide opportunities for her vision to develop. The family began to collect objects that Sharon might be able to see and placed them above and to the side of her bed to encourage her to look for them.

By Sharon's second year, when she began to attend a day program several mornings a week, her parents were sure that she could see much more than light and forms. She sometimes smiled when one of her brothers silently tiptoed toward her from the side, and she bounced and waved her arms when her mother removed her yellow bath wedge from the closet a few feet from Sharon's bed. Along with Sharon's teacher, her parents developed a list of daily routines in which they could include familiar, visible objects to help Sharon connect visual images to real events and people. Although the ophthalmologist could not be very clear about exactly how much Sharon was seeing, her family now felt sure that vision would be an important way for Sharon to learn and communicate.

As Sharon's mother turned her daughter on her side on the bed and prepared to change and dress her, she thought of how far Sharon had come over the last 4 years. Although her mother would never have wished to have a child with severe disabilities, Sharon had opened new worlds for her family. Her mother had formed important friendships with other parents of children with disabilities, and she had learned that her two older sons could capably take some responsibilities in helping to care for Sharon. Perhaps most important, raising Sharon had strengthened her parents' marriage because both parents learned that they could cope with the special challenges of parenting Sharon. There was no doubt that Sharon had enriched all their lives.

Sharon babbled loudly as her mother sat her against her own stomach and began to unfasten her daughter's pajama top. Her mother asked, "Hey, what's new, little girl? Going out to conquer the world today?" Sharon answered with a smile and a squeal of delight. To her mother, that was enough. Sharon's story contrasts with that of Michael, a boy with seemingly minor problems who can communicate with words.

MICHAEL

Sitting at the kitchen table, Michael's mother was reading his report card. She was relieved to note that, for the first time, he had no failing grades. He had received a C in reading, and she hoped that this was a sign that Michael was finally beginning to comprehend the puzzle of the printed word. Perhaps this term she would not have to leave work as often for school conferences. Her boss was becoming concerned about the work she had missed for meetings with Michael's teachers, but as a single mother, she believed that she played an important role in her child's education.

Thinking back, she could remember what an energetic, active boy Michael had been before he entered kindergarten. At that time, his parents thought the only difficulty that might affect his learning was his visual impairment. She and Michael's father had known that their son's vision was poor before he was 3 years old; the doctor had told them that the condition was called *progressive myopia,* that Michael might need to hold things close to his eyes, and that he might have problems in spotting objects in the distance or in seeing detail when watching movies. Following the diagnosis, Michael had been given glasses to be worn all day; although he was a rough-and-tumble child, he never broke or lost his glasses and always remembered to put them on first thing in the morning. As a preschooler, Michael played actively with other children and never seemed to miss much of what was going on in his neighborhood. Although he got into more than his share of fights with other children, his father dismissed these, saying that his son was just all boy and that Michael knew how to stick up for himself.

Two years earlier, when Michael entered kindergarten, many major life events seemed to happen at once. Shortly after Michael's baby sister was born, his parents divorced, and his mother went to work for an insurance firm. So much had to be done that at first Michael's mother did not pay much attention to the notes from his teacher. Her son was unable to listen and follow directions; his handwriting was slow, and he made many letters backward or upside down; he could not pay attention in class; he could not tell his name from the names of other children whose first initial was M. The teacher talked about keeping him in kindergarten for another year, but Michael's mother did not want to see her son left behind his classmates. She remembered how uncomfortable she was at having to meet with the teacher and the principal, but she did go to talk with them. When Michael's mother explained that things were very difficult at home and that Michael's vision might be making his work more difficult, the school agreed to pass him along to first grade and to try to get him some help from a special teacher of children with visual impairments.

First grade began with similar difficulties: Michael was in the slow reading group, although he loved number problems and would often choose games and books with mostly numbers to work in after school. The picture brightened a little when Ms. Jackson began to visit Michael each week. As an itinerant teacher of children with visual difficulties, Ms. Jackson worked with Michael to encourage him to use his vision efficiently. She taught him a special way of printing and asked the low vision specialist to prescribe a monocular, so Michael would be able to copy from the chalkboard without leaving his seat. However, even Ms. Jackson said that Michael's school problems did not seem to be caused by his visual condition, and she suggested that Michael have a more thorough learning assessment to determine whether or not he might also have a learning disability.

Michael's mother remembered how difficult it had been for her to agree to have the school psychologist evaluate Michael. She knew that Michael's vision was poor, and she expected schoolwork to take him a little longer. But what if there was another reason—something wrong with Michael's thinking or learning abilities? What if he was retarded? The idea was very frightening to her, and when Michael was evaluated as having a learning disability, she at first felt angry and annoyed. Her child was not slow; perhaps the diagnostician had not taken the time to make Michael comfortable enough to show the things he could do.

She even felt a little angry when she went to another conference to help arrange special education services for Michael. But she also was desperate; her active, playful child felt like a failure in school, and many mornings he would complain of a stomachache when it was time to leave for school. At the meeting, Michael's first-grade teacher suggested that he spend 2 hours in a resource room each day to work on language arts and that Ms. Jackson continue to work with him in using his vision effectively. Michael's mother agreed with some hesitation. In only a few months, however, Michael had begun to regain some of his interest in learning and the stomachaches had disappeared completely.

As she glanced at her son playing in the living room with a set of racing cars, she laughed a little at her own apprehensions. Michael was beginning to enjoy figuring out new words now. He was hunched over the racetrack, printing a sign that read "Races today!" He had to lean forward until his eyes were a few inches from his own printing, and he had an extra *o* in the word *today*, but he had printed the sign on his own initiative. Six months ago, he had tried to avoid reading and writing even when he was playing. Now he recognized the importance of printed words in daily activities; this morning he had even read her the name of the prize robot contained in the cereal box. As she got up to watch the beginning of the races, she was grateful that there were ways to adapt learning for children like Michael who might take a different route to success in learning. Michael's visual problems are very different from those of a young girl down the street who might become blind in a short time.

CHING LAN

Although Ching Lan had been wearing glasses since she was 4, and had received the services of a special teacher for children with visual impairments since second grade, her parents were not prepared when the doctor told them that Ching Lan, now 11, was losing her vision rapidly. He said that Ching Lan could be totally blind in as short a time as a few months and certainly would be blind in a few years. As they sat stunned by the news, they suddenly remembered what another doctor had told them when Ching Lan was a baby: "I'm not sure how much she sees or how long she will retain her sight. She will be fine for several years, but the time will come when she will start to lose her vision." That time had come!

They had hoped their doctor was wrong. After all, he was only human—there might be some kind of mistake. Ching Lan seemed to get along fine in school, and she seemed to enjoy playing outdoors with her friends just as much as she always had. They made an appointment with another doctor, who had been recommended by a mother they had met at a recent meeting of the National Association for Parents of Children with Visual Impairments (NAPVI). Perhaps a different doctor could give them better news. After the new doctor examined Ching Lan, his prognosis was the same: "I'm sorry, but her condition is degenerative, and we can't be sure how rapidly the loss of vision will progress." He offered to explain the condition to Ching Lan, but her parents said they would do it themselves.

As the days passed, however, they found themselves putting off talking with their daughter. What would it do to her if she knew? Would she become depressed and unable to function in school? Would her friends still play with her? Would she lose the ability to do things for herself, such as dressing or making her own sandwich for lunch? New worries came to them each day, but they were reluctant to share them with Ching Lan; she seemed so young to have to deal with such a problem. However, they did tell her teacher and asked him to talk with Ching Lan if she said anything to him about not seeing as well as she once did.

Several weeks later, Ching Lan came home from school one day with less enthusiasm than usual and acted a bit strangely. She went to her room, saying she was tired and would rest before dinner. At dinner, her parents were surprised when she said, "Did those doctors say anything about me losing my vision? I know I must be because everything gets harder to see each day, and I can hardly do my schoolwork."

Finally her father said falteringly, "The doctor did say that your eyes were not doing as well as they have been."

Ching Lan sat for a moment and said, "I knew it, but you didn't tell me because you didn't want to talk about it. Well, I've known it for a long time, and my teacher and I talked about it. He showed me a big television that I can use later that will make the printing in my books look very large. It even makes my fingernails look big!

"The kids all help me, too, and when I drop something that I can't find, they tell me where it is until I get close enough to see it. That doesn't bother me because I never could see some things if the sun was shining, or the light was too bright, or they were far away. Last week, John Martin hid my pencil, but I heard right where he put it down and I found it right away!"

Ching Lan's mother wanted to take her daughter in her arms and tell her how sorry she was that Ching Lan would not be able to see for much longer, but she could not bring herself to do it because she knew that Ching Lan would realize how sad she felt. When Ching Lan was very young, soon after the doctor told them of the vision problem, her mother remembered how much she had worried about what might have caused the problem; she tried to think about whether she had taken any medicine when she was pregnant, and she even asked her husband's sister if she knew of anyone in her family who had a problem with their eyes. However, after a while, she began to see how much Ching Lan could do, and she thought less often about why her daughter's vision was different. Maybe they would come to accept this change in the same way.

As Ching Lan continued to talk, her mother noticed how much wiser than her years she sounded: "Ever since I noticed that I couldn't see as well, I've been practicing. Sometimes I close my eyes and try walking around by myself, and you know what? Just by listening really well, I can tell a lot about what's going on and where the other kids are."

Ching Lan's father thought about how much his daughter enjoyed playing ball, and he recalled that lately she had been asking him more often to throw a grounder. It occurred to him now that she had been learning to use her hearing to locate the ball. He wondered whether they would be able to enjoy games of catch when she had no vision, and he thought sadly that they might not. However, he remembered all the other things that Ching Lan enjoyed outdoors. She had joined a girl's track team during the summer, and, in the future, she should be able to run with a guide or to follow a sound ahead of her. He wondered whether she could ever keep up with her schoolwork and whether she might need to attend a special school away from home, but Ching Lan seemed confident about the changes she would have to make.

"I think you should go and talk to my teacher," she said to her parents. "He says I may still read print for a long time. I can use a magnifier to make the letters bigger, and later I can learn to use that television—it's called a closed circuit television—to help me see more letters at a time. Besides, when I can't see well enough to read anymore, my teacher's going to let me start reading with my fingers, like Peter Stevens does. My teacher says that when I learn braille, I can read with my eyes until they get tired and then read braille to rest them. And you know what? When I close my eyes and pick things up, I can already tell what they are."

Her parents were relieved that Ching Lan understood so much more than they realized. They told Ching Lan that she had explained a great deal about her schoolwork that they had not understood. They reminded her that there would be times when she would need to ask other people to help her, and that she should be much more careful about crossing streets and doing many other things that she was accustomed to doing quite easily. Ching Lan mentioned the mobility instructor who came to the school to work with some of the other students. She told her parents that the instructor might teach her how to listen carefully for sounds around her and to use a cane so that she would be safer and would know when there was something ahead of her. "Maybe when I get older, I could even get a guide dog!" she suggested eagerly. Her mother smiled. "I'm just getting adjusted to the cat you brought home last year. Let's take a little time to think about a dog!"

Later that evening when they were alone, Ching Lan's parents were able to think rationally. They realized that Ching Lan had never been like other children with regard to her vision. She used the sight she had and apparently didn't worry about what she didn't have. Adjusting to a gradual loss in vision wasn't the same for her as it would have been for them. If she could take this in stride and modify her thinking in such a positive way, they would stop feeling sad for her. She was fortunate to have a quick mind and a keen sense of curiosity, which would help her continue to enjoy learning in new ways; they knew that not all children with visual impairments were able to learn as easily.

SUMMARY

These word pictures of five children who are visually disabled illustrate the range of feelings, learning, and functioning associated with different characteristics and conditions. Some children may be born totally blind and never feel the need for vision

(Carlos); others may have very little vision, which they must learn to use (Lucy); quite a few have severe impairments in addition to visual impairment (Sharon); some have mild neurological problems in addition to the visual impairment, which make learning inconsistent and unpredictable (Michael); and a few may have adequate but impaired vision and suddenly begin to lose it (Ching Lan).

Medical people are often matter of fact about the condition of the eyes and their functioning, and are either unable or uninclined to make helpful suggestions to parents as to how they can help their children. Unfortunately, some medical personnel are unaware of the educational and other types of intervention available to help parents and their children with visual impairments. Except for their visual impairments, these children may have few other qualities in common with each other in relation to their social, emotional, mental, or personal development. Each child's individual potential for learning to function optimally within the family, school, or the broader social environment may be fostered or inhibited by the attitudes of the people and the factors within those settings.

Carlos's behavior, for example, was similar in many ways to that of any totally blind 3-year-old who had learned to function with available resources and was oblivious to what was not available. Carlos had learned to use his other senses in his own ways. Carlos's mother adjusted her interactions to his patterns of learning. She obviously included him in her activities in the home and patiently explained things to him. It was evident also that she managed him and corrected him as she would any child. When he wanted to help, she let him; therefore, he learned to recognize household objects and the sounds and feelings associated with them. Although her expectations of him were never beyond what he was capable of doing, he had been included in her everyday life.

However, their life had not always been smooth and optimistic. At first, Carlos had cried frequently and had been very active. His parents soon understood his need for more attention and tried to include him in their activities. Because of their encouragement and attention, he was able to organize his world as he experienced and understood it, and he was able to achieve a feeling of comfort within it. As Carlos gained greater control over his actions and some knowledge about what he wanted to do, he was able to find his own ways to solve problems. Carlos could not miss what he never had (vision), but he did require frequent interpretation through verbal explanation to help sort out his experiences; he used this information to expand his repertoire of behavioral responses and to structure his knowledge about the world.

During his early development, Carlos was dependent on others for reinforcement to help him gain confidence in himself, but by the time he entered school, he had acquired enough knowledge of his environment to be able to function comfortably with considerable independence. The attitudes he developed about himself and his relationships with others were determined largely by the attitudes of his parents toward him and their acceptance of him as he was. At first they were anguished, insecure, and sometimes sad—normal feelings under the circumstances. However, determination, love for their son, and confidence in their ability to meet life's problems enabled them to learn the meaning of accepting realities that they could not change. They read everything available about children who are blind and adjusted their lives and interactions with Carlos as his needs seemed to indicate. There would always need to be special arrangements for him to learn some things, and throughout his life he would require time and greater effort to learn certain functional skills.

Carlos's parents were very grateful that such excellent help and services were available to parents of children with visual impairments. Without the support and suggestions of the counselors and teachers, Carlos might have been delayed in his development and learning simply because his parents did not know how to help him learn.

In contrast, Lucy was thought of as a seeing child because her parents hoped and looked for evidence of her ability to see. There were some commonalities between Carlos and Lucy in that both were functioning in relation to the resources they had, never having known the sight they should or could have had. Lucy's parents learned to make minor adjustments to help her clarify the distortions and confusions that arose constantly. The many contradictions in her vision presented conflicting evidence about the nature of her vision, but such inconsistencies exist in many children with low vision. Few definitive predictions can be made about these children's potential for learning and development, and none can be made about how efficiently they will be able to use vision in the future.

People around Lucy came to be observant and perceptive of her efforts to use her vision and continually encouraged her to use the vision she had. For Lucy this stimulated an interest in searching for clarification of a distorted and sometimes bewildering world, a world in which she needed to learn to feel comfortable and secure. Her behavior indicated that she was a seeing child and could continue to develop greater visual efficiency as modifications were made for her, and she, in turn, made the adjustments compatible with her ability. She learned also that in some situations she could not rely solely on her vision and needed to ask for assistance or acknowledge her visual limitations to others. She even came to understand that as she progressed in school and the work became more visually demanding, she might learn braille to supplement her visual reading when she became too tired.

Although Sharon's development and learning had been and will continue to be slow, she is beginning to show evidence of responding to her environment and to people with whom she is familiar. It is virtually impossible to predict very much about Sharon's future, but she will require a great deal of assistance with personal care throughout her life. Her communications and interactions with others may improve as she grows older, but total independence is probably not something ever to be anticipated.

In children who have less noticeable or less serious visual impairments, such as Michael, parents and others tend to think that everything will remain stable after the initial diagnosis of progressive myopia and the prescription of glasses, forgetting that progressive means "continuing to progress." The possibility of other problems for Michael was not even considered. Although he was not as focused or as able to concentrate, he was just as active but not as motor advanced as other preschool children with whom he played. The minor differences were attributed to his vision. Even when he began kindergarten and the teacher's notes should have sent up red flags, his mother was coping with so many other problems that she found it emotionally difficult to attend to the teacher's concerns. When the vision specialist requested a thorough evaluation, his mother had to begin to face reality, despite the pain she felt for herself and for Michael. She thought back to the things she had noticed but failed to acknowledge about Michael, finding it easier to pretend that everything would be all right. Michael's mother had to come to terms with her negative attitudes about the thought of her son needing special education, instead of thinking that it was a reflection on her parenting skills. When she was able to reason with herself and to accept the concern and help of the teachers and the psychologist, Michael improved in school, and Michael's mother developed a very positive way of thinking about special services for children who need them.

Like Michael, many children who have learning difficulties do not receive help until they begin to fail in school or have such obvious difficulties that the problems can no longer be set aside. Subtle differences in attention, lack of tolerance for certain kinds of games, and a slight lack of coordination in motor activities are of concern in preschool children, and should be described in detail to medical or educational personnel as soon as they are noticed. Children often know that they cannot do the things their playmates can do, and they find their own ways of coping with their frustrations, such as Michael's repeated fights. Many marked and obvious impairments are reported at once, but the less noticeable differences may do great damage to the child's self-esteem before help is provided.

The flexibility and tremendous capacity for adjustment inherent in all children cannot be overemphasized. Ching Lan clearly illustrates these abilities to adjust. In her case, the challenge was primarily for her parents and teachers to reinforce her positive attitudes and motivation, being careful not to interfere in her adjusting to her gradual loss of vision by stressing their concerns or by imposing their adult fears on her. The gradual transition from performing as a seeing child to functioning as a child who is blind meant that she would have more time to adjust to her visual loss and could use her diminishing visual capabilities for support as she began to develop new approaches to learning. Her ability to use remembered visual imagery to help her associate and integrate new learning patterns and skills, in addition to having been around other children who were totally blind and whom she accepted as her friends, made it easier for her to continue to consider herself as a competent person who would be able to find ways to cope satisfactorily.

Throughout the text, specific factors from each of these children's cases will be recalled and related to appropriate discussions. At times, the child (in referring to his or her impairment) may be identified by name. More frequently, the readers will be free to make their own associations and inferences.

Consistency in Words, Clarity in Concepts

Words are not reality, nor can they describe reality; however, words can change our understanding of reality. Words used as labels or as terms to describe others often assign people to groups to which they may or may not belong, thereby ignoring other individual characteristics that may differentiate each individual from other members of the group. Labels or descriptive words used in referring to a child can sometimes imply that there is something undesirable about the child, creating a difference greater than what actually exists in reality. The first attempts to differentiate between the terms *impairment*, *disability*, and *handicap* were made by people in rehabilitation (Hamilton, 1950; Myerson, 1963; Sussman, 1969; Wright, 1960). These terms have been adopted and refined by people in both rehabilitation and education (Scholl, 1986; Sigelman, Vengroff, & Spanhel, 1984) and may now be considered to mean the following:

- An *impairment* can be defined as an identifiable defect in the basic structure or function of an organ or a body system as diagnosable by a medical doctor or other clinician. The defect may or may not interfere with the individual's learning or functional ability.

- *Disability* is the term used in the Americans with Disabilities Act of 1990, and for this reason it has become the preferred term in legal documents and in disability-related literature. It means the extent to which the impairment interferes with or limits the person's functions and activities. An impairment may contribute to a disability in one or more of five areas: health, social–attitudinal, mobility, cognitive–intellectual, and communication (Sigelman et al., 1984). Often the disabling effects of an impairment can be minimized or completely erased through medical or environmental intervention.

- A *handicap* results when the "individual is placed at an actual or perceived disadvantage" (Sigelman et al., 1984, p. 3) in functioning because of the impairment. A disability does not have to become a handicap unless individuals accept the limitations imposed by others, or the individuals impose limitations upon themselves.

HISTORICAL TERMINOLOGY

Since as far back as the early 1800s, there has been a lack of precision in the use of terms relating to those who have visual impairments or who are totally without sight. This inconsistency is apparent in the use of terms by doctors, optometrists, psychologists, rehabilitation therapists, and educators. Differences and divergent roles in each discipline have been influenced by regional attitudes, cultural practices, and clinical focuses (Corn & Koenig, 1996; Myerson, 1963). These myriad attitudes and roles reflect the confusion that has resulted from the lack of agreement in terminology, even among professionals who directly associate daily with people who are blind or who have impaired vision. Table 2.1 lists terms that have appeared in the literature in the last 150 years, all of which describe people with visual impairments. These terms are grouped according to their use in general and specific disciplines.

Education programs since the early part of the twentieth century have been designated by a number of imprecise and confusing terms. However, in recent years there has been a trend to be more thoughtful in the use of words that could give a negative connotation to programs and to the children with special visual needs for which they are designed. Both federal and local legislation have promoted the idea of consistency in the use of terminology that is factual but not prejudicial to the individuals being served. Some important questions that arise and need to be considered by educators include the following:

How much vision is sufficient vision to perform specific learning tasks?

What other factors may constitute limitations in visual or tactual learning?

What other critical variables influence individual visual behavior in children and youth?

Why do some children with severe visual impairments function at markedly higher levels than others whose impairments are much less severe?

What is the relation (if any) between impairment in component parts of the visual system and what the child can learn to see?

Is the limitation in visual functioning primarily because of an impairment in the visual system, is there a neurological–cognitive impairment, or is there impairment in both systems?

Giving consideration to and resolving as many of these questions as possible is imperative before placement decisions are made and before Individualized Education Programs are finalized.

TABLE 2.1
Terms Related to Visual Impairments

All disciplines	Rehabilitation
congenitally blind	legally blind
adventitiously blind	medically blind
visually handicapped	economically blind
residual vision	vocationally blind
Clinical	**Education**
partially blind	educationally blind
visually disabled	functionally blind
subnormal vision	visually impaired
remaining vision	low vision
visually defective	braille blind

INTERDISCIPLINARY TERMINOLOGY

At least three major disciplines—medicine, optometry, and education—are involved in identification, diagnosis, and service delivery to those with visual impairments. People who fill various roles and have specialty training can be defined as follows:

- A *general ophthalmologist* is a medical specialist who treats diseases and provides surgical care to the eyes. The primary emphasis is on diagnosis and medical or surgical treatment of the condition, when possible, and on measurement (with the use of cycloplegias) of the refractive and accommodative status of the eye to determine visual acuity at a distance of 20 feet or beyond. If specifically requested, some ophthalmologists also will provide near vision acuity, especially for children.

- *Pediatric ophthalmologists* are those who specialize in infants and young children and are most likely to work closely with parents and teachers in monitoring the functional visual progress in children.

- A *general optometrist* is a specialist in physiological optics and refraction and is licensed as a clinical practitioner to examine eyes, prescribe and provide lenses and optical devices, and sometimes perform visual therapy. The primary emphasis is on visual functioning at both near and far points, on describing the disorders of function, and prescribing lenses, devices, or both, to minimize the effects of the condition. Although in some areas, optometrists can legally use cycloplegias for measurement of refractive status, if medical or surgical intervention is indicated, referral is made to an ophthalmologist. Increasingly, ophthalmologists and optometrists are working cooperatively in low vision clinics to provide the most comprehensive service to both children and adults.

- *Clinical low vision specialists* are either ophthalmologists or optometrists who specialize in working with people with low vision and in prescribing care and devices to maximize the use of vision in all functional aspects (Pugh & Erin, 1999).

- An *optician* is a specialist who grinds and fits lenses, and designs and manufactures optical instruments according to the prescription of the ophthalmologist or the optometrist.

- *Low vision therapist* is a term used in some sections and is certified by the Association for Education and Rehabilitation of the Blind and Visually Impaired (AER) as well as some international organizations to denote a person who may be a professional in one or more of the following areas: education, orientation and mobility, rehabilitation, or health care. The low vision therapist is trained to provide instruction in the functional use of low vision, including the use of low vision devices. The low vision therapist works in interdisciplinary low vision service settings in schools, rehabilitation centers, nursing homes, and day care centers. They work very closely with other professionals such as eye specialists, teachers, mobility instructors, and counselors.

- A *teacher or consultant of students with visual impairments* is a certified teacher with knowledge and skills in the education of students with visual impairments. "They provide instruction to students who are blind or visually impaired in the areas of communication, literacy, daily living, and social emotional skills, academic support, and career education. In addition, they provide skills for students to access the common core or other curriculum provided to all student without visual disabilities" (Pugh & Erin, 1999, p. 82).

- *Orientation and mobility (O&M) specialists* are people who are university trained and certified in orientation and mobility. They provide instruction in tools and techniques employed by people with visual impairments to orient themselves and move independently in their environments. Some mobility specialists are certified also as low vision therapists and work specifically with low vision children in night travel and in the use of monoculars for distance viewing in identifying landmarks, recognizing objects at different distances, and in scanning the environment. They may teach the use of optical devices in transit and the visual skills needed for possibly seeking driver licensure if state requirements can be met.

The communication and cooperation of individuals in these disciplines is important if people with visual impairments are to receive optimal educational and clinical services. However, each of these disciplines has tended to use terminology characteristic of the specific discipline until recent years, when interdisciplinary cooperation and a greater concern for consistency has brought the various definitions into closer similarity. Classification of levels of vision has also lacked uniformity among the different professionals. In 1977, August Colenbrander chaired a worldwide committee that recommended a new classification system, which was adopted by the World Health Organization and is based on the extent to which a person is disabled visually. The original system was refined and published as *Guide for the Evaluation of Visual Impairment* (1999) (see Table 2.2).

TABLE 2.2
Classification System for People with Functional Vision

Classification	Level of Vision	Level of Disability
Normal	Normal vision	Normal reading speed Normal reading distance
	Near normal vision	Normal reading speed Reduced reading distance
	Moderate	Near normal reading speed with devices
Low vision	Severe	Performs visual tasks at a reduced level of speed, endurance, and precision, even with aids
	Profound	Has difficulty with gross visual tasks; cannot perform most detailed visual tasks, including reading
Blind	Near blind	Vision is unreliable; relies primarily on other senses; no visual reading
	Blind	Totally without sight; relies exclusively on other senses

Note. From *Guide for the Evaluation of Visual Impairment*, by A. Colenbrander, 1999, San Francisco: Pacific Vision Foundation. Copyright 1999 by A. Colenbrander. Adapted with permission.

This is an abbreviated adaptation of his entire system, which has been updated from his previous classification system (Colenbrander, 1977). His suggestions make it much easier for clinical (medical and optometric) and educational personnel to communicate because the focus is more on how the individual can perform visually; for those who desire more exact measurement criteria, these criteria are also included in the monograph. Professionals from all disciplines are thinking about and working toward lessening the impact of visual disability by improving the affected person's abilities and by reducing the environmental demands for performance of visual tasks.

TRENDS IN TERMINOLOGY

An analysis of the terminology of special education in general survey books published in the last several years revealed few inconsistencies. All the title chapters used the phrases *visual impairments* or *visual loss*, even those written by people outside the field. In some discussions, the term *visually impaired* was used as a generic descriptor of the population, and in most cases, *blind* and *low vision* were used as subtitles. In the revision of the Individual with Disabilities Education Act (IDEA), the only terms used are *visual impairment* and *blindness*. This trend in terminology seems to have reached a rather consistent level in recent publications, both in general special education and in the specific field of visual impairments, when referring to infants and toddlers and to school-age children.

For subgroups, the terms *blind* and *low vision* differentiate those people without sight from those who can use vision for a variety of functional purposes. Corn and Koenig (1996) defined *functional vision* as "vision that can be used to derive input for planning and performing a task" (p. 8). At present, there is no universal accepted definition of low vision, although several are offered in the next section.

Perhaps through the efforts of people with impairments and the professionals who work with them, the same type of positive change can occur in the terminology used by the media and general public that has already taken place in the educational literature. Teachers can have some influence in bringing about such a change.

ADDITIONAL TERMS AND DEFINITIONS

Some of the terms discussed previously, as well as others, are defined in different ways by specialists in various disciplines. The legal definition of blindness (20/200 or less in the better eye after correction, or a field of less than 20 degrees) is a purely clinical one based on arbitrary acuity measurements. It does not take into consideration that approximately 80% of people included in this definition have some, if not considerable, visual capacity, and only about 20% or less are totally blind. This definition is used primarily for purposes of eligibility for rehabilitative services for adults. It has no relevance to children and youth with congenital or acquired visual impairment, and is seldom if ever used as eligibility criteria for educational services. Any impairment that affects functional–learning capacity and selection of the most efficient medium or media are the primary determinants for the needs of school-age students.

The term *functionally blind* is used frequently in an educational sense to indicate students with or without usable vision who need to use tactile or auditory methods, or both, for primary learning activities. They may, however, be able to use light and object perception as cues to move in selected environments.

Low vision is an especially difficult term to define because none that have been suggested give a clear picture of all the individual variables that must be considered. Not one of the following examples has been accepted universally:

> Children with low vision are those who have limitations in distance vision but are able to see objects and materials within a few inches or at a maximum of a few feet away from the eyes. (Barraga, 1983, p. 23)

> A person with low vision . . . has difficulty accomplishing visual tasks, even with prescribed corrective lenses, but . . . can enhance his or her ability to accomplish these tasks with the use of compensatory visual strategies, optical and other devices, and environmental modifications. (Corn & Koenig, 1996, p. 4)

> Low vision is a vision loss that is severe enough to interfere with the ability to perform everyday tasks or activities and that cannot be corrected to normal by conventional eyeglasses or contact lenses. (Jose, 1992, p. 200)

Generally, most children with low vision can use their vision for many school learning activities, including visual reading, although some may need to use tactile materials, and possibly even braille, to supplement printed or other visual materials. For some purposes, and under varying conditions relative to light, contrast, and personal characteristics, such children will always need to be made aware of what they are able to see and given assistance and encouragement in looking at educational materials and other objects (as in the case of Lucy). Even if braille is decided upon as the primary reading medium, under no circumstances should children with low vision be referred to as blind or deprived of visual materials or instruction in the use of vision for whatever purposes in which they are interested and capable.

Visual acuity refers to a clinical measurement of the ability to discriminate clearly the fine details of objects or symbols at a specified distance. To date, no relationship between acuity measurements and functional use of vision has been established. People with very low clinical acuity measurements may function visually at a very high level, whereas some people with much higher levels of visual acuity may behave as if they had no vision.

Visual impairment denotes any optically or medically diagnosable condition of the eye(s), visual system, or brain that affects the structure or functioning of the tissues and results in less than normal vision. Impairments may be of a rather minor nature, may even be correctable, or may be quite severe and incorrectable with lenses or treatment. The impairment may be in the central part of the eye, such as the lens or the area around the macula, in which case the person could have very good peripheral vision but have trouble seeing fine detail. Conversely, the impairment might be in the outer retina in the periphery and cause what is known as tunnel vision; the person may have very clear central vision at a specific point of focus but be unable to see to either side. The impairment also might be in the optic disk or nerve, which would interfere with the transmission of the retinal stimulation to the brain. The problem can be in the brain either in the reception area or in the ability to interpret what is received in the occipital cortex. Other impairments may include differences in color, light tolerance or needs, levels of contrast sensitivity, or combinations of these impairments.

Visual efficiency is the most inclusive of all terms relating to vision and is contingent on many personal and environmental variables. Visual acuity at a distance and at near range, control of eye movements, accommodative and adaptive capabilities of the visual mechanism, speed and filtering abilities of the transmitting channels, and speed and quality of the processing ability of the brain are all related to visual efficiency. A. Corn (1989) presented a theoretical model to explain the development of efficient visual function. For educational purposes, visual efficiency is the most important consideration (Barraga, 1983) because it determines the degree to which the student can perform specific visual tasks with ease and comfort, as well as in the minimum amount of time. Visual efficiency is unique to each individual and cannot be measured or predicted clinically with any accuracy by medical, psychological, or educational personnel.

SUMMARY

To label as *blind* children who are able to see many things is to imply that they are not expected to see, and in a short time they will begin to function as if they were blind and perceive themselves as visually incapable. When a person ceases to look, the ability to see is lost. Such ambiguous terms as *partially seeing* or *partially blind* seem to suggest a relationship between the quantity of an attribute and the quality of functioning in the individual; this is a totally false inference, which is the reason these terms have become obsolete.

However, to disregard all descriptive words would be foolish and possibly detrimental to these children's safety and their special learning needs. The words used should relate to development and learning in children, as well as the potential for more efficient visual functioning in all individuals with low vision. Using the terms *blind* and *low vision* appropriately is a realistic cue to teachers, and to society in general, of what to expect from students. It is important for professionals to communicate the meanings of the terms used, especially when talking with families and other team members who may not be familiar with the terminology. Rosenblum and Erin (1998) found that negative terms can have a powerful influence on attitudes. *Visually impaired* and *low vision* were both rated as positive terms by professionals and special education students; both have educational significance and are used throughout this book.

For teachers to say what they mean and mean what they say, the following educational definition is offered:

> A child's visual impairment becomes a disability when it interferes with optimal learning and achievement, unless adaptations are made in the methods of presenting learning experiences, in the nature and quality of the materials and devices used, in the lighting and contrast in the learning environment, or in combinations thereof.

Early Encounters and Interactions

The knowledge explosion regarding development and learning in infancy and early childhood indicates that this crucial period may have a tremendous influence throughout people's lives. Certainly the interest in and study of infants and young children, especially those most vulnerable to developmental and learning problems, have emphasized the potential of early intervention as a preventive measure to lessen the impact of sensory, motor, endocrinological, or mental impairments.

Physical impairments, such as hearing or vision problems, structural or motor problems, or dysfunctional organs, may not interfere directly with the physical development of the body, but may influence developmental aspects by limiting the natural use of the body, which is essential for organization and function. Likewise, a negative impact on learning and functional behavior may not occur as a direct result of the physical impairment, but the quality and scope of learning may be limited by the reduction in environmental interactions of both a physical and a social nature. With some physical impairments, the actual structure of the body and its capacity to develop may be inhibited to some degree, if not totally. Sensory impairments place a direct limitation on the capacity to learn incidentally without intervention or assistance. Although there is validity in making some distinction between the terms *development* and *learning*, a strong relationship exists between them, and most agree that they are interdependent. The human growth cycle encompasses both physiological maturation and learned behavior, and the ideal for each child is that these two dimensions be in balanced concert as the child seeks to become emotionally secure and able to function socially, physically, and mentally. Without a stabilizing emotional environment, children may experience interruptions and gaps in both physical and mental development.

GENERAL CONCEPTS OF DEVELOPMENT AND LEARNING

The process of development and learning in all children begins at birth and is related to and, to some extent, dependent on the mutually satisfying interactions between infant and caregiver, infant and environment, and infant and other children in play (Baird, Mayfield, & Baker, 1997). The critical variables in interpersonal interactions and encounters as foundations for development and learning involve what happens to the child within the family. Affective development, as well as social and cognitive development, is contingent for the most part of the family's attitudes and personal involvement with the child, who is constantly striving to become a complete human being. On this topic, Barraga (1983) wrote the following:

> With his first breath at the moment of birth, an infant has the capacity to become a receiving, participating, interacting human being who enjoys a reciprocally satisfying relationship with his immediate environment, and eventually a fulfilling involvement with an ever expanding world. (p. 117)

Studies have shown that the duration and variety of vocal, tactile, and kinesthetic stimulation provided by caretakers are related to overall development and that the mother's level and quality of preverbal interaction with her baby relates to the child's later linguistic and cognitive competence (Dote-Kwan, Hughes, & Taylor, 1997).

Attachment or bonding to another human being has long been considered basic to future feelings about oneself and others. The mutuality of the interplay between an infant and caregiver establishes a bond of communication in which each initiates an action, waits for the response, and then either repeats the action or expands it to elicit a different response. Eventually a pattern emerges in a rhythm of interaction and alternation of initiators, and the maintenance of particular actions occurs for shorter or longer time periods (Sameroff, 1993). The bonding and attachment process can be observed during feeding (especially nursing), reciprocal gazing, gentle holding and mutual touching, and vocalizations. These interchanges provide evidence of spatial relationships between individuals, smooth or awkward body movements, strength of the initiator, and feelings related to the action (Tronick, Als, & Brazelton, 1980).

The early reflexive movements that appear to be generated from within the infant's body soon become integrated with responses generated by external stimulation from the caregiver. Some experts theorize that early movement in infants is motivated by a need to reduce tension. If this is true, and bonding and attachment are of critical concern, then the parent's primary role is to create a feeling of comfort and mutual communication by touching, patting, stroking, manipulating, and talking to the infant during interaction. A continuation of this cuddling provides a basis for establishing trust and security, and may supply the framework from which the infant organizes responses into a cognitive map of self in relation to someone else and of knowledge of a larger environment (Murphy, 1972). Cohen and Beckwith (1979) found evidence that a mutually reinforcing relationship between caregiver and infant can have an effect on the infant's performance at 9 months of age, and can be related significantly to performance on infant assessments at 2 years of age. Mutual activity between caregiver and infant stimulates curiosity and language acquisition and provides motivation to explore further. Increased exploration permits the infant to gain some control over body movements and to refine actions.

An infant's responses to nurturance and play have a strong influence on the quality and nature of the interaction. Because babies who are blind cannot maintain eye contact or see facial expressions or other positive indications of adult satisfactions, they are less likely to interact in ways that are motivating to parents. Passivity, or lack of expected responses, could lead parents to think their baby is not enjoying the cuddling and play. Parents must learn to look for other indicators of pleasure in infants who are blind and make a greater effort to engage their infants in social interactions other than those related to vision. There needs to be alternating vocalizing and listening time. Parents must respond vocally to infants' vocal utterances, but never interrupt them.

More touching and handling of the baby who is blind is necessary to help the infant feel the interaction rather than see it. Without eye contact, parents at first may feel estranged. It is important to learn to read these vocal and tactile responses, which may convey even stronger feelings of attachment than visual responses. If an infant who is blind fails to develop strong affectional ties and pleasure in human contact, emotional development may stall at a primitive level, creating a need to seek and exploit alternative sources of comfort to relieve separation anxiety.

For the baby who is visually impaired, body play or manipulation helps the infant learn new patterns of body movement and minimizes the need for sterotyped and rigid tension-reducing movements (e.g., aimless waving of arms, rocking the body back and forth, poking the fists into the eyes, or shaking the head), which become resistant to change after several months. According to Eichel (1979), such mannerisms are the result of the lack of appropriate stimulation. Children usually do not exhibit them when engaged in active play. Emotional security, meaningful activity, and lessened anxiety seem to eliminate the need for these movements and the frequency of their occurrence. The common labeling of such behaviors as *blindisms* is erroneous because the same actions may be observed in sighted babies who have been deprived of emotional needs and adequate nurturance caused by isolation from caring adults for long periods of time. It might be more meaningful to describe these behaviors as tension-reducing actions.

If babies begin to feel that they cannot influence their own world or have some control over what happens, they are likely to begin to retreat from the world and those in it. A certain cognitive satisfaction relates to the development of a strong self involved in making things happen and in mastering the environment, to say nothing of the mediating effect it may have on later cognitive development. Piaget (1966, 1973) suggested that feelings supply the energy necessary for action and for specifying goals for behavior; these "feeling oriented" actions may be related to the emergence of conscious thought much earlier than one would think. In time, the infant, the toddler, and eventually all young children learn that they can do many things. Joint attention between parents and infants, both physically and vocally, has been associated with a shared effect and provides a means of integrating cognitive development with the interpersonal skills of communication (Mundy, Kasan, & Sigman, 1992). These interactions provide the basis for a strong self-concept and a feeling of pride in each new learning experience.

EARLY DEVELOPMENT AND LEARNING IN THE CHILD WITH A VISUAL IMPAIRMENT

The emergence of a strong identity of self may take longer to develop, and may be achieved through different means, when a child has a visual impairment. Parents are naturally distressed when they learn their child is blind or has a serious visual impairment. Although most parents experience similar feelings, these parents often feel guilty about acknowledging their disappointment, even to themselves or each other. The anxiety and insecurity of not knowing how to accept this baby with an unexpected (and unasked for) difference may cause them to overemphasize the diagnosis of the impairment and forget, momentarily at least, that this is a real, live baby who needs them and their love in the same way that a baby with normal vision would. Not knowing exactly what to do and being afraid of doing something wrong, parents may have a tendency to leave the infant alone, providing only basic physical care while struggling with their own feelings. This abandonment of sorts defeats the infant's need to achieve the bond, or human attachment, that is so vital to development. The following sections discuss some factors that appear to be most crucial to the early development and learning of children with visual impairments.

Body Manipulation

For the infant who has a visual impairment, body play must replace eye contact to communicate parental concern and love—the facilitators of developing a self-concept. More than the usual amount of time should be spent cuddling, holding, touching, stroking, and handling the baby. At the same time, soothing, comforting sounds and words from the parents will help establish love bonds through a "tactile, auditory language" (Fraiberg, Smith, & Adelson, 1969) instead of the usual attachment stabilized through eye contact. Parents who resolve their ambivalent feelings early have more energy available to devote to establishing an infant–parent feedback system. Although a "self-righting" tendency in the developmental process appears to be evident, the negotiation proceedings between the infant who is visually impaired and the caregiver can be observed to be more explicit, repetitive, and amplified. A parent needs to be sensitive to infant reactions in order to be the follower as well as the leader in the dialogue. As suggested by Baird, Mayfield, and Baker (1997), parents may need to be taught how to interpret the infant's facial expressions, body movements, and verbal or nonverbal responses as either positive or negative, and how to react accordingly. It takes longer to reach a heightened stage of mutual exchange, and the end goal is achieved when the infant reaches out for the parent or object, or offers sounds

Human interactions provide the basis for the infant's future learning; therefore, a reciprocation of signals and responses between the baby and the parents is essential. If the child who is visually impaired does not experience this interaction, personal security in relating to others, and eventually to the outside world, is impaired.

Sound Stimulation

Parents of the infant who is visually impaired might have to find new ways of expressing their own feelings of pleasure when interacting with their baby. In a few short months, as parents satisfy their hunger for cuddling, holding, touching, and handling, the baby will begin to respond and show feelings of pleasure and comfort. In addition, the infant learns to make an association between the human voice and the tactual intimacy. Once this association is made, the human voice, heard from a distance and without physical touching, begins to unite the child with the world, forming a basis for experiencing feelings from voices and environmental sounds. Parents can continue to talk about every sound that is heard and every movement that is made, allowing sounds and actions to begin to have meanings to their baby, meanings that are acquired incidentally through vision by babies who can see.

Visual Development

If there is indication that an infant is responding to light, every effort to encourage the development of the use of available vision should be made. Use of moving lights, objects which reflect light, and brightly colored objects can be presented with bright light on the objects in a dimly lit room. Hanging objects, such as carefully chosen mobiles, directly above the baby and to either side of the crib may be helpful, as in Sharon's case. The more an infant looks, the more he or she is likely to foster development of increasing visual capacity, is a valid concept for parents and teachers to remember.

Language and Communication in Early Childhood

Development of appropriate language can depend on the child's ability to make connections with people, events, and relationships in the environment; therefore, the young child with a visual impairment might be at risk for delayed or different language development. A baby first understands the turn-taking aspects of communication when reciprocal communication with the parent is mastered. At the earliest stage, this depends on gaze and eye contact; each partner orients toward the other when conversing, and long before the infant understands oral speech sounds, he or she can participate in this communicative exchange.

For the child with a visual impairment, however, the absence or diminution of vision may interfere with this process. The child's attending signals, such as quieting vocalization or ceasing physical activity, may be misinterpreted by the parent, who then decreases or simplifies speech, hoping to receive an active signal from the child. In the absence of a responding eye gaze, the parent chooses language, which offers the best possibility of a response.

Many caregivers tend to use declarative sentences ("Eat your carrots.") or questions ("Are you eating your fruit?") when talking to young children with visual impairments. Adults also may label objects and repeat these labels in order to reassure themselves that the child understands what is being said (Kekelis & Andersen, 1984). This may be one reason why many young children with visual impairments use different language patterns when they begin to speak. Compared with children with normal vision, those with visual impairments may use commands and questions more often, and they may more often repeat words and phrases (echolalia) during speech. Also, they may be less spontaneous than sighted children in using referential words and gestures for objects out of reach (Urwin, 1983). A stimulating language environment (talk, listen, give choices) has a more positive impact on young children with visual impairments than does the socioeconomic level of the parents or the presence of materials or physical things (Dote-Kwan et al., 1997).

Parents and caregivers may be concerned about the distinctive features of the language of the child with a visual impairment, and they may attempt to correct the spoken language. However, this can result in the child's decreased willingness to use language freely to interact with others. The primary goal in language development for the young child is to increase the use of meaningful language; conversation that relates to events and people in the environment and that enables the child to interact successfully with others helps to develop stable relationships and fosters this goal.

With strong human attachments and having heard meaningful language, the child with a visual impairment is better equipped to cope with the world of mysterious objects that he or she encounters, often accidentally. Objects seem to come out of nowhere and disappear into nothingness once contact with them is interrupted (Fraiberg et al., 1969). Sustained by a feeling of security and encouraged by supportive others, children view the world as a friendly rather than a fearful place, and as toddlers they are ready to explore, to learn to control, and to act on the world beyond their own bodies. Feelings and desires in all children are related closely to movement and action, and because sound and tactile sensations do not have the same arousing and motivating effects as do visual sensations, without consistent interaction and stimulation, the child who does not see well may become passive. Inactivity, occasioned by no one to talk with and nothing meaningful to touch, creates the child's need to perform the undesirable repetitive and stereotypical movements referred to previously. Interestingly, none of these stereotypical behaviors is noticed in children in Africa who are blind; mothers of these children carry their infants on their backs all day, talk to them, and include them constantly as part of the complete world of family life. None of these stereotypical behaviors were observed in Carlos, who was apparently emotionally secure and trusted himself and others. Conversely, for Michael, who was quite insecure in his interactions with others, aggressive behavior was his typical response to peers.

Social–Emotional Need

Infants and toddlers with visual impairments may have feelings of rejection or of living in a world void of stimuli if left alone for prolonged periods with no tactual or auditory contacts. If they do not receive warm and accepting feelings from adults, most of the time they will resort to self-stimulation. The immobile baby who does not have a visual impairment can satisfy this need for sensory input by looking at things, learning to focus the eyes, and trying to reach out and touch objects; during these periods, the baby is learning eye–hand coordination. Not equipped with this ability, the child with a severe visual impairment relies on sustained sound contacts to keep in touch with the distant world. When vision diminishes later in early childhood, as in Ching Lan's case, transferring from the use of sight to reliance on other sensory stimuli requires time to adjust mentally to interpreting the meaning of sounds, odors, and tactile encounters. This learning process is not totally unlike that of the developmental pattern in young children.

During the first 18 months, toys should have a strong tactual appeal, with a variety of pleasant textures; rough surfaces are more desirable than smooth ones (Zimmerman, 1985). Later, when the baby is more active, toys capable of making sounds may be added to encourage the child to follow the sound with the hand, and later to move toward the sound. This ear–hand and ear–movement coordination becomes critical in later months, when sound localization and spatial orientation are important for purposeful movement. Carlos, at age 3, used sound and spatial cues very effectively as he located his toys and moved about the house and even outside. Remember, however, that he also frequently sought verbal or tactual reassurance, or both, to feel continued security and to maintain contact with others.

In Ching Lan's case, sounds quickly became auditory cues, and attention to sounds provided a frame of reference for interpretation of actions. Touch becomes the means of verification and clarification of more definitive information than sound can provide. Attention and practice hasten the learning process, as do personal security and emotional acceptance of the world perceived through different senses, which is so aptly demonstrated by Ching Lan.

Parents and siblings form the basic psychological (social–emotional) climate for the development of positive behaviors through emotional interactions. Close relationships with loving others enable a child to satisfy the need to be loved. The resulting inner satisfaction makes it possible to cope with personal feelings and to respond to feelings elicited by others (Lowenfeld, 1981). Carlos had strong social and emotional interactions in his first years, which prepared him to reach out and interact with other people, and to involve himself actively with his entire environment. No doubt, the speed with which Lucy was able to integrate herself with her sighted nursery and kindergarten friends could be attributed to the time and attention given to her by her parents in the first years of her life.

It would be misleading, however, to suggest that either Carlos's or Lucy's emotional development is complete or will ever be fully realized. Psychosocial development must be fostered and expanded throughout life to maintain one's mental health. Although stresses and frustrations are a natural part of life for everyone, for the child with a visual impairment, the alternatives available for coping with stresses and for reducing tension and anxiety might be restricted by environmental conditions and societal attitudes and expectations. Consequently, chances for developing and maintaining a flexible, adaptable self-concept are strengthened when the child's early years in the family and in school have provided stable patterns of interaction. The same is true for older children who lose their sight through accidents or progressive eye conditions, or who have learning problems in addition to visual impairments. Family and friends can impede or hasten personal adjustment and acceptance, a fact evident in Michael's behavior once he received the assistance he needed.

NEED FOR EARLY INTERVENTION

Support systems for parents and young children with visual impairments are still very limited in some areas, although federal legislation mentioned earlier is an attempt to address this need. A team approach involving a teacher, orientation and mobility specialist, physical therapist, occupational therapist, pediatrician, ophthalmologist, psychologist, social worker, or others seems to be the most desirable means of providing services to parents and young children (Moore, 1984). Moore suggested a home program for the first 2 or 3 years. Parents can be taught early stimulation techniques and strategies (such as was done for Carlos's mother), thus gaining confidence in their abilities as well as the ability to cope more easily with their own negative feelings. However, the effectiveness of such a plan is contingent on the home teachers. Many teacher education programs are beginning to recognize the need for courses that teach how to work with parents so that they understand the principles of the early intervention teacher. Teachers must think of themselves as guests in the home, and parents need to think of themselves as the primary learners. Teachers are the primary source of information for parents and can become synthesizers of information from clinical and social services professionals. As they work with parents in the home, teachers can demonstrate how to use everyday materials under natural conditions and emphasize the value of these materials over toys and unrealistic approaches.

The orientation and mobility specialist can assist the parents in learning how to encourage safe exploration and movement in the home, allowing the child to begin early development of echolocation as a precursor to later independent travel. The team members might rotate visits as long as they are in close communication with each other; they must act as liaisons and advocates between the parents and other team members. The child is the focus, but the parents are the learners, and through such a system, the parents gain greater confidence in their ability to be their child's best teachers.

Without this early intervention, infants and young children may develop very slowly in social and emotional areas because their parents may not realize the importance of attention to these concerns. Some of the possible effects of depriving children with severe visual disabilities of constant interaction with others need to be given careful attention. First, lack of communication, both preverbal and verbal, may have a retarding effect on all dimensions of development, especially on social communication through speech and language. Passively exposing a child with severe visual impairment to an auditory environment such as family conversation, household noises, radio, or television, without personalized interpretation, may have negative consequences. For example, echolalic, or repetitive, speech develops frequently in children who are blind and left to listen without reciprocal verbal interaction. This imitative speech pattern might be exhibited by verbatim repetition of jingles or commercial tunes. Oral imitation of sounds or words without understanding them does not indicate language acquisition, nor does such behavior foster sequential development in higher cognitive levels.

The focus on visual development is a very important one, as mentioned previously. As babies begin to move about, it is important to help them to focus on objects in their visual path, to teach them to reach and touch desirable objects, or to use the light, object perception, or both, to avoid other objects. Use of any developing vision may be a strong impetus to move toward something and become aware of shadows cast by larger objects. Awareness of, and coming into contact with, everything in the environment, both tactilely and visually, gives meaning to words and more complex language, and eliminates the need for repetitive or echolalic speech, which may delay the development of cognitive skills such as those needed for communication with others.

More recent evidence suggests the need for teaching play behaviors to children with visual impairments, allowing them to play realistically with other children (Rettig, 1994; Troster & Brambring, 1994). Play, even in 4- and 5-year-olds, is influenced by lagging language and cognitive skills and often remains repetitive and unimaginative. Parents and teachers can help preschoolers to acquire more functional, realistic, and symbolic play that is characteristic of their sighted peers, which is necessary for crucial social interactions.

The sounds and words heard and repeated from passive exposure never become important as a means of social communication with another person. Interpersonal communication through language is one of the strong forces in the socialization process because feelings are both expressed and received more vividly through verbal interaction. For the child who cannot see facial expressions, gestures, and other subtleties conveyed through body language, the feelings communicated vocally are most meaningful.

Without the bonding and attachment to loving, caring people, children may develop bizarre behavior patterns as means of getting attention and attempting to satisfy their unmet needs for nurturing. In fact, later in life, some children are able to manipulate adults so adroitly that they exercise almost complete control over their environment, although the attention they receive is not the type that helps them develop socially. Could it be that these children feel that they are puppets who are maneuvered through life without understanding how or why?

SUMMARY

Failure to recognize the importance of bonding, attachment, and communicative interaction in the personal and social development of a child who is visually impaired may have lasting inhibitory consequences on the person's psychosocial aspects of personality throughout his or her life. When children share feelings and thoughts with an adult and that adult responds in an accepting manner, children realize that thoughts and feelings can be accepted by others and are significant to them. This does not mean that the adult should bombard the child verbally, talking about things without appropriate tactile or visual contact, but rather that the adult should listen as the child reveals personal impressions and should talk only to verify or to correct inaccuracies in the child's perceptions. Experiencing frequent communicative interaction helps children learn that they can acquire information on their own and are considered of value and worth to another person.

Satisfaction in human relationships frees children to recognize that they possess a self independent from another person. They can search actively to encounter and relate to the world of concrete objects and even begin to exercise some control over it. As movement and activity increase in the preschool years, more and more independence fosters development in another dimension, sensory–motor, which is the topic for the next chapter.

Movement, Exploration, and Spatial Awareness

Chapter 3 focused on the necessity of bonding and human attachment for the development of feelings of security and trust in the infant and young child. Once established, a sense of security provides a stable basis for the desire and motivation to reach out and extend beyond the self into the world of objects. Chapter 3 also suggested that rhythmic involuntary movements seem to be related to the infant's neurological or physiological need to relieve internal tensions through involvement with external stimulation. Both reflexive and intentional movements at an early age may permit motor patterns to be internalized kinesthetically (Furth, 1969; Hebb, 1949) and assist in "programming the central nervous system to seek and search" (Foulke, 1981, p. 100).

EARLY MOVEMENT

Although unintentional at first, reflexive movements in infancy provide body contact with the environment. Later, the baby becomes aware of the object world as a basis for self-initiated, goal-directed movement. These early movements begin to have meaning when infants internalize them and are able to structure and control future movements of their bodies. Functional exchange between the moving infant and the environment provides the sensorimotor integration that is essential for the development of mental images from which perceptual development ensues (Ayres, 1981; Furth, 1969). Movement helps one to define, integrate, and understand the body as a tool for information gathering; "action learning is considered a vital component in the cognitive development of visually impaired children" (Stephens, 1972, p. 107). Unless children experience the world through their bodies, they will not grasp true concepts and the words they hear will have no referents (Hall, 1981).

After patterns of movement have begun to be established, and the infant has become aware of the surrounding world, motor activities might become goal oriented. There is a purpose for the child's movement, such as to make contact with a person or object, or to change the position of the body or a single body part. These primitive actions form the groundwork for later coordinated movements of manipulation, locomotion, and skill development. The concept of body and objects as factors in movement begins before 2 years of age according to some specialists (Hill, Dodson-Burk, & Smith, 1989).

MOVEMENT AND VISION

When vision is present, it is the first sense to make contact with the environment beyond the body. From the time an infant with sight opens his or her eyes, light is all around, and stimulation of the visual sense from this point on is virtually constant. As early as the first weeks of life, infants attempt to focus on and respond to patterns and colors. It has been theorized that visual stimulation excites the infant, and indeed, babies do tend to engage in very active movement when looking at unusual visual patterns in both black and white and in color.

The extent to which vision is actually a stimulating and facilitating factor in perceptual and cognitive development is not known precisely. Whether vision promotes movement, or movement promotes visual search and control, is not yet determined; however, there are many indications that sensorimotor development proceeds with greater rapidity when the reciprocal action between vision and movement is optimal. According to Amerson (1999), "sensory input affects motor output, and movement affects what is received through sensory channels" (p. 18). Clearly, movement toward an object is more likely to happen when the object can be seen, and certainly the child's movement through space is more likely to happen when there is something of interest in the immediate distance toward which to move.

Vision, even without movement, offers opportunities for looking at the world and provides a wide variety of vicarious experiences that become part of the child's knowledge of the world. Vision not only extends the quality of information available but also provides unique sensory data that are never quite as accurate when gathered through another sense. Specific details of form, color, and spatial relationships among objects can be perceived only through vision. In addition, vision provides an instant concept of the totality of what one sees and is thought by many to be the prime unifier of all other sensory information acquired during the early months and years. Visual images held in the brain provide a constant reference system for recall, even after the actual objects are no longer visible. An impression of the constancy of the world and the objects in it is achieved readily through the visual sense but remains variable when perceived only through other senses. Vision permits children to learn to imitate actions very early, thereby enabling them to refine the coordination of the body by repetition of observed movements. Interrelationships of motor and visual systems affect development of social, communication, and cognitive skills (Amerson, 1999).

MOVEMENT IN CHILDREN WITH IMPAIRED VISION

If there is a strong interrelationship between movement and learning, then when a child is blind or severely visually impaired, movement might be the most accurate replacement for vision in clarifying information about the world. When children are visually impaired, external visual stimulation for spontaneous movement, exploration, and spatial awareness will diminish over time or will be totally lacking from birth. The manner in which children organize perceptions and learn through other senses will be different from, although not necessarily inferior to, those of children who have vision. For example, play styles of sighted children are quite different from those of children who are visually impaired. Appropriate interaction cues must be taught to children with impairments, and sighted children can be taught to interact patiently with them and to use more verbal communication (Zanandrea, 1998). A movement program designed specifically for infants and young children with visual impairments might strengthen the connection of body movement to the "scheme of things in their world" and provide a greater variety of perceptions (Palazesi, 1986, p. 574). Because the needs and problems of the child who is totally blind differ somewhat from those of the child with low vision, we discuss the two separately. We discuss the child who is totally blind, using Carlos as an example. For the aspects of movement and exploration unique to the child who has low vision, we refer to Lucy.

Body and Movement in Children Who Are Blind

The body in action defines space and organizes it into a perception of personal space even without the advantage of visual spatial perception (Van Weelden, 1967). Some suggest that space exists for people who are blind only to the extent that the body or some part of it has moved through space. Movement involves both the proprioceptive and the muscular systems; the action stimulates the proprioceptive sense, which is essential to the development of muscle tone—the foundation of coordinated movement. Movement also creates a kinesthetic awareness, or a feel, that is perceived and internalized. Knowledge of this nature may be referred to as muscle sense. The responsibility for parents, who are the first educators, is to foster as much as possible this internalization of kinesthetic information by moving the baby's arms and legs up, down, and in circular motions to imitate reaching, turning, and stepping, movements used in later exploration and independent movement. The role of the parents or caregivers is very important early on because they are the mediators who determine the child's access to the environment from which exploration follows, and without which no meaningful interpretation of the world is possible for the child without vision (Davidson & Simmons, 1984). A controlled, or specially designed, environment for infants who are blind provides an early basis for developing an awareness of spatial relations. Through movement within a limited space, they may be able to achieve a preunderstanding of a concept of objects and that they can produce object-based sounds (Nielsen, 1991). The selective use of carefully designed push toy devices at a very early age may assist in environmental awareness of objects and in directing movement in children without vision. In fact, a continuum of mobility devices from push toys to precane instruments to the long cane might be helpful to encourage independent movement in preschool children (Leong, 1996; Pogrund, Fazzi, & Schreier, 1993; Skellenger & Hill, 1991).

Body Image

Cratty (1971) first emphasized the need for developing body image in children who are blind because, he said, the body is the center platform from which all knowledge of movement and space is acquired. People who are blind must know about their own bodies, the movements possible, the potential for exerting control over movement, and the body's relationship to other objects and people in space.

In the infant who is blind, the first awareness of body parts comes through movement of the extremities (hands and feet) to touch another body part or something in the environment. Any movement of the body promotes the development of motor patterns. If this structured manipulation is not done for the infant by adults, primitive, involuntary motor behaviors may persist into childhood as purposeless mannerisms, a subject discussed in the previous chapter.

Using the hands to find the head, feet, shoulders, and other body parts stabilizes the infant's orientation in near space, which is critical to freedom of body movement through extended space. The hands become finely developed instruments of investigation essential for tactual exploration and the manipulation skills required in later learning. The feel of motion helps to replace the inability to see motion. The parent's constant use of words to identify the part of the body being touched is necessary to develop an awareness in the child that there are names for different body areas. This use of words helps to establish a kinesthetic image of the body as a related and constant whole capable of being regulated at will. In advocating a motor development program for preschoolers with visual impairments, Palazesi (1986) suggested daily 20-minute movement sessions with a patterned sequence of activities, beginning early in the child's life.

The tactual–kinesthetic awareness and stabilization of the object world are the next hurdles in the beginning of motor development of the child who is blind. The parents should make available every small and large object that is safe to touch, explore, or manipulate when the child begins to show interest in both inanimate and living things. Removing objects from the house to protect the objects from falling or breaking creates a sterile environment from which no information is available. Confining a child who cannot see to a crib or playpen after being allowed to crawl or toddle about creates another obstacle to learning. Encouragement and freedom to explore and move about are indispensable for providing a range and variety of experiences necessary for all facets of development and also for future success in academic endeavors.

Permitting the child who is blind to encounter the same bumps, bruises, falls, and other natural consequences of independent actions that all children experience is difficult for some parents. The common inclination is to protect the perceived helpless child from a seemingly hostile world; however, to do so communicates feelings of inadequacy and incompetence and makes the child needlessly dependent.

Two important skills are developed through freedom to move about the house: the use of the total body as it moves through space to encounter stationary (and usually large) objects, and the use of the hands to explore objects that are either stable or that move with contact. Parents can help by verbally describing body actions and objects to assist in interpreting the nature of things and the body functions required to control the movements among them.

Without the ability to see and imitate the body movements of others, the child without vision must experience movement in the muscles before a specific action can be perceived or verbal instructions from others understood. Hearing actions described has no meaning to young children who do not see unless they are simultaneously performing the action with their bodies (Duehl, 1979).

Many of the postural deviations and infantile patterns of movement observed in numerous children who are blind can be prevented by the use of simple instructions, such as "head up," "shoulders back," "long steps," and "swinging arms." There are specific exercises designed to accentuate body image in stationary positions as well as in locomotion. For example, *Movement and Fundamental Motor Skills for Sensory Deprived Children* (Kratz, Tutt, & Black, 1987) contains a variety of suggestions for physical activities, dances, and games for children with visual handicaps.

Thinking back to Carlos and how easily and with specific purpose he was able to move around the house and outside, one might infer that his parents taught him about his body and its use from early infancy. They may have done this by moving his body in all possible ways, turning it in every position, moving individual limbs and parts through space to develop his kinesthetic sense, and by stroking and touching his body with different textures to stimulate awareness of the multitude of possible sensations and perceptions. Carlos's parents worked to teach him to hold his head up in order to gain muscular control of the head and neck because a child without vision has no reason to hold the head in an upright position in order to see. In addition, his parents probably played many hand, finger, and other body part games with him, which enabled him to learn to position his body in relation to theirs. By the time Carlos was 4 or 5 months old, his parents were probably propping him in a sitting position and playing with him on their laps to promote the strengthening of head, neck, and trunk muscles, as well as helping him expand his world by hearing sounds from different distances and locations and by learning to manipulate objects with his own body. When he was able to sit alone, by 6 or 8 months of age, he was probably given a controlled space in which he could find many interesting objects (Nielsen, 1991). According to Fraiberg's (1977) studies, babies who are blind exhibit exploration and recognition qualities through handling and manipulating objects at as early as 8 months of age. From observing Carlos, it seems apparent that he was given much guidance and frequent demonstrations of how to use objects, in addition to explanations of the effects of his actions on them. For children without vision, nursery rhymes that use body manipulation substitute for picture books. Again, if he had not been encouraged to search and find objects or had not received adequate body manipulation, he might have become inactive and passive and sought stimulation through his own body, which would have caused him to exhibit meaningless, stereotypical movements.

The objects offered the child for play in the first year or so should be simple in form and shape, varied in texture and weight, and capable of some auditory feedback to encourage the child to develop ear-hand-brain coordination as a substitute for eye-hand-brain coordination developed by normally seeing children. If children are encouraged to use hand and finger movements to lift, press, and move toys and objects that change form, they gain perceptions that are necessary for more refined tactual discrimination and recognition, which are discussed later in this chapter. Such structured play gave Carlos the knowledge necessary to mentally organize and reorganize the objects in relation to himself and his ability to act on them, and also taught him a reality and a constancy similar to that acquired by children who are able to view the objects visually.

Having gained some control of his body, a perception of space from movement through it, and a perception of objects in relation to himself, Carlos developed at a normal rate the muscular coordination and strength to hold his body in an upright position (for the most part) and to walk and move in purposeful directions. As he began to move, he was evidently able to perceive the position of his body in relation to echoes bouncing off walls and near and far objects, enabling him to avoid them as he moved. At first, of course, Carlos was given much guidance, encouragement, and physical contact. His parents might even have stood him on their feet and walked with him to give him the feel of his body moving through space. Familiar toys that make sounds were probably used to get him to move toward those toys to touch and manipulate them. Because of previous experiences in having his body moved and in learning to move it himself, his kinesthetic memory developed, giving him the ability to determine his position and to use selected external cues from the things he encountered, permitting him to begin to move on his own.

Spatial Orientation

According to Hill, Rosen, Correa, and Langley (1984), "orientation is the process of utilizing sensory information to establish and maintain one's position in the environment" (p. 58). With practice, the child who is blind learns to assimilate these signals into a meaningful conceptual model of space. Lydon and McGraw (1973) suggested that the following four aspects of spatial concepts form the basis for concept development in children who are blind: (1) action space, with the body as a fixed point from which to anchor movements; (2) body space, in which short distances can be measured in relation to body movement; (3) object space, which is the area within which awareness and location of an object can be perceived without actual contact; and (4) map space, which is the mental organization of certain spatial areas in relation to the body. In one study of the development of space concepts in children who are blind, Birns (1986) investigated the age at which topological and projective space concepts were achieved. Topological space was defined as "spatial relations that remain constant whatever changes there may be in size, shape, proximity, or order of figures" and projective space "included concepts of rotation and perspective—or the projection of how an object will appear from another viewpoint" (p. 577). Birns concluded that children who are blind achieve topological space at about the same time as sighted children, but that 50% of those studied had trouble making the transition to projective space.

With the help of very early intervention, Carlos completed a cognitive map of himself and his surrounding world and was beginning to develop a style of learning that was unique for him. If he had lacked the opportunity to form these perceptions from birth and throughout the early learning years, Carlos would most likely not have acquired freedom of movement and purposeful manipulative skills that were evident from his behavior. He had learned to move and function efficiently without vision.

Because of the recent infant and preschool federal legislation, the role of the orientation and mobility specialist is expanding. No in-depth curriculum has been accepted yet, but the emphasis is far broader than simply cane travel; the focus now is toward basic skills (rather than premobility skills) used with or without a cane (Pogrund & Rosen, 1989). For very young children (toddlers), push toys, miniature grocery carts, hula hoops, and beach balls may be the first tools for independent movement. The possible benefits of this early teaching of independent movement are enormous and include better postural patterns, whole body muscle tone, vestibular stimulation for balance, and an increase in the awareness of textures and objects in the environment. For this concept to be most effective, there is a need to include parents, early childhood teachers, and all therapists who work with young children. For youngsters with low vision, there is some evidence that they may feel more comfortable in using their vision for near and distant landmarks than for looking at their feet to see where they are going (Hill et al., 1984).

When a child who is blind enters a more structured school learning situation lacking the early movement and manipulative skills more easily acquired before 5 or 6 years of age, the retarding effects are likely to be long lasting and possibly permanent. In such cases, achieving ease and efficiency in independent travel may never be possible, and the negative influence on developing abstract cognitive skills may be noticeable throughout life (Gerhardt, 1982; Hall, 1981).

Assuming that Carlos had taken walks with his parents and accompanied them on shopping tours, he would have developed numerous perceptions of the vast world of space and the information available for use in later learning. If his parents described to him such landmarks as lampposts, mailboxes, buildings, curbs, and gutters, then he would have learned how the environment was constructed, "how to manipulate it, and how to move freely in it" (Hill et al., 1984, p. 62). Ability to relate spatial layout of structures in the environment has been linked to more effective use of the cane for independent travel. Talking about the differences in the textures of soft grass, gravel, cement, or sand while walking on or through them would help develop a vocabulary necessary to progress in academic subjects. Unless such words as *inclines*, *slants*, *hills*, and *valleys* are felt through body awareness, they have no meaning to children who cannot see. Expanding knowledge through using the body, combined with verbal interpretation, is the key to continuous refinement in motor skills for children who are blind. Many frustrating problems could be avoided through greater focus on use of the body with freedom and confidence.

Using Low Vision or Visual Imagery for Movement

Warren (1974) postulated that "having vision simultaneously with the motor function allows registration of the motor function and its effects in a visual framework" (p. 61). In a later publication (1984), he concluded that "it may be documented that the child with some visual function is at least potentially at an advantage over the totally blind child" (p. 78). Being able to realize that potential, however, requires early, concentrated attention to learning how to use the impaired vision. One can see from the descriptions of Lucy and Carlos that there are obvious differences in the potential for motor development of a child who has limited visual capacity and a child who is blind. Despite the discrepancies in Lucy's behavior in relation to her use of vision, and despite the confusion in her movement patterns, the fact that she moved her body when she was visually aware that objects were present indicates that she was using the functional vision available to her to guide movement. Lucy's spontaneous awareness of visual space was, and could continue to be, limited to very small areas surrounding her body; however, because she was able to see objects and movement within this space, she could develop an awareness that there was something beyond her body.

The more her parents encouraged and enticed her to continue to move and explore, the more accurate she became in her movements and the more curious she became about the blurred world she saw, a world toward which she could move to gain a clearer impression. Crawling or toddling toward a wall mirror may have contributed to body awareness and body image. In this movement, Lucy learned to gauge distance, even though she could not actually acquire a clear visual picture of what was in the distance. An orientation and mobility instructor suggested that Lucy use a large push toy to prevent her body from bumping into doors or large objects or stumbling over objects she could not see clearly. This enabled her to correct herself without assistance and prevented bruises and unnecessary falls. This greater freedom of movement forged motor patterns into her nervous system, which would be key factors in developing increasing independence in the outdoor environment.

Lucy, never having had normal vision, saw the world as clear, rather than as the blurred image that those with normal vision would describe of her perspective. Of course, Lucy's parents were concerned and exercised some caution, with good reason. Because of the lack of detail in her distance vision and the blurred nature of the environment she was experiencing, Lucy's safety was an important consideration. Perhaps her parents and mobility instructor suggested that she listen in order to help clarify what she could not see, and that she learn to anticipate possible dangers, so that her movements would be cautious without being fearful. An orientation to and a relationship with the environment were more easily achieved by Lucy than by Carlos. Lucy's limited vision, with the use of monoculars, permitted her to stabilize her concepts of both near and extended space into integrated visual and motor patterns. Her visual–motor organization may have been fostered by games such as rolling, bouncing, hitting balls, crawling, and walking up and down flights of stairs with and without assistance; such skills required her to use vision for accuracy in spatial position or prediction of spatial distances.

Selecting playthings for nursery-age children with low vision is a matter for careful consideration. Texture and shape are important for children with low vision, but color and light-reflecting qualities are equally important; in fact, toys that have highly visible differences are often preferred over those that make noise. Some children enjoy shiny, light-reflective toys, while others find them unpleasant.

Even children who have close range vision do not see well enough at a distance to recognize toys or to imitate other children's use of them. Children with close range vision seem to interact differently with objects: They try few manipulations with the toys and require assistance in determining their functional use (Gerhardt, 1982; Olson, 1982; Parsons, 1982). In a definitive scientific study by Parsons (1986), qualitative differences in play patterns between sighted and low vision preschool children were identified. The children who had low vision spent much more playtime involved in stereotypical behaviors, such as mouthing and banging toys, and less time in functional play, using toys for their intended purpose. Other differences noted were in styles of play, ability to play independently, and capacity to stay focused on the functional use of toys.

Studies of children, youth, and adults blinded at different ages suggest that a relationship exists between the length of time vision was present in early life and the subsequent ability to perform increasingly complex tasks requiring spatial awareness and manipulative skills (Valvo, 1971; Warren, 1984). Differences also were recorded in the knowledge of positional concepts, as well as success in orientation and independent movement in mobility, and in making judgments of spatial distances (Fletcher, 1981; S.E. Miller, 1982; Overbury, Goodrich, Quillman, & Faubert, 1989). Personal observations indicate an observable difference in movement patterns between children who are congenitally blind and those who had vision for as limited a period as 18 months to 2 years, which lends validity to Piaget's (1973) idea of an internalized sensorimotor integration through early movement experiences.

Because Ching Lan had limited but adequate vision during her developmental years, it is reasonable to assume that her movement and exploratory patterns were well established before she began to rapidly lose her vision. She had good visual imagery of space, understood the relationship of her body within space, had seen her body in various positions and therefore knew what her body could do, and had developed stable motor patterns and skills. The primary concern for Ching Lan is adapting to the use of other senses, which will alert her about the world, and guiding her movements as she recalls her visual perception of spatial relations. In fact, she indicated that she began doing that when she became aware that she was losing vision. She would continue to update her perceptual cues and use a variety of computational strategies to travel from place to place (Reiser, Guth, & Hill, 1982).

Provided that her parents and teachers encourage her to continue independent movement, her self-confidence should return with some ease, even after her vision is totally gone. However, if she develops anxiety and fear because her parents and teachers impose restrictions and are overprotective, her adaptation to the use of her other senses will be much slower, and some of her motivation for adaptation might be lost. Calling on previously established visual imagery and associating this imagery with new patterns of tactual and auditory information, Ching Lan will begin to interpret how things feel or sound in the way that they looked, and a modified picture of the world will soon emerge.

Because Ching Lan already knew the names of the parts of her body and had the language associated with body position within her repertoire, she was especially attuned to following verbal instructions in relation to her new exploration and movement, and she could interpret and associate the descriptive language of others using her remembered visual imagery. Continuing recall of visual imagery in the case of those who have lost all their vision is crucial. The more visual recall required of the person, the longer and more vivid the visual images will remain. Like any other facet of thought, unused memories will soon lose their clarity. During the adaptive period, it is especially important that verbal instructions be used to assist Ching Lan in her movements, and that her parents, peers, and teachers refrain from physically moving or guiding her, except when she requests assistance or her safety is threatened. Independence and self-confidence are much more easily acquired if children who lose all vision are assumed to be able to follow instructions and are permitted to move independently, according to instructions. Applying the notion that success promotes success, the more that one moves and travels independently, the more rapidly confidence and efficiency will become a reality.

Although Michael had a visual impairment of a moderate nature, he was much like Ching Lan in his early years in using vision in relation to movement. His problem was more a perceptual than a visual problem, which may have affected his abilities to always know how to interpret what he was able to see and to develop stable visual imagery. Michael needed encouragement to give his full visual attention to whatever he was doing, and he needed a great deal of support to strengthen his self-confidence and increase his self-esteem. Many of the suggestions about Ching Lan can apply to Michael, especially if his nearsighted condition begins to progress more rapidly, which may mean that he needs to have more time to process information and to interpret sensory information.

DIFFERENTIAL PROGRAM PLANNING

Children who are congenitally blind and whose early experiences have been similar to Carlos's can enter physical education activities with sighted children with minimal assistance and encouragement when given the opportunity to participate. As soon as they learn stationary landmarks and are shown the routes to follow, children who are blind from birth will learn to travel alone within the classroom, around the building, and on the playground with efficiency and confidence. Given the assistance of an orientation and mobility instructor, they will be ready to begin some independent travel within the neighborhood, and to and from school, on foot or by public transportation, by the time they complete elementary school or sooner. With travel instruction in high school, children who are blind and who possess good motor development have the potential for efficient independent travel in unfamiliar areas.

However, not all children who are blind enter school with established patterns of motor development. Those who have been restricted because of parental fear or lack of knowledge about how to raise a child who is blind may know little about their own bodies and even less about the realities of the environment. Such underdeveloped children might require as long as 2 years, or possibly more, of physical therapy, intensive exercise, daily excursions outside, and regular field trips, in addition to a concentrated program of concrete learning experiences in language and developmental concepts (Dodds, Howarth, & Carter, 1982; Hill et al., 1984; Palazesi, 1986). Many children progress rapidly and are able to grasp formal abstract concepts almost as readily as those whose early development was less delayed. Others might have multiple disabilities in addition to blindness, which might limit learning potential—a topic addressed in the next chapter.

Unlike Lucy, some children with low vision enter school having no awareness of their visual potential and behave as if they were unable to see anything. Their parents, having been told the child was blind (using medical–legal criteria based on acuity, restricted field, or both) have made no effort to stimulate the child visually or to encourage the use of low vision. For these children with low vision, a program similar to that proposed for underdeveloped blind children, with special emphasis on visual development in relation to movement, would be advantageous. In every experience and activity in the program, the child is encouraged to look in order to learn to coordinate visual and motor systems, and to begin to bring increased clarity and order to a world that may have been confusing. Although not all children with low vision will become primarily visual learners, increased visual efficiency will enhance their movement patterns, motor coordination, and conceptual development (Barraga, 1980c; Dodds & Davis, 1989; Hall & Bailey, 1989).

Because both Ching Lan and Michael had vision during their preschool and early school years, their movement patterns developed normally as a matter of course. However, because of some lag in his motor development, Michael began to encounter some difficulty in speed of movement as he grew older. Not only will Ching Lan retain a mental picture of the world of objects and space, but she also will unconsciously use the movement patterns internalized in her body, even when she no longer has sight. The primary focus in teaching such children will not be on their learning how to move, but instead will concentrate on the feel of movement, visual recall of spatial concepts, and adaptation to the use of ear–brain coordination (rather than eye–brain coordination) to orient themselves within space and to guide and direct movement.

SUMMARY

There are obvious differences in freedom of movement, mobility within limited environments, and future independent travel among children who are congenitally totally blind, those with low vision, those who lose vision after having had good vision, and those who have learning problems in addition to visual impairment. These differences must be considered in relation to the learning process and the teaching technique, for which appropriate adaptations must be made. Spatial orientation and concept formation require a long and tedious learning process for children who are totally congenitally blind. They will learn to use other senses, but must be constantly encouraged and supported by adults who carefully plan sequential experiences as the children gradually acquire skills. The concepts acquired will necessarily be different from those acquired through the use of vision. The potential for independent travel at a later age is directly proportional not only to the early learning experiences provided by parents and teachers but also to the extent to which the children are encouraged to reach out and be independent and knowledgeable in movement from the beginning.

Exposed to these experiences, the child who has limited visual impairment will be able to enhance his or her knowledge of the world and patterns of exploration more easily. Independence in movement will come with less effort and greater efficiency as opportunities for practice are provided. As in the case of a child who is blind from birth, independence in travel for children with limited visual impairment is closely related to the appropriate learning experiences and encouragement provided in the early years.

Children who lose some or all of their vision after having established their concepts of the world and their movement patterns must learn to adapt these patterns by using other senses. The process of adapting may be slow in the beginning and is related to psychological factors within the children and those around them. Independence in travel can be maintained through appropriate teaching procedures that stress the acquisition of different skills for movement and travel. Mobility training programs must be designed specifically for each individual in relation to previous development and learning. No doubt, increased use of electronic travel aids will occur in the near future (Ferrell, 1984; Harris, Humphrey, Muir, & Dodwell, 1985).

The trend in the field of orientation and mobility is toward working with children in the preschool years, and to begin teaching the use of the cane at earlier ages than was thought appropriate a few years ago. Experimentation with and research about younger children and individuals with multiple disabilities is increasing, and the validity of this approach is likely to be substantiated in the next few years.

Children with Visual Impairments and Multiple Disabilities

Like increasing numbers of children, Sharon (described in Chapter 1) experiences several disabilities that affect her development and learning. Although children with both visual impairments and disabling conditions in other body systems are not a new subject, in the past few years they have received greater attention. As early as 1969 (Lowenfeld, 1969), surveys indicated that a growing percentage of children who were visually impaired had other medical or physiological conditions not related to the functional or developmental conditions discussed in previous chapters. During the 1970s, increasing evidence indicated that half or more of school-age children with visual impairments had clinically and medically diagnosed conditions in one or more body systems other than the visual system (Kirchner & Peterson, 1980; Kirchner, Peterson, & Suhr, 1979). Current estimates by teachers of students with visual impairments indicate that approximately 50% of students receiving educational services because of visual impairments have other disabilities (Sacks, 1998). Gates (1985) attributed the increasing number of children with visual and multiple disabilities to three factors: etiological causes such as retinopathy of prematurity and maternal rubella; medical advances that have saved the lives of children, but in the attempt may have created other problems including visual impairments; and current trends in service to previously unserved children.

Most of the children with visual impairments described as multiply disabled who received educational services before the early 1970s were in fact able to learn to care for their own needs such as toileting and feeding (Erin, Daughtery, Dignan, & Pearson, 1990). Not until after the passage of the Education for All Handicapped Children Act of 1975 (EHA; P. L. 94-142) were children, such as Sharon, who have severe multiple disabilities that may prevent them from caring for themselves as adults, included among those served in educational settings. Before that landmark legislation, these children were often ignored by educators—considered hopeless and therefore not entitled to inclusion in educational settings; they may have been institutionalized at birth; they may simply have been kept at home, given total care, and considered to be incapable of learning. The rubella (German measles) epidemic of 1963 and 1964, which resulted in a population of several thousand children who were deaf and blind, and the passage of the EHA (renamed the Individuals with Disabilities Education Act in 1990) have provided the strongest impetus for alternative thinking and adapting service delivery systems to accommodate children with personal and educational needs who had not heretofore had access to special or public schools.

There are greater numbers of students with neurological difficulties associated with prematurity and anoxia incidents, many of whom have cortical visual impairment, a complex condition that affects memory, perception, and mental capacity as well as visual ability. As educational services for visually impaired individuals have expanded to address the needs of students with multiple disabilities, the goals of education have changed also. Teachers of students with visual impairments must integrate educational goals with functional activities that will enhance students' quality of life. There must be an increased emphasis on community-based instruction to ensure that students can generalize what they have learned during real experiences, and legal requirements for transition planning now support early preparation of students with disabilities for adult experiences (Sacks, 1998).

TYPES AND CAUSES

Visual impairments combined with other disabilities may result in a variety of conditions. These conditions may be genetic, may be caused by prenatal or perinatal factors, or may result from trauma after birth. Medical technology has provided a future for many children who may not have survived at all 20 years ago. It is up to families and professionals to ensure that these children, regardless of the severity of their disabilities, are provided with the opportunity to reach their potential.

Physical and Sensory Disabilities

Many children with multiple disabilities are affected by cerebral palsy. Of children who have cerebral palsy, 25% to 50% have visual impairments that may affect their educational progress (Hardy, 1983). Children with cerebral palsy have experienced damage to or dysfunction of the brain that causes them to process motor signals differently than other children. This may mean that their physical tone is too high (hypertonic) or too low (hypotonic), or that it alternates between too high and too low. It may be virtually impossible for children with cerebral palsy to control certain muscle groups and they may have difficulty with gross motor skills such as walking, sitting, or rolling as well as with fine motor skills such as handling a pencil or picking up coins.

Children with cerebral palsy most commonly have two types of visual differences. One is a strabismus, or a muscle imbalance of the eyes. This lack of ability to fuse the images from both eyes could result in a condition known as amblyopia, in which the child relies on the vision from only one eye or uses each eye for different distances. For the child with cerebral palsy and strabismus, careful observation is important to determine the best physical position to permit the child to see tasks well and to have maximum physical control over use of materials.

The second type of visual impairment common with cerebral palsy is neurological in nature and is related to the brain's role in interpreting visual information. There is some brain dysfunction, usually in the area of the visual cortex in the lower back part of the brain. Children with this condition may show a puzzling combination of behaviors: (a) their vision may fluctuate from one minute to the next; (b) they may turn or look away from objects toward which they are reaching; and (c) they do not normally show nystagmus or visual mannerisms (Jan, Groenveld, Sykanda, & Hoyt, 1987). According to Ferrell (1987), cortical visual impairment is the leading cause of visual disability in children with multiple conditions. Spina bifida is a second type of neurological disorder that occurs often with visual impairment. An opening in the spinal column allows spinal fluid and myelomenigocele to emerge, often accompanied by hydrocephalus, or fluid buildup, within the brain. Children with this condition often have visual impairments, commonly strabismus, that result from pressure within the brain (Zambone, Ciner, Appel, & Graboyes, 2000).

Some children with visual impairment are considered multiply disabled because they exhibit major developmental delays that persist, sometimes in spite of high-quality intervention. These children might lag behind in language, with echolalia and meaningless or irrelevant speech dominating their spoken output. They might show asocial characteristics that cause some to be described as autistic-like; these characteristics include limited initiations of interactions with others, rigidity in following certain routines, stereotypical behaviors, and preference for repetition in environmental stimulation. Such children are often diagnosed as mentally retarded by the educational systems that serve them. Although they clearly function within the ranges of retardation according to clinical definitions, their unique patterns of behavior suggest a more complex problem imposed by the combined effects of visual deprivation and cognitive inability to process and interpret their environment.

Children who were formerly called deaf-blind are now being described as dually sensory impaired by some professionals (Goetz, Guess, & Stremel-Campbell, 1987). The largest group of children with both hearing and vision losses in the 1960s and 1970s were those affected by maternal rubella; now these people have reached adulthood, and their primary needs are for appropriate living and occupational arrangements. Of students who are currently described as dually sensory impaired, many have pervasive neurological impairments caused by conditions such as cytomegalovirus (CMV), anoxia, toxoplasmosis, meningitis, maternal rubella, or a recently identified condition known as CHARGE association. CHARGE is a grouping of anomalies that might include colobomas, heart conditions, and hearing loss, not all of which appear in every child. In addition, a few children experience hearing and visual impairments without additional disabilities, often related to conditions such as Usher syndrome or to traumatic injury.

A few children who need educational services sometimes have complex health problems that may limit their life spans and their levels of physical activity. Children affected by acquired immunodeficiency syndrome (AIDS) are vulnerable to infection of any kind and need flexibility in programming according to their day-to-day comfort and capacity. The visual effects of this condition might include viruses such as CMV, a common virus that can settle in the retina and destroy vision in the affected areas.

Learning Disabilities and Behavioral Disorders

Many students with visual impairments also have milder difficulties related to learning or behavior. Because these may be less apparent than physical disabilities, they can be overlooked during educational assessment because psychologists and other educators can assume the problems are a result of the visual impairment.

Some studies report that as many as 60% of students with visual impairments have learning disabilities (Erin & Koenig, 1997). Learning disabilities related to reading, writing, auditory or visual processing, mathematical functions, organization, or attentional difficulties may also be present with a visual impairment, although they may not be a result of the visual disability (Silberman & Sowell, 1998). They may not be identified because psychologists and diagnosticians may not be skilled in diagnosing these difficulties and may assume the learner's difficulties are associated only with the visual impairment. For these students, a structured and well-organized learning environment is critical (Silberman & Sowell, 1998).

In addition, students with visual impairments can also exhibit emotional or behavioral disorders across the same ranges as students without visual impairments (Mar & Cohen, 1998). Self-injurious and self-stimulatory behaviors, attention difficulties, disruptive behaviors, and difficulties in social interactions may not be directly related to the presence of a visual impairment. However, the child who is blind or has low vision may use different ways of expressing emotions (e.g., verbal opposition rather than physical or passive withdrawal rather than physical aggression). Intervention strategies used with students should address differences in motivation and reinforcers related to visual impairment; for example, a blind child is more likely to change behavior for a reward such as music or a physical activity than for a visual reinforcer such as a sticker in a book.

Additional disabilities have various functional effects on children. Although it is helpful to know about the impact that specific conditions can have, there is no way to predict function based on etiology alone. Each child is an individual, and many factors influence what he or she can do.

THE IMPACT OF A VISUAL IMPAIRMENT

Peter was 3 years old, and his mother was becoming more concerned. Even though the doctor said that there was no problem except for blindness, Peter's mother knew that he was not like other children with visual difficulties in his preschool class. At playtime, Peter would sit in his favorite rocking chair and hit a block against the arm of the chair; he would rock back and forth, smiling and making nonsense sounds. When a teacher encouraged him to play with the other children, Peter would scream, "No playtime!" and throw the block angrily. At home he often wanted to be left alone; when his mother called him to dinner or to get ready for bed, he would cry and sometimes bang his head.

The teachers at school used words such as *developmentally delayed* when they talked about Peter's progress. His mother wondered secretly whether he might be retarded, even though no one had used that word. She had tried to follow all the suggestions in the books she had read, and she encouraged Peter to play with other children and to become curious about the world around him; however, his preference for repetition and his dislike of other people was making it more difficult as he grew older. Perhaps his difficulty was not only blindness—or was it? Some children have developmental and learning differences that cannot be associated with diagnosable medical or physiological conditions. The sensory deprivation, along with isolation from natural experiences and human interactions, can result in behavioral deviations and influence normal psychological development.

The presence of a visual impairment with additional disabilities causes several difficulties that may affect learning. Some of these difficulties are rooted in the concept of sensory deprivation: the idea that the failure to receive and use input from the senses will eventually result in a long-term inability to use those learning channels. A child with multiple disabilities may not only lack experiences that are primarily visual, but also may not have the ability to confirm or replicate experiences through movement, through hearing and speech, or through recalling similar experiences.

A classic experiment by Held and Hein (1963) illustrates the problem experienced by many children with multiple disabilities. They studied the effects of visual deprivation in kittens by raising two kittens in the dark for the first few weeks of life. After the kittens were exposed to light, they placed them in baskets at opposite ends of an arm on a small structure like a merry-go-round. One kitten was moved passively, while the other one was active in using his legs to move both his basket and that of the other kitten. The active kitten developed visual perception, whereas the passive one remained virtually blind. This is further evidence of the probable relationship between the motor and visual systems in perceptual development, an idea suggested in Chapter 3.

The experience of the passive kitten is similar to the experiences of children who cannot interact freely with their environment by moving within it because of a physical disability. They might learn to experience the world as an event unrelated to them, and they do not learn that they can have an effect on the environment. As they grow older, their motivation and their real ability to interact may diminish. It is critical that the learning experiences for children with multiple disabilities involve plenty of opportunities for them to act on the environment and get results. A smile and a hug from a parent when they vocalize or a piece of wanted food when they request it with a sign or gesture are examples of results that can convey the message, "You did it!"

The intensity of stimulation in the environment can be another area of concern as a child develops. All people vary in their toleration for various levels of activity around them, but children with neurological differences often show greater ranges of toleration (Rogow, 1988; Smith & Levak, 1996). Some children are hypersensitive to stimuli and dislike tasting new foods, touching sticky or moist substances, changing ac tivities, or being lightly touched by others, even in an affectionate manner. Som even reject any stimulation simply because they cannot handle it or they do not kno what to attend to when there are environmental distractions (Morse, 1991).

Other children seem to tolerate any type of stimulation to the point that they d not have preferences or do not try to alter the environment to their liking. The chil who listens placidly to the radio at the highest volume, who does not show excitemen even at a party or an event when excitement would be appropriate, who does not laug when tickled, and who does not complain about pain or discomfort is a child wh might need to learn to notice even gross differences in the activities and stimu around him or her.

The absence of vision may increase the intensity of these reactions. The child ma have no way of predicting when a new stimulus is presented and might become hyper sensitive or passive as a defense against the lack of control over external events. Agai the critical objective is to provide a means by which the child can act successfully o the environment in a satisfying manner. This takes much patience, and may requir consistent, long-term conditioning for it to become a reality.

Some children with visual impairments show repetitive or stereotypical behavior such as head bobbing, eye poking, light flicking, or rocking. These are more commo among children with multiple disabilities, who are often more difficult to discourag because they may lack social awareness. Scholl (1986) suggested a variety of causes fo these movements: the need for sensory stimulation, the effect of movement limita tions, lack of social experiences, inadequate relationships with adults, and lack o knowledge about appropriate behaviors. McHugh and Pyfer (1999) hypothesize a rela tionship between early motor deprivation and the appearance of rocking among stu dents who are blind. The four students who were observed in McHugh and Pyfer study rocked at different times of day, during functional tasks as well as when bored o tired. Huebner (1986) suggests consideration of the causes and effects of the behavio when planning interventions; she emphasizes the importance of providing a variety o opportunities for activity to the young child as a preventive measure.

The interaction of vision loss with other disabilities can also affect the appropri ate development of language. Among some children who are blind, inappropriat speech patterns can become predominant. Many children demonstrate echolalia (re peated speech), including delayed echolalia (repeating something heard in the past and mitigated echolalia (using shorter rote phrases within original speech units (Rasmussen, 1985). Other children who are blind demonstrate a low frequency of ut terances, which may indicate a lack of understanding that they can have an effect o the world through communication; still others do not develop speech but may lear to use other forms of communication such as sign language and gesture. A few wi continue to communicate at a prelanguage level, through vocalization, intonatio and movement.

It is important that language be considered primarily as a means of communica tion and expression, and that language intervention not be merely an attempt to shap the formal processes of speech production. For the child with multiple disabilities, language is a critical connector to other people; the important message to be conveyed is that language is a means of building social relationships. Rogow (1978, 1988) recommended the use of social routines and play activities, such as nursery rhymes, to establish early communication; by associating movement and action to these routines, the child learns to expect and share social interactions, even though his or her expressive language is limited.

The presence of additional disabilities may also affect a child's ability to use any functional vision effectively. Some children who are physically disabled have to exert effort to attain their best visual position and to maintain head control in order to fixate on an image. Children with cognitive or learning difficulties may experience problems in interpreting visual information, particularly if their acuity is poor and they have no previous experience with the shape or configuration of an object. Many children with neurological differences experience perceptual confusion. If they do not know which stimulus is significant, they are unable to make visual comparisons (Bailey & Downing, 1994). They may not understand constancy of depth, shape, and size, and may not be able to select important information from a busy background. These children may respond best to simple, high contrast visual stimuli in a setting that allows them to experience the same stimulus frequently. Later, when the image is familiar and meaningful, more complex visual situations can be introduced while teaching organized search strategies (Rogow, 1992).

A visual impairment can multiply the limitations imposed by other disabilities. Children with such limitations are at risk of becoming passive observers of the world around them. To prevent this, professionals and parents must carefully evaluate and identify capabilities, and set goals that will promote the child's interaction with the environment. For example, if a child has some useful vision, it needs to be nurtured and stimulated, even though his or her other disabilities might impact how the child is able to use functional vision.

ASSESSMENT

Valid assessment of the child with multiple impairments requires the skills of many individuals. Assessment is particularly challenging because the team must gather information that provides a representative picture of the child's abilities, and yet must maintain the integrity of the whole child without presenting a fragmented perspective.

Although it is generally accepted that the team is the foundation for effective programming and assessment, the composition and structure of the team may vary. A *multidisciplinary* team includes specialists who work individually with a child on goals specific to the special skill area; this structure closely approximates a medical model of service delivery. On an *interdisciplinary* team, each member works individually with a child but also maintains regular communication with other team members through meetings and documentation. A *transdisciplinary* team, more recently preferred in infant and early childhood programs, provides services directly through one or two primary team members and the parents; others act as consultants on this team (Campbell, 1987; Silberman, 1986).

Assessment of the young child with multiple disabilities might involve the use of a developmental instrument or scale. This approach provides information about the child's attainment of skills in comparison with the age at which a child usually achieves them. Very few of these instruments are standardized for use with a child having both visual and multiple impairments. *The Callier-Azusa Scale* (Stillman, 1979) has been developed for children who are multiply disabled or deaf-blind; it includes an inventory of items from six areas and is intended to be completed by someone who is observing the child regularly over a period of time.

In using a developmental scale in assessing a child with multiple disabilities, the professional should be aware of its disadvantages as well as the information that can be gained. As a child with disabilities grows older, physical change is less rapid and learning becomes more greatly influenced by environmental factors. It cannot be assumed that a child will acquire skills listed on a developmental scale in the exact order in which they are listed, especially if it is a scale not intended for children with visual limitations. Differences in priorities, experiences, motivation, and capabilities will determine what a child achieves. The older a child becomes, the less helpful a developmental instrument will be in determining goals.

Assessment of children with severe disabilities has recently broadened from a focus on the use of specific instrumentation to include environmental influences on the child's learning and behavior. Known as an ecological approach, this perspective itemizes the skills a child needs in order to function in the immediate environment and in the next environment the child will encounter in his or her life (Nietupski & Hamre-Nietupski, 1987). It provides guidelines for the development of objectives which can be easily translated into program activities. For the child with a visual impairment and additional disabilities, it provides a highly individualized approach to assessment that will help the team to identify what the child can accomplish in the immediate environment, such as reaching for a toy.

The accurate assessment of vision in the child with multiple disabilities is a particular challenge. Standard screening instruments and procedures often are not appropriate, particularly if a child cannot indicate preference or make a choice. Although some clinical procedures, such as preferential looking and the *Parsons Visual Acuity Test* (Cress, Spellman, DeBriere, Sizemore, Northam, & Johnson, 1981), offer response options that are appropriate for the child with multiple impairments, careful observation will continue to be the best indicator of a child's visual abilities. Responses such as blinking, turning the head, or brightening toward a visible object might be the only evidence that a child is aware of changes in the visible environment. Observation across time, in various settings, and with different caregivers will provide a more representative picture of the child's functional vision. Only a few resources exist that assist the professional in assessment of vision in the child with multiple disabilities; among these are *Look at Me* (Smith & Cote, 1982) and the *Functional Vision Screening Inven-*

ory for the Child with Severe Handicaps (Langley, 1980). Erin (1996) provides a description of procedures for functional vision assessment of students with multiple disabilities, with emphasis on functional applications. The *Individualized Systematic Assessment of Visual Efficiency* (ISAVE) (Langley, 2000) provides a framework for assessment and use of vision in students with severe and multiple disabilities.

A Low Vision Project International, directed by Dr. Jill Keeffe of the department of ophthalmology at the University of Melbourne in Australia, has published two very important volumes to add to the material available for assessment purposes. The first volume is *Screening for Impaired Vision*, and the second volume is *The Effects of Low Vision and Assessment of Functional Vision* (Keeffe, 1994). The material is being used worldwide and is a valuable resource, especially for developing countries.

Assessment of the child with multiple disabilities involves collaboration among families and professionals in order to gather information about a child's function. It is important that a teacher of students who are visually impaired be a part of the assessment process to ensure that the student's needs related to visual impairment are addressed appropriately during assessment and planning (Lewis & Russo, 1998). In most cases, use of a standardized instrument is inappropriate because of the highly individual patterns of development demonstrated by children with multiple disabilities. Compared with items on standardized instruments, criterion-referenced instruments and skill inventories provide information that is more easily translated into program objectives. An ecological approach encourages maximum flexibility in developing an appropriate plan for each student and ensures the development of skills that will allow the student to function in the immediate environment.

INTERVENTION AND PROGRAMMING

Recent trends in programming for the child with multiple impairments emphasize integrated approaches that teach skills to help the child to be a functional member of his or her community. The concept of the team as the core of program planning acknowledges that the child with multiple disabilities requires the specialized knowledge of a variety of individuals; however, in some settings, a transdisciplinary team is preferred because it involves only one or two professionals along with the family as primary implementors of the child's program; other professionals act in support roles (Silberman, 1986).

Early intervention is vital for the infant with multiple disabilities; the effectiveness of this intervention depends strongly on the family's involvement. Mori and Olive (1978) described the importance of encouraging families to interact with their infants and to allow the infants to participate in normal family activities, including being cuddled and played with by friends and family members. Infants and preschoolers should be encouraged to use all of their senses to learn about the world around them, with experiences and objects presented in meaningful contexts. Use of varied textures, odors, and sound effects in the environment can generate awareness of differences in the world, even before they are ready to initiate cause-effect actions. *Reach Out and Teach* (Ferrell, 1985) provides direction for parents and professionals in planning activities for the preschool child with visual and multiple disabilities. The handbook and manual clearly convey the challenges that confront a child with a visual disability as well as the satisfactions of meeting those challenges; through the use of illustrations and step-by-step activities, families and caregivers can encourage active learning.

As the child grows older, the emphasis is on the mastery of functional skills, that is, the skills that will enable an individual to meet the demands of his or her immediate setting and the requirements of future settings. Priorities are set according to these specifications as well as student strengths and interests, family preference, and age appropriateness.

Although goals might be specific to designated skill areas or domains, integrated programming is the key to mastery and application of skills for most students. Instead of scheduling a single time of day in which a child will work on a skill, adults must provide opportunities to practice a skill throughout the day. For example, if a goal for Mary is to perfect a pincer grasp (grasping with the thumb and index finger), the teaching strategy can be applied at group time when she places a sticker on a chart; at snack time, when she picks up a raisin; later in the day, when she is given a penny to place into her bank; and at the end of the day, when she helps to clean up paper clips from the work table. Practice on one skill for extended periods of time usually is not as productive as frequent work on the same skill for shorter periods and within tasks that are meaningful at different moments.

It is also important that the students experience an activity at the time of day when it would naturally occur and in a setting as much like the actual setting as possible. Because many students who are blind or have low vision are not aware of incidental events in their world, instructors cannot assume that they will associate details from a simulated situation with details from a real situation. Although a classroom store may be a motivating method of reinforcing a child's completion of work tasks, a visit to a real store is a more accurate learning experience and provides opportunities for finding out new information: "Do you know that their cash register talks?"; "How did you know you were getting close to the frozen foods?"; "How much money will you need to buy those raisins?"

Time awareness is an important feature of learning to organize the world for the child with multiple disabilities (Smith & Levak, 1996). Because these children have no understanding of clock time, they may feel that they operate in a world in which random events seem to happen in an unpredictable order. Not only is it vital to establish a routine and follow it consistently in programming, but it is also important to include antecedent activities that will give children clues about what will happen next. This can be as simple as letting a child carry a placemat to the lunchroom, or as complex as giving a child a braille list of events planned for that day. When students do not understand the effects of their own behaviors as communication, they must have immediate and repeated experiences to build that awareness. One way of building that awareness is through the use of activity boxes, enclosed spaces where small manipulat able objects are suspended. These boxes allow students who are blind to contact and explore materials repeatedly to learn that objects continue to exist and that they can interact with objects (Dunnett, 1999). This approach provides immediate contact and maximum control to the young child who is blind and who has not yet learned how to explore the world spontaneously because he or she is not aware that objects and materials are nearby.

The *Prelanguage Curriculum*, based on a program developed by Van Dijk (1965), emphasized communicating to the student about time through the use of a calendar box. Using this strategy, the student begins by associating a related object to an event that will take place and by wearing or carrying that object during the duration of the event. The student moves from that level of recognition of routine through the complex use of calendars to establish a sense of past, present, and future. This teaching approach, which emphasizes the development of language through movement, moves a child from the stage of relating to an adult through the spontaneous use of language.

The Van Dijk curricula have influenced more recent approaches used with children who are deaf and blind and who usually require highly specialized educational programming. Children who are deaf and blind, also described as having dual sensory impairments, often have usable vision, hearing, or both. Because of the isolating effects of a dual sensory loss, which are combined with neurological differences in some children, programming goals emphasize communication and socialization. Many children who are deaf and blind show autistic-like characteristics and are not motivated by human contact and approval; therefore, one of the greatest challenges for the educator is to create motivating and functional learning activities that encourage the child to make contact with others.

Communication methods used by individuals who are deaf and blind will vary according to several factors. The child's functional ability, motivation, and the previous or current existence of hearing and vision all have an impact on the communication modes used by those with both vision and hearing impairments. For many children, a total communication approach will provide the most intensive information about the meaning and structure of communication; this includes the use of speech, sign, gesture, facial expression, and any other modality that conveys information and ideas.

Vocal communication may be an option for those who are highly motivated or who have usable hearing. This may be taught using some variation of the Tadoma method (Kates & Schein, 1980), in which the individual learns speech by touching the throat and lips of the speaker. Alternative manual systems include the one- or two-hand manual alphabets; American Sign Language, with the hand of the receiver lightly covering the hand of the signer; printing on the palm of the hand; and communication boards or augmentative systems that utilize braille or tactile systems. Technological advances have increased the options for this population: The Tellatouch, in which the sender types a message that is conveyed to the receiver through a braille cell, and the recently available mechanical hand developed at Stanford University for Smith-Kettlewell, provide a broader array of options for the individual who requires an alternative form of communication.

For the child who is not able to use a complex language system, there are approaches that can make the immediate environment more understandable and predictable. The use of anticipatory cues, particularly touch cues for children with little vision, can make them aware that they will be touched or moved. The shaping of natural gestures, devised by children themselves, can enforce the relationship of a body or hand movement to a predictable event. The establishment of a routine and the presentation of choices within that routine will build the foundation for the development of communication and language.

Like children who are deaf and blind, children with other multiple disabilities require highly individualized educational programming. Prepared curricula for young children with visual disabilities may serve as supplemental resources in developing a program that will differ from child to child according to family preference, service availability, age, and functional level. *Growing Up* (Robinson, 1982) and the *Oregon Project* (Brown, Simmons, & Methvin, 1978) are intended primarily for the child who is visually impaired without additional disabilities, but both specify activities and milestones that can help in program planning for the child with multiple disabilities.

Several recent curricula and resources can support the educational team in their work with students who are multiply disabled. Some specialized schools, including the Texas School for the Blind and Visually Impaired and Perkins School for the Blind, publish curricula that are designed specifically for educational planning with students who have multiple disabilities. Smith and Levak (1996) have developed a resource guide for teachers of students with visual impairments who are also serving students with multiple disabilities, and it includes guidelines for assessment that include students who have severe and multiple disabilities.

Some children with multiple disabilities will be able to develop academic skills, often with the use of adapted materials or methods. Braille reading may be introduced as a functional skill for the student who is blind and who may not have the cognitive ability to master higher order reading skills; the association of sight words in braille with significant objects and possessions reinforces the concept of braille as a means of communication, and braille can be used to identify responses on an augmentative communication device for some students. The use of braille should not be ruled out as a part of the total communication system simply because a child does not appear to have the cognitive capacity to read complicated materials.

Heller, D'Andrea, and Forney (1998) described adaptations in reading and writing that allow students with multiple and visual disabilities to maximize their literacy potential. Students with multiple disabilities may have the potential to be braille readers if teachers provide adaptations in methodology and materials. D'Andrea (1997) identifies adaptations for braille readers with multiple disabilities, including those with learning difficulties, physical disabilities, intellectual disabilities, and deaf-blindness. The use of functional activities, simplification and stabilization of materials, adapted braille writers, and the association of meaningful experiences are among the adaptations D'Andrea suggests in teaching braille to students with complex learning needs.

Programming for the child with multiple disabilities and a visual impairment must also include assessment and programming in orientation and mobility to encourage self-initiation and independence in movement and travel. Although some people do not learn to plan complex outdoor routes or to use public transportation, the ability to travel efficiently within familiar environments will enhance an individual's ability to manage the daily routine. Children whose physical disabilities prevent independent locomotion may still gain the skill to communicate choices regarding where and how they are to be moved; they can comprehend directionality, learn safety measures, give accurate instructions to others, make choices, and learn concepts that support the understanding of their own body movement.

A variety of adapted techniques and devices have been applied to encourage greater control in moving through the environment for the individual who is severely disabled (Coleman & Weinstock, 1984; Del Frari, 1978; Uslan, Malone, & De l'Aune, 1983). Harley, Wood, and Merbler (1981) also emphasized the use of flexible teaching approaches in working with individuals who have severe impairments. Uslan et al. (1983) especially encourage consideration of the cane as a travel device for many such individuals, and they caution that a lack of physical activity can be of particular concern with this population. In developing independence within the environment, the individual with multiple disabilities and a visual impairment may be disadvantaged by overprotective caregivers, a lack of experience in initiating activity, and the inability to recall locations that are not visible or immediately available to other senses. It is important that a certified instructor (certified by AER) be involved in the assessment and planning of orientation and mobility programming for the individual with severe disabilities. It is important that orientation and mobility instruction be presented in meaningful units that identify specific adaptations for travel within the student's own environment. Bailey and Head (1993) describe the use of task analysis for teaching orientation and mobility skills in real contexts for students with multiple disabilities and visual impairments.

Children with multiple disabilities who have useful vision should be encouraged to use vision contingently to affect the environment (Utley, Duncan, Strain, & Scanlon, 1983). This can be done most effectively in functional activities in which the child is required to use vision to complete a task (e.g., hanging a coat on a hook or stacking cups) (Goetz & Gee, 1987). To be applied meaningfully, goals in functional use of vision, as in other program areas, must be integrated into daily routines and generalized across settings, people, and materials. If the functional use of vision is not encouraged, the child with multiple disabilities is at risk of increased isolation from the environment and a decreased sense of control over the events around him or her.

Although the emphasis in vision usage should be on functional activities, there is some support also for the value of providing specific visual stimulation, including environmental management, for students who have more severe disabilities. Mamer (1999) found improvement in visual attention and fixation in adolescent students with severe multiple disabilities, and the students themselves reported increases in visual following after intervention.

A new curriculum from the American Printing House for the Blind, Inc., ISAVE (Langley, 2000), provides a framework for assessment and use of vision in students with severe and multiple disabilities. It addresses the interaction of vision and physical function in students who have other disabling conditions.

SUMMARY

The population of students with multiple disabilities and visual impairments is becoming more diverse and complex. Educational programming must provide the opportunity for children to learn that they can have an effect on the world around them. The selection of functional goals, the integration of skills into natural environments, and the generalization of skills into home and community settings offer the opportunity for effective learning for the child with multiple disabilities. Through this approach, the isolation imposed by a visual impairment in combination with multiple other disabling conditions can be minimized and each student can have the opportunity to reach his or her potential.

Tactual, Auditory, and Visual Development and Learning

Chapter 3 discussed that children's social–emotional development and feelings about themselves and others are directly related to the quality and extent of their human interaction. Chapter 4 developed the idea that motor development and learning are facilitated by exploration, movement, and knowing how to control one's body in order to respond purposefully to the environment and to objects within it. Chapter 5 described children with a myriad of additional disabling conditions, along with some notions for assessment and programming for the development and learning problems they exhibit. This chapter presents a comprehensive discussion of learning and cognitive development through the senses.

INTRODUCTION TO SENSORY LEARNING

The development of cognitive ability—that is, knowing and thinking—involves the use of the senses because the mind cannot perceive anything that has not first been received through the senses (Arnheim, 1969). What one feels, hears, sees, tastes, and smells is internalized and stored as a model corresponding to the environment, thus determining what one knows about the world and one's relationship to it (Bruner, 1966). Information coming through the senses must be received, interpreted, combined, and stored in the brain. The acquisition of language facilitates the integration of discrete sensory impressions to permit the learner to bring order to the material stored. Language also acts as a medium of exchange with others for clarifying and verifying sensory receptions. The ability to note the likenesses and differences among touch sensations, sights, sounds, tastes, and smells determines the relationships later developed between ideas. Integrating the diverse bits of concrete information received through the senses into a unified group of concepts about people and things provides the functional knowledge for thinking and talking about abstract ideas. The process of sorting, coding, and organizing sensory data and concepts to make all the characteristics and operational functions fit together is a complex mental task. Each child learns this process in a unique manner, which Piaget (1973) called a "cognitive style of learning."

Seeking, selecting, ordering, and programming information evolves as a consistent, individual pattern that each child uses in learning. The notion of unique learning patterns emphasizes the need for individualized instruction for maximal learning. Given this concept, parents and teachers should understand and accept each child's preferred learning strategies as appropriate (Keogh, 1973). Some theorists hypothesize that cognitive style might be well established by the age of 3 but that it is amenable to alteration or modification for many years. Numerous studies have demonstrated that style affects learning success and achievement. In fact, studies of youth and adults who lose their vision indicate that after vision loss, adaptation to the use of alternative senses can be achieved more readily when sensory training exercises are focused specifically on individual senses. Those who were able to use this approach in the performance of tasks in their own homes and daily lives were able to make the mental adjustments with greater ease.

LEARNING PROGRESSION

Before trying to understand the specific problems in cognitive learning experienced by the child with a visual impairment, one must first distinguish between the terms used to discuss sensory learning and the type and quality of information received through the various senses. Whichever sense is used to gather information, the term *discrimination* refers to the ability to note the differences or likenesses within and among tastes, smells, sounds, touches, and visible objects or materials. For the baby, discriminations are gross in that there is attention to only a fraction of the available features at any time. With more and more sensory input, discrimination becomes increasingly refined. Recognition is an indication that what is sensed has been encountered previously. That memories and discriminations are being stored and recalled is one of the first indications that learning is taking place (Barraga, 1986).

Discrimination and recognition enable children to develop perceptions about what they see, hear, touch, smell, or taste; that is, when they are able to give meaning to, understand, and interpret incoming information through the senses, they are perceiving that information and are able to use it. Perception is an active process in that the learner is constantly seeking, attending to, and accepting information that is needed or desired and is ignoring sensory input that is useless or unnecessary (Foulke, 1968). Bower (1977) suggested that the sensory and perceptual systems may be coordinated rather than differentiated in the early months, but both systems seem to register modality specifics after perceptions become organized. Perceptual selection is determined by whether the information received fits with previously sorted data to give a different type or level of new understanding. Piaget (1973) referred to this process as "cognitive accommodation and assimilation." At this stage, the child has the capacity to seek and accept stimulation of one specific sense to the exclusion of other sensory input.

A minimum level of stimulation—a threshold—is required in each sensory system before the impulses can cross the connecting nerves and be directed to the appropriate receiving station in the brain. For example, stimulation of retinal cells by light rays leads to the transmission of impulses through the optic nerve directly to the occipital lobe of the brain. Sound waves arouse no activity in the retinal cells, but are directed through the auditory nerve to the nerve endings in the inner ear and on to the auditory reception center. It should be understood, however, that the intensity of the stimulation in any sense is not necessarily related to the strength of the sensation received in the brain. Physiological maturation and the consistent flowing of stimulation across the nerve fibers seem to affect the quality of sensory reception. For this reason, it is difficult—if not impossible—to determine accurate acuity measurements in any sense organ in the early years. Hence, acuity measurements alone do not give valid information about the usefulness of a particular sense for learning.

TACTUAL–KINESTHETIC SENSE

The tactual–kinesthetic (touch and movement) senses are often referred to as the skin senses and may be given less significance than they deserve. Active involvement with the environment and with the objects in it is dependent on effective use of the tactual–kinesthetic sense, which is stimulated by mechanical, thermal, electrical, and chemical stimuli. The hands and other parts of the body can push, press, grasp, rub, and lift in order to get information. The fingertips, however, provide the most distinct impressions, with a degree of accuracy exceeding even that of visual impressions (Fieandt, 1966). Measurement of the acuities of the skin senses is an almost impossible task; touch sensitivity varies over the body surface because different parts of the body have fewer or greater numbers of receptors. There is no way to separate kinesthetic information from touch information, which is why we use the term tactual–kinesthetic. Knowlton (1987) suggested that teachers can make students aware of efficient methods of acquiring tactual information by presenting simple learning tasks at first and then gradually proceeding to those requiring finer and more complex discriminations, a concept already emphasized in prebraille reading materials. When one is unable to use the visual sense, or when vision is severely impaired, information gained through the tactual–kinesthetic sense provides the individual with the most complete and reliable information. Getting one's hands on an object may be thought of as analogous to seeing the object with one's own eyes. Some theorists suggest that there is a developmental trend in the ability to use the proprioceptive and tactual–kinesthetic senses throughout the learning years (Gipsman, 1981).

AUDITORY SENSE

The auditory sense functions through nerve endings that are deeply embedded within the inner ear and surrounded by fluid. Stimulation through the sense of hearing is more difficult during the early months of life because the reception area for hearing is located deep within the center of the brain. Probably little usable information is available through the sense of hearing before 3 to 6 months of age (Fraiberg et al., 1969).

Although infants may show involuntary responses to sound, actual discrimination and recognition of sounds are not possible until several months after birth. Hearing acuity is related to the vibration of receptor cells in the cochlea caused by the intensity of the sound waves traveling through air and fluid, the frequency of vibrations, and the masking effects of the environment. There can be no fixed unchanging level of sensitivity of the auditory system to any single sound or groups of sounds (Ludel, 1978). When the human voice at very close range provides pleasurable auditory sounds, infants may begin to note other sounds. Soon they begin to imitate sounds, especially the human voice, when encouraged by vocal play with adults. This imitation is an important process because information fed to the brain through the auditory sense forms the basis for future sound repertoires necessary for speech production and language development.

VISUAL SENSE

Because the visual sense provides a greater quantity and a more refined quality of information in a shorter period of time than does any other sense, vision is often thought to be the mediator between all other sensory input and is sometimes attributed with stabilizing the child's interaction with his or her world (Barraga, 1986). Most of what young children learn incidentally (without direction) is learned through the visual sense. For this reason, the most efficient use of any existing visual capacity is critically important for children with visual impairment, regardless of the degree of severity. When there is sufficient light to provide contrast between objects or to permit motion to be seen, there is potential for the child to use this visual information in meaningful ways. Visual acuity measurements are influenced by a wide variety of factors, such as the type of stimulus target, the light surrounding it, the distance from it, and the time needed to bring the target to focus and to respond. Unless these conditions are optimal, and the target is appropriate to the developmental level of the child, the acuity measurement may be irrelevant when considering children with an impairment in the visual system. The role of vision was summarized by Sonksen (1983) as "guardian of the personality, tutor of the senses, monitor of movement, and builder of concepts" (p. 88).

OLFACTORY AND GUSTATORY SENSES

The olfactory and gustatory senses react more readily to chemical qualities in the environment, about which little is known; thus, thresholds and acuities cannot even be estimated at this time. The information received through the sense of smell may be very different from the information received through the sense of taste, even in response to the same stimulus. Thus, these two senses may give conflicting and confusing information, especially when they are involved simultaneously. The gustatory sense (without the use of olfaction) provides little specific information about flavor but gives a wider range of information about texture, contour, and size through the tip of the tongue and the sides of the mouth. The tip of the tongue is thought to have the most sensitive of all nerve endings in the body. In fact, people have even been able to read braille quite efficiently with the tip of the tongue. For teachers, the overriding consideration is not the sensitivity or acuity measurement of any sense but whether the child can respond to selected sensory stimulation and receive and interpret its meaning for use in learning and functioning.

The senses probably do not provide isolated bits of data, but the extent and manner in which information received through a single sense is transferred to another sense have not yet been determined. Some research indicates that attempting to use two senses simultaneously is inhibitory because of the interaction between them. Anater (1980) found that auditory information presented simultaneously with haptic information (information gained through touch) did not interfere with storage or recall of the information acquired through touch. Apparently, haptic information is processed independently of auditory interference. Possibly, children can translate information through one sensory channel into another modality for storing and thinking, but they do not need to in order to remember it. Regardless of the unsettled controversies about multisensory learning and intermodal transposition of information, there is little question that every available sense needs to be used by children who have impairments in any one or more of the other senses. If the available senses are not developed, learning is likely to be fragmented and inaccurate.

TACTUAL LEARNING

The progression of sequential learning is similar for all the senses. In children with visual impairments, however, greater attention may need to be given to a task-analyzed approach to presentation of the skills in smaller increments and in an orderly progression. Early studies suggest that children's development in tactual discrimination follows a pattern of using large-to-fine hand movements (whole hand to fingertips), from the early use of active touch to the later use of passive touch, and from simple to more complex. Later studies have provided more definitive information about the tactual, kinesthetic, and haptic systems, and their effectiveness in making discrete discriminations and recognitions of objects and materials with different characteristics.

When studying 20 children with blindness at each of three grade levels from kindergarten through second grade, Kershman (1976) was able to identify the following hierarchical order in which tactual skills were acquired by this group:

1. Large solid geometric shapes
2. Flat figures (puzzle pieces) smaller than geometric shapes
3. Embossed-dot geometric figures smaller than flat figures
4. Raised-dot figures
5. Braille figures

Heller (1985, 1989) found that people who had never had vision were as efficient in tactile pattern perception as those who had been blinded, leading him to conclude that visual experience might not be necessary for tactile perception. Familiarity with braille did not seem to guarantee good performance with tactile pictures, although tactile skills and tactual perceptual experience did have some effect. He had concluded earlier that simultaneous use of vision and touch by people with low vision seemed to enhance recognition of embossed patterns; he suggested that persons with severe low vision use their vision to guide their tactual exploration.

When discussing the intelligent hand, haptics was defined by Klatzky and Lederman (1988) as a "perceptual system incorporating inputs from multiple sensory systems" (p. 121). They postulated that both tactile and kinesthetic systems were involved, including skin, muscles, and joints. They considered haptics as an encoding device in its own right and not simply a poor substitute for vision. In an earlier study, Klatzky, Lederman, and Reed (1987) found that haptics were able to identify specific characteristics of objects in this order: shape, hardness, texture, and size. Klatzky, Lederman, and Metzger (1985) called touch an "expert system," compared with a sensory substitution system for the deaf, citing the Tadoma method of understanding speech as evidence that tactual systems can process complex spatio-temporal patterns at rates close to those of auditory speech perception.

Millar (1985) was concerned about the perception of complex patterns by touch, especially for those who would be reading braille. She concluded that perception of global outlines was not the basis of fast perception of dot patterns by touch (braille). The production or perception of outline shapes did not seem to be related in any way to reading efficiency in terms of rate of reading. One possibility might be that the important features of touch perception are not shape features, but rather depend on dot density relations, an idea suggested by some of the very early braille recognition studies.

Some children who are blind or who have profound low vision may resist touching objects and so are said to be tactile defensive. According to Mamer (1995), they may be only tactile selective; they may resist touching unusual textures or unfamiliar shapes. Careful presentation of selected objects may be necessary, such as presenting fur rather than feathery objects, or putting the fingertips rather than the palm of the hand on objects. Other possibilities are rolling the body over objects, or touching objects with the feet or the back of the hand. Touching objects in water, another presentation option, gives an entirely different sensation.

Let us use Carlos as an example as we discuss some of the above conclusions in light of what is known to be the sequence of development in tactual learning. This approach might be useful to teachers as they plan prereading programs for children who are blind.

Awareness and Attention

Tactual–kinesthetic development begins with awareness and attention to differences in shapes, hardness, texture, and size, as well as temperatures, vibrating surfaces, and materials of various consistencies. As Carlos holds objects in his hands, pressing and lifting them, he becomes aware that most of them are shaped differently, that some are rough and some are smooth, that some are heavy and some are light, and that he can mash a few of them, but that many are hard to the touch. When he plays with such materials as clay and dough, he begins to understand that there are different consistencies. Putting his hands and body in water of varying temperatures, and moving himself and objects in water or in sand, make him aware that substances are not all alike and do not all behave in the same way. It can be said that he is attending to the quality of the tactual information (Griffin & Gerber, 1982). With students who are blind, the preference for specific textures, which is shown very early in life, seems to influence the accuracy of their discrimination (Zimmerman, 1985).

As they touch objects that vibrate and those that do not, they learn that some provide stimulation and others do not. Children who are blind learn that they receive information from objects and at the same time are able to alter and adapt some objects through tactual–kinesthetic handling, whereas they are unable to change others in any way. This beginning level of tactual learning is especially important for children with multiple impairments to assist them in learning safety and survival skills necessary for their daily living. Of course, as these explorations are taking place, an adult needs to be vocalizing the concept words that are appropriate to the experiences.

Structure and Shape

The second level of tactual–kinesthetic understanding relates to knowledge of the basic structure and shape of objects encountered. By moving his hand across objects, grasping and holding many shapes, and manipulating objects of various sizes, Carlos acquires information about protrusions and indentations, as well as general contour and variations in size and weight. Interaction for maximum learning during this stage is best achieved through well-known objects that are part of his daily life, such as bars of soap, cups, plates, glasses, shoes, and socks. As Carlos discriminates objects, it becomes appropriate to introduce language to teach recognition of specific things. Cupping his hands around something gives him a bit of gross information about it; moving his hands around the object and tracing the shape of it gives him successive information about the variations to enhance recognition by name. This early handling and exploring might help isolate distinctive components of objects, discriminate likenesses and differences, and "provide a means for mental reconstruction of the objects" (Simpkins, 1979b, p. 100). Again, adult direction and discussion of objects and actions will hasten learning and help him clarify questions. At the same time, he is increasing his expressive language as he interacts verbally with adults or even another child.

The Relation of Parts to the Whole

Once Carlos is able to recognize simple, everyday objects by name, the next level of tactual–kinesthetic perception is possible. Whole objects that can be taken apart and put back together will help him learn the relationship of parts to the whole. At this point, it is important that he manipulate actual three-dimensional objects, such as toy cars that can be taken apart and put together, blocks that fit together, and household objects that have parts to be assembled, such as an unplugged mixer or food processor. Putting lids on pans, keys in locks, and screwdrivers into heads of screws are examples of object manipulation relating parts to wholes. These activities also foster concepts of mental space because "spatial concepts are internalized ideas based on actions" (Simpkins, 1979a, p. 86).

Grouping objects according to texture is another appropriate skill to learn. For example, Carlos's mother might present him with clothes that have the same texture, silverware that is all alike, blocks of the same texture, and buttons that feel alike. Learning would focus on differences in size, length, and weight of objects, and the uses to be made of them. Such activities increase skill in using the hands in manual inspection to detect specific cues for identification. Concurrently, Carlos becomes aware that he can exercise control over objects and make them work in desired ways. Through this handling, he begins to form concepts of groups and categories. Practice in making finer and finer discriminations and maintaining the ability to recognize parts and wholes of objects prepares the child who is blind for more complex tactual–kinesthetic learning related to academic work.

More complex manipulative experiences permit the child to develop tactual strategies for fitting parts to each other and into a recognized whole. Carlos developed such strategies because he was able to fit blocks together to complete a unified structure such as a toy house. Synthesizing tactual and haptic impressions permits the child to make accommodations to new elements touched and to assimilate these rapidly in relation to information already stored. Such concepts of physical characteristics are not easily perceived without vision. For students who have multiple impairments, this may be the highest level of tactual–kinesthetic information possible because they are less likely to be able to understand the more abstract concepts required to interpret graphic representations.

Graphic Representations

Presenting two-dimensional objects in graphic representation is the next stage in tactual–kinesthetic development. Such representations can be made with string or wire, or by using a tracing wheel or stylus on foil, plastic, or paper. The graphic representation of a real object might bear little tactual resemblance to the actual thing, and what is perceived might not fit with previously stored information. The spatial arrangement in a graphic representation is often quite unlike the spatial perspectives gained by handling the three-dimensional object. For this reason, it is useless and confusing to present any two-dimensional replications unless the real three-dimensional object is well known and has been handled many times. Even then, it might be necessary to accompany the graphic representation with the actual object at the first exposure to graphic forms. Approaching the presentations in this manner helps to minimize missed or distorted concepts. Selecting simple structural patterns such as geometric forms, which can be handled by the children while they examine the two-dimensional graphics, permits the children to gain successive tactual impressions gradually. As fingertips and muscles move in certain patterns, the children learn to associate the real object and the flat representation. For example, once a child recognizes round objects or forms easily, then various sizes of roundness can be presented graphically for the child to examine. Carlos has not yet reached this stage, but gradually increasing his experiences to include many shapes and structural forms will provide the basic experiences necessary for later learning (Barraga, Dorward, & Ford, 1973).

Such graphic replications as raised lines, curves, simple geometric forms, and object outlines of very well-known objects should be introduced slowly. It is important to provide only one piece of information at a time and to ensure that the concept is not confused by focusing on a less important aspect of the object, (e.g., the hole rather than the doughnut itself). Once the basic information has been interpreted, then each additional element can be added in successive graphic representations. For example, if one is going to prepare material for a child to perceive the human figure tactually, the first step would be to present a straight line and seek the child's understanding of the relationship of the line to the straight postural position of the human body. Adding a circle for the head would be the next step; then one would add lines (both straight and angular) to represent arms and legs, emphasizing the contrast between the straight lines of the body and the roundness of the head. Adding lines to represent fingers and toes would complete the figure. In contrast, if the child were given the entire graphic of the body at one time it could be very confusing. This confusion is termed *tactual noise* (Hammill & Crandell, 1969).

Also appropriate at this time is to teach children to make their own graphic drawings. As they make a line with a tracing wheel or with a tool on a piece of heavy aluminum foil or on a raised-line drawing board (heavy plastic on a hard rubber mat), children begin to realize how the hand and arm moves in order to make certain lines or forms. Making pictures that they can feel with their own hands is exciting for children, and this excitement provides motivation to examine everything on paper or in books that is tactually perceivable. This desire and skill prepares them for understanding abstract tactual representations, such as maps of floor plans or room arrangements or even maps for mobility (Bentzen & Peck, 1979; Easton & Bentzen, 1980; Fletcher, 1981).

Braille Symbols

The highest level of tactual–kinesthetic development is discrimination and recognition of symbols in the form of braille characters that denote letters, words, and eventually stories of the child's own experiences. Symbol recognition through the visual sense requires a high level of visual coding and association, but the tactual discrimination and recognition of symbols in the form of braille characters is an even more abstract level of perceptual–cognitive association. Children who are totally blind not only must recognize the symbols tactually, which in itself is a high-order task, but also must interpret their meanings in relation to other surrounding braille characters and in the context of the material being read. Each braille symbol is temporal in nature and can be perceived only when the fingertip is touching it. This places a burden on tactual–kinesthetic memory and requires the child to make immediate decisions in relation to recognition, memory, association, and interpretation (Harley, Henderson, & Truan, 1979).

If Carlos's early preschool experiences continue to provide a wide variety of tactual–kinesthetic exposure and manipulation, then his readiness for academic learning through reading will be more advanced than that of a child who did not have preschool activities that provided the appropriate development in learning through touch. If the child who is blind has not reached a high level of tactual–kinesthetic perception before entering prereading programs, the teacher's role may be quite different from that which is normally expected in a school setting, because braille reading would need to be deferred. The appropriate experiences for developing perceptual skills to the refined stage of symbol recognition need to become part of the child's readiness curriculum and, in rare instances, require several years before the child is ready to begin learning more formal types of academic skills, such as reading. However, with the new federal mandates for preschool programs, by the age of 3 years the likelihood of this occurring should be eliminated in the near future.

Such mechanical skills as hand movement, finger position, finger dexterity, wrist flexibility, light finger touch, and tactile perception and discrimination have been identified as precursors to efficient braille reading (Wormsley & D'Andrea, 1997). Although learning to read braille is much more mental than physical, the mechanics of tracking and the lightness of touch are important skills for the child to develop (Mangold, 1978).

The tactual-reading process is more complex than the visual-reading process because of the numerous braille characters (63 possible combinations in the 6-dot cell) and because of the contractions used in embossed material in the abbreviated Grade 2 braille found in school texts, magazines, and other materials. Many braille symbols have multiple uses, and the interpretation of their meaning depends on their relationship to other characters; their position in the cell; and the initial, medial, or final position within the word or sentence. Braille symbols representing the same letter or word may be different within a single sentence; hence, decision making in braille reading requires a high level of ability in cognitive abstraction. Only those children who have achieved the mental flexibility and processing necessary for this task can be efficient in tactual reading as a primary means of learning (Harley et al., 1979). Children who are functioning below average mentally may learn to recognize letters, and safety or single-object words, but may not be good readers of running text unless special materials are prepared. The braille symbols should be introduced gradually: At first, only those standing for a single letter are appropriate; later, symbols representing whole words can be incorporated. Thorough understanding and recognition of each group of symbols is imperative before adding a more complex group. There is little evidence to suggest that discrete tactual symbols are useful with children who have multiple disabilities.

Fortunately, *Patterns*, the only beginning reading series designed and written specifically for braille readers, is now available from the American Printing House for the Blind (APH) (Caton, Bradley, & Pester, 1982). Teacher reports indicate that the braille-reading efficiency of students who began at the readiness level with this series shows the series' value to both students and teachers, although some disadvantages have been reported by a few teachers. Ongoing research is leading to refinement of this series, with additional worksheets becoming available on a continuing basis. Work is being completed on a series for adventitiously blinded children, youth, and adults.

Children with severe and profound low vision, such as Lucy, also need tactual–kinesthetic learning. Even though Lucy has some visual capacity, and she has begun to use it early in life, her development of touch needs to be given the same attention that was given to Carlos. Touching and feeling objects will help to clarify and support the unclear images she receives visually. Maximum haptic development in the child with low vision will unify all sensory input and enable the child to form more stable concepts.

Decisions about reading media for children who have low vision need careful consideration. Some children who, unlike Lucy, do not indicate by their behavior that they are truly visual learners may need to have the opportunity to learn to read using both ink print and braille (Mangold & Mangold, 1989; Mangold & Roessing, 1982; Rex, 1989). After learning to read both print and braille, some learners with low vision will show a definite preference for one medium, whereas others may continue to use both media throughout their school years, depending on lighting, availability of material, and fatigue factors. In fact, reading both ink print and braille could increase overall learning efficiency for some students; teachers have observed that average and above average learners use both media with little difficulty (Barraga, 1980c). Below average learners and most students with multiple impairments who have usable vision will do better concentrating on visual reading (when possible) because of the abstract nature of the braille code. Decisions must be made on an individual basis according to the physical and mental characteristics of each student, the age and grade level, and the stability or instability of the eye condition. Students who need ultrahigh magnification to read any visual material must use braille for primary learning, but continue to read ink print when the devices are available to them. Some guidelines and assessment procedures to assist in making objective decisions regarding reading media have been developed by APH and can be obtained upon request.

In the case of Ching Lan, who was losing her vision rapidly, previous visual learning and her understanding of visual images made the transition to loss of vision less traumatic. She did have to learn when she could continue to rely on vision or when she needed to supplement her available vision with auditory cues, tactual cues, or both.

Although Michael showed himself to be a completely visual child, his learning difficulties posed some of the same problems for him as severe low vision might for another child. He could see at close range but had problems understanding what he was seeing, especially if it was not known to him or was of a complex nature. Even with his moderately low vision, he seemed to use touch as a means of confirming what he was seeing. His speed of visual processing might be likened to that of a child who had much poorer vision and was slow because of trying to see more clearly or to integrate the fragments into a meaningful whole.

AUDITORY DEVELOPMENT AND LEARNING

Some have suggested that the ears of a person who is blind are comparable to the eyes of a sighted person for providing information. There is some truth to this, but one must exercise caution in accepting this idea without qualification. Because of the nature of the auditory sense and the continuous presence of inescapable sound in the environment, the human being has little physical control over auditory input but instead must learn to exercise mental control—selective perception. This masking of sound occurs through a process that is at first unconscious, and then later becomes conscious attending to sound, according to its meaningfulness to the individual. The mere presence of sound does not necessarily mean that everyone listens to or hears the same sound.

Although sound and auditory input are primary sources of contact with and orientation to the environment for children who lack the ability to see in the distance, excessive auditory stimulation of meaningless sounds may evoke verbal repetition or echolalic responses to sound and can actually inhibit the use of meaningful auditory input as a means of learning. Auditory stimulation for the sake of producing noise must not be confused with meaningful auditory input translatable into learning experiences; for example, constant sound from a radio or television might interfere with auditory development in children with severe visual impairment who are not engaged visually with objects or people in their environment. Parents and teachers should direct specific attention to the sequence in auditory development, the use of hearing as a primary learning medium, the promotion of efficient listening skills, and the relation of auditory learning to language development as instruments for thinking.

The sequential pattern for the formation of auditory perceptions and concepts (Gleason, 1984) is similar to that of tactual–kinesthetic and visual development, although the appropriate application of these sequential ideas to the child with visual impairments is clearly different for hearing than for touching or seeing.

Environmental Sounds

The first level of learning through the sense of hearing is the awareness of sound at the reflexive level, in which responses are unintentional and cannot be taught. This is soon followed by the attention and alerting level to specific sounds. The infant might be both soothed and startled by some sounds, whereas other noises appear to have little effect. Part of the explanation for this is that only sounds of great intensity, in either volume or pitch, penetrate the infant's auditory receptive system; this is actually a built-in protective device because the infant has not yet learned to mask disturbing or confusing sounds.

To bring soothing sound into awareness, the child with visual impairment should have the opportunity to hear many pleasing and comforting sounds, such as soothing music and soft human voices. These sounds create an unconscious awareness and attachment to the environment, in addition to conveying affective feelings of warmth and comfort. Even in a young infant, before attention is given to specific sounds, the human voice is a sound that provides a feeling of communication and attachment, probably substituting for facial expressions and gestures, which do not exist for children who are blind. Without exposure to the human voice in the first few months of life, children who are totally blind may feel as if they are living in total isolation (Fraiberg et al., 1969). Continuous and appropriate vocal stimulation in the early months may help children who are blind learn to use this auditory contact in much the same way that sighted children use eye movements to follow the actions of those around them. Placing bells or other pleasant sound producers on objects the infant touches or on another person helps to stabilize the idea that there are many sounds within the environment. In the early months, it is appropriate to urge the infant to listen to specifically pleasing sounds when being moved about by someone else.

Specific Sounds

Although the infant who is blind might show awareness of sound and attend to a few specific sounds, the second level of development—response to and localization of specific sounds—probably does not occur before approximately 4 to 6 months of age (Fraiberg et al., 1969). Responses to specific sounds may be in the form of smiling, turning the head, listening intently and silently, and, later, attempting to imitate vocally. This behavior suggests that the child is beginning to maintain contact with specific sounds and to localize the source of the sound. Turning the head in response to specific sounds indicates that "listening to hear" (Piaget, 1973) is the intent. Also, at this stage, ear–hand coordination (again, comparable to eye–hand coordination in the sighted child) is possible, and can be taught by using sound toys, music, speech, and distinct environmental sounds. The manipulation of objects simply to hear sound may be observed, indicating the beginning of recognition that a certain hand action produces a particular sound. Knowledge that sound can be associated with an object implies that the baby can be taught to reach for sound, such as searching for a toy or moving toward an appealing sound, which occurs at approximately 1 year of age.

Sound Discrimination

Discrimination among familiar household and outdoor sounds, voices, and musical tones is the next level in auditory development for the child with visual impairment. By this time, babies may move in relation to household sounds to find their sources. Parents should encourage this activity and permit the child to explore sources by attending, localizing, and moving toward the sound until tactual contact is made. This enables them to note the variations in frequency, intensity, rhythm, and duration of auditory signals. Attention can be focused on relevant sounds, such as the telephone, doorbell, washing machine, or dishwasher.

At this discrimination level, it is also appropriate to name the sources of sounds, which establishes the knowledge that sounds come from different objects in the home, and permits children to associate sounds with things they will hear every day and can touch. By noting the differences in environmental sounds and voices, children are learning to connect their own actions, and those of others, with particular sounds. As these associations become more frequent and refined, they may be able to make discoveries for themselves by attending to sounds as orientation cues for movement, a skill necessary for independent travel in ensuing years.

It is important that parents or caregivers name the source of the sound and encourage vocal mimicking. Such guidance in auditory development permits children to organize their behavior in relation to a specific goal or their movement in relation to sounds. For example, children with severe visual impairments who begin to recognize people by the differences in their voices or their footsteps may actually associate the voices or footsteps with the anticipation of an event. One child with profound low vision, upon hearing her father's footsteps, learned to say her first connected words, "go-car," associating the footsteps with the anticipation of going for a ride.

In this discrimination stage, sound begins to replace vision for perceiving distance relationships and might also serve as a primary motivation for movement as children are learning to walk. Movement, in relation to sound, can also provide (perhaps unconsciously) incidental development in the use of sound echoes to indicate the presence of objects. The level of sound as children approach an object becomes a referent for distance, in addition to guiding direction in movement. The greater the range and variety of sound from sources children can move toward and also touch, the more rapidly discrimination and familiarity of sound will proceed, and the more stable the base for interpreting sound sources will become.

Sound Recognition and Association

As words begin to have meaning to children, the next level of auditory development—recognition of sounds related to specific words and connected speech—is possible. As children are learning that objects have names, they may also learn that sounds and their own actions have words to describe them. To assist in this process of recognition and association, parents should talk about their child's movements and actions, interpret in words what is happening when there is a response to certain noisemakers, and clearly differentiate between the sounds of words. Children may soon respond to tonal variations by smiling when they hear happy words and praises, and by sobering when scolded. There is some indication that imitative speech (when hearing words and jingles) occurs more rapidly in children with visual impairments than in sighted children because, without the full use of the visual sense, attending to auditory input develops acuity and a greater sensitivity to sound. There is no indication that children with impaired vision have any greater capacity for auditory perception than do sighted children, but their constant use and heavy reliance on the auditory sense permits development to proceed rapidly.

During this vocal period, children with visual impairments are developing linguistic strategies that will be the basis for their speech and language development during the school years. Mistakes in the use of personal pronouns, confusion in the use of *I*, and lack of the use of the verb *see* have been noted in some children with little or no vision (McGinnis, 1981). Adverbs of location and prepositions are used with less frequency. Adults need to exercise care in the construction of their verbal explanations in order to minimize imitative errors.

It is important when children respond to sound that parents give them the opportunity to listen carefully without interruption and to touch the sound source whenever possible. If touching is not possible, parents should provide verbal interpretation of the object. Talking to children with visual impairments as they move and play is more important than talking to sighted children, because the only way the children with visual impairments have to interpret their own actions is by having others talk to them about what they are doing. As mentioned earlier, passive auditory stimulation from radio or television without meaningful verbal discourse with adults often results in echolalic speech or verbalizations that have no real meaning and do not contribute to cognitive development. Playing word games, reading nursery rhymes, and singing action songs while holding or moving children can strengthen sound association and memory.

Comprehension and Interpretation of Verbal Instructions

The next stage of auditory perceptual development involves an understanding of words and phrases so that children respond to instructions of increasing complexity and length, from one-part commands to two- and three-part directions that are related. They then learn to respond to instructions of actions that are unrelated (e.g., "Please close the door and then sit down." or "Put your toy on the shelf and hand me a tissue please"). During this period, listening may be taught most easily by focusing children's attention on the action they are being asked to perform. When they have achieved the ability to filter out irrelevant or meaningless sounds, and to attend to musical themes and to speech that provides directions and instructions, children may begin to formulate their own speech for feedback to themselves and to others. Adults will recognize discrepancies in meaning as well as inaccuracies that have occurred because children hear without being able to verify by looking. For example, adults can play games that focus on identifying voices of specific people by questioning, "Who is that?" Adults also can make tape recordings of environmental and household sounds and ask children to talk about what is being heard.

Translating vocal instructions into purposeful actions is one of the highest levels of auditory–perceptual processing, and it is a critical skill if children with visual impairments are to work in groups with sighted children in preschool. It is also a major determinant of academic success for children with visual impairments who are a part of a regular class in a school setting. Given the proper opportunities to develop through the previously mentioned stages, children with visual impairments should be able to respond and carry out actions according to instructions given to them. Young children who are unable to do this should be given greater attention to determine whether they understand the meanings of the words they hear in relation to their own movement and actions. Children with poor body image and the inability to understand how to control body actions may have greater hesitancy in acting on instructions. Unless children can translate auditory input into meaningful options or associations that can be used immediately, there is little indication that auditory input is being related to mental processing. For children with visual impairments, the cognitive translation of auditory language provides mental stimulation that may be equivalent to sighted children's motivation through visual–perceptual skills. Children form images in relation to spoken language. This imagery creates a basis for recall and for higher level abstract thinking when the words are no longer heard. For example, when instructions are given to move the body to a specific position or to walk in a particular pattern, children have to think about what has been heard and translate this into body actions. Later, when the same or similar instructions are heard, movement patterns associated with the words are remembered. Michael gave evidence of some problems in this area by his slow actions; fortunately, he had enough vision to help him to confirm what he was hearing or to imitate what he could see. Hall (1981) said that children with visual disabilities often form fewer and less detailed images of their environment, unless they have experienced actions with their own bodies. Words that can be heard, felt, or experienced are concrete words and can be used as referents. Practice in translating what is heard into personal meaning may stimulate the search for meaning in other spoken messages.

Auditory Skills and Listening in Learning

Once children with visual impairments enter regular classrooms, one of their primary channels for learning is hearing; consequently, achieving the highest level of auditory processing and listening efficiency is essential for further cognitive development. Paying attention to the outlined sequence in auditory development and perception will help adults avoid the mistaken assumption that simply because the child can hear, he or she is able to use listening efficiently for academic learning. Processing through the auditory sense without the preparatory perceptual skills is almost impossible.

Teaching listening skills is sometimes considered an important part of the educational program for students with visual impairments. For this training to be useful, students must be taught how to listen to something (Cobb, 1977; Gleason, 1984). How material is presented on tape or records is of crucial concern if aural learning is to be effective for students who must rely on it for the bulk of their information input, especially in high school and vocational programs.

Acquiring information tactually by reading braille is slower on the average than print reading or listening (Nolan, 1966). As students progress through school, they may find that auditory input is more efficient, especially for literature and history courses. How material is presented on tape is a factor in long periods of listening; for example, too slow a rate may cause the brain to "go to sleep," and the listener may lose attention more rapidly than when the reading rate is faster than normal. For some learners, attention wanders and processing is fragmentary when the reading rate is either too slow or too fast; the use of technology with variable speed adjustments has been helpful. Research in aural study systems (Nolan & Morris, 1973) and the perfection of reading machines with vocal output are changing the availability of printed material for students and those whose careers require constant reading.

VISUAL DEVELOPMENT AND LEARNING

Developing maximum visual–perceptual ability in children with visual impairments is of major importance because more than three fourths of all school-age students with visual limitations, even those who have other disabilities, have some usable vision. The tendency in the past to equate the extent of visual impairment with the individual's limitation in seeing has been found to have no basis in reality, and neither does the assumption that visual acuity has any relationship to the capacity for visual development or for actual visual functioning (Faye, 1984; Jose, 1992).

Another erroneous assumption is that children with impaired vision should be protected from eye strain and that using the eyes might in some way damage the vision that is present. Faye (1984) suggested that whatever vision a child has should be used to maximum capacity, which from a perceptual and learning point of view means that the more children look and use their vision, the more efficient they will be in functioning visually.

Vision is related not only to the structure and function of the eyes but also to the many parts of the visual system and brain, as well as other body systems. Figure 6.1 identifies the components of the total visual system and the particular function of each in relation to the entire process of visual interpretation. The physiological structures in

light enters EYE refracts rays that	focus on cells in RETINA where neural energy is generated	and transmitted along	nerve fibers in OPTIC NERVE to	reception area	in BRAIN where visual information is interpreted

FIGURE 6.1. Components of the visual system (capitalized words) and their functions in visual interpretation.

the eye, such as the pupil and the lens, facilitate or impede rays of light from reaching the sensitive retinal cells. The location and spread of the activated cells help determine the strength of the burst of energy sent along the optic nerve to the brain, where the person receives the electrical charges as fragments of visual information, organizes them into a visual image, and relates the image to messages received from the other senses for full interpretation.

In recent years, the patterns of visual development in children have been studied extensively and findings indicate that visual acuity, visual skills, and visual perception may progress at a faster rate than was previously thought. From a comprehensive review of the literature on vision (Barraga, Collins, & Hollis, 1977; Hall & Bailey, 1989) and more recent research (A. L. Corn, 1989; Hall, Kekelis, & Bailey, 1986; Heersema & Hof-Van Duin, 1990), a model of visual development can be proposed that begins with optical control, which leads to visual stimulation, which prepares for actual visual learning (see Figure 6.2). In addition, this model suggests the periods of optical and visual–perceptual development; concept development and maximum organization of visual imagery; and storage and recall of visual information. The model also incorporates aspects of concept development and periods of growth spurts in the brain. This model is derived from recent research that has studied the functioning of the visual system before birth and throughout life. An examination of this model permits the teacher, clinician, and rehabilitation professional to approximate the visual developmental age of the person with a visual impairment as it relates to the pattern of optical training, the nature of the function in visual stimulation, and the behaviors indicative of actual visual learning from which visual imagery and memory can be evaluated. Therefore, it enables them to develop visual goals and adaptations that will enhance learning.

How to promote the continuing development of the visual system and functional behaviors has been the concern of some investigations. For example, Hall et al. (1986) found that visual behaviors could be taught most effectively by concentrating on three: visual attending behaviors, which would include the refinement of optical skills using the eyes to focus in a variety of spatial areas; visual examining behaviors, which would be the equivalent of stimulating the use of vision with an array of objects, colors, shapes, and eventually pictures of the same things; and visually guided behaviors involving the motor system in reaching, grasping, manipulating, marking, assembling, and finally making choices from a selection of visual materials. These behaviors prepare the person to use vision for learning and making decisions about the appropriate responses to the multitude of visual stimuli encountered in the environment. Bell (1986) postulated that programs to ensure the stimulation of visual pathways led to the development of anatomically based compensatory neural mechanisms that foster the maximum development of the visual system. The sequence of visual behaviors and functions may be assumed to develop in a similar pattern for all children; however, the model shown in Table 6.1 uses visual age, rather than the usual chronological age, because this denotes the maturity of the visual system itself in regard to its functional control and the cognitive maturity needed to use the system for purposes of learning. Without stimulation, optical control and subsequent learning through vision cannot be accomplished.

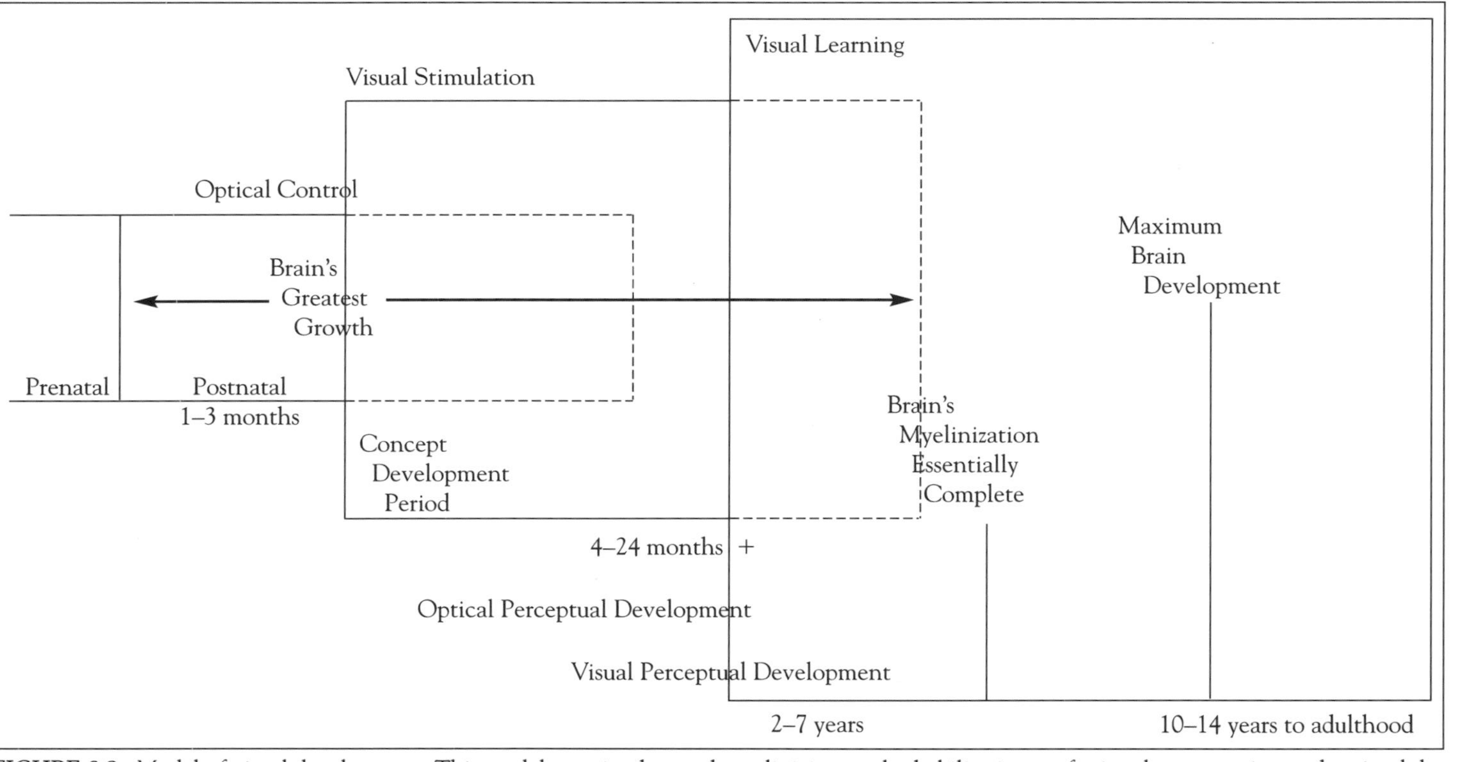

FIGURE 6.2. Model of visual development. This model permits the teacher, clinician, and rehabilitation professional to approximate the visual developmental age of the person with a visual impairment as it relates to the pattern of optical training; the nature of the function in visual stimulation; and behaviors indicative of actual visual learning from which visual imagery and memory can be evaluated.

TABLE 6.1
Sequence of Visual Behaviors and Functions

Visual Age	Optical	Stimulation	Learning
1 to 3 months	Focusing Fixating Tracking Convergence	High contrast, bright colors Complex patterns Moving objects Close to distant	 Discriminates faces, colors
3 to 7 months	Movements smoother Explores Acuity sharp Shifts eyes Eye–hand coordination	Small objects to reach Changes in facial expressions Suspended objects Face pictures Peek-a-boo Actions to imitate	Grasps, looks Imitates faces Manipulates objects Chooses Places objects Chooses faces Anticipates action Makes faces
8 to 12 months		Finger paints Looking and hiding games Expanded games Hidden objects	Makes marks Plays games Searches Initiates play Gives to others
1 to 2 years		More objects Picture books	Uses objects Matches objects Stacks blocks Scribbles Imitates actions
2 to 4 years		Geometric forms, colors Simple puzzles and shapes Crayons Pictures of forms Picture puzzles Magazines	Matches colors and forms Matches shapes and places Draws circles Matches form to picture Selects by name
5 to 7 years		Action pictures Complex scenes Abstract shapes Letters and words Signs, books in different styles Word-play games Chalk and pencils	Sequences Spatiality Copies Associates with pictures Names shapes of letters Perceives sameness Matches words Writes letters and words in all styles

Visual Skills

Such optical skills as fixation, tracking, focus, accommodation, and convergence are achieved by the majority of children with normal vision in their day-to-day functioning when they have a visually stimulating environment. However, the child with a visual impairment may have difficulty in developing these skills if the impairment is severe enough to interfere with normal visual scanning. When very little light can enter the eye or reach the nerve centers in the retina, muscular control may be difficult, especially when no image can be formed from the blur. Studies (Barraga, 1980a; Bell, 1986; Downing & Bailey, 1990; Hall & Bailey, 1989) have concluded that use of impaired vision can be taught, even in children with multiple disabilities. The earlier this stimulation and training is begun, the greater the likelihood that efficiency in use of vision will continue to improve for many years and facilitate overall mental development.

Several programs are available that present a step-by-step process to be followed from the earliest months of life to the time when the child with low vision (or the adult who begins to lose vision) can function visually at the highest possible level (Barraga, 1980a; Bell, 1986; Downing & Bailey, 1990; Erhardt, 1987; Goetz & Gee, 1987; Harrell & Akeson, 1987). Each program has some differences, but they all include a variety of stimulating materials for use in numerous environments, focusing on a multitude of visual responses, initiated behaviors, and visual–motor activities beginning with the very simple and gradually becoming more complex.

Although skillful use of the eyes might not, by itself, enhance visual learning, it certainly increases the possibility of perceptual development through the visual sense. Of course, actual seeing cannot occur until messages transmitted through the eyes are received in the brain and interpreted. Even when visual information is blurred, distorted, or incomplete, as long as the brain is able to combine the images with auditory and other sensory information, the person can use vision as a contributing sense in cognitive development. Medical specialists and educational researchers have shown that poor vision does not necessarily cause poor learning—what the brain is able to do with the visual information it receives determines how well the person will be able to function visually (Barraga, 1964; Bateman & Weatherall, 1967; Faye, 1984).

Visual–Perceptual Development in Students with Low Vision

The extent to which the impaired visual system will enhance the capacity for perceptual–cognitive development in individuals is virtually impossible to predict because an infant or young child may have "a recorded visual acuity of light perception and later show some useful vision" (Seidenberg, 1975, p. 118). For example, Lucy's only visual response at first was to bright light, but she later showed evidence of having limited vision at a distance and in some circumstances.

Barraga et al. (1977) and Rogers and Puchalski (1988) assumed that from the evidence available, learning through an impaired system occurs slowly, but follows the same sequential pattern as visual development in a normal system. However, the visual skills and perceptual organization are seldom, if ever, spontaneous or automatic in a system with an impairment other than a refractive error. The sequence of perceptual development may emerge quite unevenly and is influenced by such factors as type and extent of impairment, mental capacity, stimulation and encouragement to look, and numerous environmental factors, some of which may be adaptable whereas others are not within the control of the individual (Corn, 1985). A broad base of visual stimulation and a wide variety of looking skills are the keys to the refinement of more discrete skills because visual development is integrated with perceptual and cognitive learning.

Barraga and Collins (1979) presented a rationale for a program of visual development and learning for students with low vision. They identified in detail all the visual functions and skills necessary for maximum efficiency, specified the types of tasks compatible with the progression of perceptual–cognitive development, and discussed the pertinent considerations in visual environments. This rationale became an integral part of the publication *Program to Develop Efficiency in Visual Functioning* (Barraga & Morris, 1980). Since that time, others have adapted the ideas and applied them to specific children, detailed them in smaller learning increments, and designed sequences especially for children with multiple impairments, an increasing challenge that is now being addressed with greater frequency (Bell, 1986; Corn, A., 1989; Hall et al., 1986; Smith & Levak, 1996). Another volume was added to this program in 1998, titled *Design for Instruction for Learners with Developmental Delays* (Barraga, Morris, & Stallings, 1998).

As the population of children with visual impairments changes and a greater percentage of infants experience neurological or cognitive damage at or shortly after birth, careful attention must be paid to their visual development. Even though visual acuity may seem to be very poor in the first few months, rapidly change during the first year, and continue to develop to greater efficiency throughout early childhood, there is some indication that improvement may take place for many years after the early damage to the brain (Groenendaal & Hof-Van Duin, 1992). For this reason, visual stimulation must begin at an early age, and visual learning opportunities must be provided for many years, even into adulthood (Tavernier, 1993). Observation and interpretation of the visual behaviors of some children has determined that they may have both ocular and cortical impairment (Jan & Groenveld, 1993); some may not even appear blind, but have short visual attention spans and actually process little visual information.

Teachers must remind themselves constantly that learning through the visual sense can never exceed the overall level of individual perceptual–cognitive development, always a concern when working with students of any age with multiple disabilities. Although it is difficult to think of visual and mental age rather than chronological age when working with this population, if we do not, we tend to expect higher levels of visual functioning and present materials and activities far too complex for the level of mental understanding. Another factor to consider when working with students and youth with low vision is that although they may have usable vision, they may not have had the concentrated, visual learning activities needed at an early age to enable them to use their vision effectively. If this is the case, regardless of chronological age, we must concentrate on visual age, and begin with activities at the lowest level, so that visual images of forms, objects, pictures, and finally symbols, as outlined previously, can be learned in sequence.

When children with visual impairments, especially those with very low vision, enter school, they may need, as part of their readiness program, to spend a long period of time in visual–perceptual development before attempting visual reading material. With the increase in infant and preschool programs, as well as earlier identification of impairments, extended time spent in visual–perceptual development may not occur as frequently now as in the past, but it still deserves sensitive consideration. Visual–motor and eye–hand coordination seem to be areas in which some children with low vision have tended to function less efficiently. In fact, an item analysis of the performance of 112 students with low vision ages 5 to 20 revealed that the most frequently missed items on the *Diagnostic Assessment Procedure* (Barraga, 1980b) were those requiring motor skills (Berla, Rankin, & Willis, 1980). The use of the visual sense in students with severe visual disabilities was long neglected, but more than 20 years of intensive research and development have resulted in more programs and activities to enhance visual–perceptual development in children, youth, and adults with low vision.

Lucy, whose parents were told it was impossible to determine at her young age the extent that her visual capabilities might improve, is an example of a child with low vision who will probably need a longer period of readiness in visual activities designed specifically to acquaint her with print symbols and enable her to relate these to visual concepts she may have experienced in her preschool years. Consequently, the program will need to be stabilized and associated very gradually as she learns to use her vision for acquiring information in school and responding by writing, typing, or using the computer. This might also be the case for Michael because his learning difficulties, along with his moderate visual impairment, indicate that he will need smaller increments and more time to understand and process symbols.

Because Ching Lan is gradually losing her vision, she will need help and guidance in continuing to retain her visual imagery and in recognizing objects that she can no longer see clearly, although she has retained visual memories of many objects. Children who are losing their vision will retain functioning for a much longer period if they are encouraged to use their vision and are helped to interpret and make decisions about the unclear visual information they receive. If the vision loss is gradual, monoculars for distance viewing, and other optical devices, such as magnifiers for near use, may be of assistance, but the time will eventually come when even these are of little value.

Children seem to use different senses in varying degrees and for their own purposes, even when all senses are intact. Some children with rather good vision look very little, whereas others with very limited vision look quite intently. Nevertheless, cognitive development follows a more stable pattern when a child has use of all available senses; only when all senses are used to their maximum capability can learning and cognitive development reach the optimum for each person. Whether the individual is totally blind, has very low vision, or has only moderately impaired vision, there need to be opportunities to explore the use of all senses and to develop a unique style of learning that gives the greatest quantity and the highest quality of usable information for cognitive development. For example, the use of optical devices may give a person with low vision the ability to exercise greater control over the visual environment by modifying the visual perspective in order to receive a higher quality of information to process cognitively.

COGNITIVE DEVELOPMENT

Piaget (1973) suggested that there are many object classes that children who are blind cannot act on perceptually (through vision, hearing, or muscular motion) but must simply know in terms of the symbolic auditory language. This may be a factor in a problem referred to earlier as verbalism, that is, using words without understanding their meanings. Studies of cognitive development in children who are blind (Anderson & Fisher, 1986; Dodds, 1983; Gottesman, 1976; Hall, 1983; Higgins, 1973; Stephens & Grube, 1982; Wan-Lin & Tait, 1987; Witkin, Oltman, Chase, & Friedman, 1971) have indicated some lag in various aspects of abstract thinking, such as conservation, mental rotation, and reasoning. Problems also have been identified in the areas of spatial concepts and nominal realism, possibly because of the relatively limited manner in which students who are blind can experience the world, which influences their understanding of objects, spatial features, and the language expressing their mental imagery (Anderson, 1984; Pereira, 1990). Boldt (1969) found that cognitive development in children who are blind developed similarly to that of sighted children; however, the ability of children who are blind to process complex auditory material suffered a tremendous lag until about age 16 or 18, placing their development several years behind that of sighted students. This finding exemplifies the fact that hearing and verbalizing appropriate words does not mean that the words are completely understood cognitively. Numerous studies have found that children who are blind are less able than their sighted peers of comparable age and intellectual ability to define the meaning of vocabulary words on intelligence tests. A broad generalization suggests that children who are blind may know and use a word, but are unable to express a cause-effect relationship, possibly because of the lack of a clear mental image to use as a referent (Stephens, Simpkins, & Wexler, 1976).

Some have suggested that children who are blind, and some children with severe visual impairments, operate from a different database, depending on experiences and verbal explanations offered by others. An anecdotal interview with a person who was gifted and blind reported by Whitmore and Maker (1985) included the following statement: "The teachers paid more attention to teaching how to use equipment than how to think about the process, particularly in math; computation skills took precedence over the concepts involved" (pp. 83–84). The suggestion followed that students who are blind need to learn underlying principles first, followed by the individual skills and strategies needed to apply the principles in meaningful ways.

There needs to be clarification between academic knowledge (e.g., of how to spell or calculate square root, of the names of presidents, or of theory of relativity) and practical knowledge (e.g., how to balance a checkbook, how to read a help wanted advertisement, of what *RSVP* means, or how to make hotel reservations) when discussing learning (Corn & Bishop, 1984). These authors emphasized that practical knowledge is what enables an adult to live successfully in society. Using the *Test of Practical Knowledge* (TPK) (Wiederholt & Larsen, 1983), Corn and Bishop found that adolescents with visual impairments in their small sample of 116 students performed poorly when compared with sighted norms in areas of personal, social, and occupational skills and knowledge. Interestingly enough, the students with low vision (those who were legally but not totally blind) seemed to have more difficulty in acquiring the knowledge than did their peers who were totally blind (Corn & Bishop, 1984). This may have been related to factors other than the amount of vision, but perhaps teachers spend more time making sure that students who are blind have skills and knowledge that teachers think is important in daily living skills, and make the unwarranted assumption that students with low vision need less direct teaching because they learn by using their limited vision. Corn and Bishop concluded that a new test designed specifically for students with visual impairments needs to be developed to complement the TPK, and that further research in this area is indicated.

It appears that children without vision, or with very little vision, cannot fully develop many concepts unless carefully planned teaching strategies counterbalance the perceptive privation. Because of limited visual input, students with severe visual impairments construct reality differently than sighted students, although not necessarily with a deficit (Sanctin & Simmons, 1977). Obviously, this difference will affect problem-solving and reasoning strategies. However, lessons designed to teach logical reasoning can be very helpful and should be a part of the specialized curriculum for students with visual impairments (Sicilian, 1988; Stephens & Grube, 1982). This logical–reasoning approach might help to minimize some of these deficits in practical knowledge by the high school years.

Concepts Applied to Children

A few studies have shown that youth who are blind have superior ability to sustain attention and to process material auditorily with ease. However, no general conclusions would be applicable to all students who are blind; the individual characteristics of each must be considered in relation to previous background and experience. The evidence presented in the word picture of Carlos suggests that his auditory–perceptual abilities were in keeping with his level of development, as demonstrated by his awareness of footsteps indicating someone's arrival, his ability to understand verbal instructions and to act accordingly, and his efficiency in localizing sound sources to facilitate easy movement in familiar surroundings. When Carlos reaches school age, there is good reason to believe that his auditory–perceptual abilities and listening skills will have developed to a level that will permit him to expand and refine them for use in mobility training and as one of his primary means of learning and interacting.

Lucy, who has questionable visual ability, will need as much careful attention to auditory–perceptual development as is given to tactual–kinesthetic and visual development. Because of the probability of limited vision throughout her school years, she will need to use auditory learning as a supplemental, if not her primary, sense for academic and environmental learning. Auditory perception and careful listening might assist her in clarifying the incomplete or blurred visual impressions she receives. Obviously, her low vision will limit or preclude the use of vision as a primary learning sense, and Lucy will be required to rely on audition as the distance sense. Sound localization will be her major safety clue in movement and travel outside her home.

Ching Lan, because of her spontaneous adjustment to the gradual loss of sight, has no doubt already begun to use sound as a key referent in her environmental interactions. As visual loss continues, her parents and teachers should direct her toward refining auditory localization and listening skills to help her bridge the transfer from visual learning to tactual and auditory learning. She must be taught to use some caution in movement, which will help her to be sensitive to her own safety.

Efficient braille reading will develop slowly for Ching Lan, during which time she will rely heavily on listening and auditory learning as she perfects her tactile skills. In her educational program, she will probably use both tactual and auditory learning; they will complement each other and enable her to continue her achievements in schoolwork and related activities.

Michael may find it difficult to attend to and process all sensory stimuli because of his learning problems, but as he matures and teachers and family are constantly sensitive to the need for orderly, small increments of new learning, he can be expected to improve his attention span, and he will find it easier to process sensory information with additional speed. Time and patience, on Michael's part and on the part of adults, may facilitate his understanding of his own style of learning, and eventually enable him to organize his world in his best interest so as to reduce the possible confusion he might experience with uncontrolled stimuli bombarding him through all senses.

SUMMARY

In recent years, more attention has been given to the role of the senses in learning and cognitive development for all children, especially for children who are visually impaired. Every child with a visual disability needs to be encouraged in the early years, and perhaps throughout the school years and adult life, to support and confirm information being received and to search out additional information through the use of all other senses. The tactual sense keeps a person in direct contact with the concrete world and provides a variety of information that is not available visually and that lacks clarity and precision when experienced only through the sense of hearing.

All children with moderate to severe visual impairments, and certainly those who are totally blind, learn to rely heavily on auditory input as a primary means of alerting them to what might not be seen and of keeping them in contact with distance information that will never be available to them visually. For people who are congenitally totally blind, auditory information will be the primary guide to movement, even in familiar environments, and will provide cues for safe movement in new environments and eventually in independent travel. Similarly, individuals who have lost vision after having used vision as the primary learning and functioning sense need to develop auditory sensitivities that will alert them to every sound emanating from the environment, and they need to use sound clues as a valuable means of associating previously seen information with what now can only be heard.

Teachers and others might find it valuable to give greater attention to reasoning activities related to academic facts and computations to foster maximum cognitive development in all students with visual impairments. In an ever changing and highly sophisticated workplace and living environment, people with visual impairments need the knowledge and skills of their sighted peers if they are to live productive and satisfying lives as truly integrated citizens.

Educational Settings and Services

Questions about where education should take place and who should provide that education have generated many different answers for as long as formal education has existed for children who are blind and visually impaired. The inception of established educational programming took place in France in the late 1700s, when Valentin Haüy began his school for blind children; this was followed rapidly by the creation of residential schools in other European countries (Roberts, 1986). Even during this era, when the concept of a separate specialized school implied a higher quality education for any child, professionals had begun to debate the viability of providing an education in a setting beyond the child's own community. Lowenfeld (1981) translated a paper written in 1845 by Jakob Wilhelm Klein, an early Austrian educator of children who were blind and visually impaired, in which Klein stated the following:

> Everybody will agree that children in their tender years, especially blind children who are so much in need of help, are best cared for in their parental homes under motherly care; and if the regular schools suffice for their education, why should they be removed from their homes and placed in costly institutions that accommodate scarcely the sixtieth part of those who are in need of education? (p. 165)

The first educational institutions in the United States for children who were blind and visually impaired were segregated settings in the strictest sense of the word. From the opening of Perkins School for the Blind in Boston in 1829 to the establishment of 48 other residential schools by the early 1900s (Roberts, 1986), most schools educated children of normal intelligence whose only disability was a visual impairment. Black students were educated separately, sometimes on other campuses. Children with additional disabilities often were institutionalized or kept at home with no education except that which the family could provide. The enrollment standards for the Texas School for the Blind cited in the bylaws of the 1869–1870 Annual Report described the populations included in the early schools for children with visual disabilities: The school would enroll no students who were "incapacitated by age, physical infirmity, mental ability, or moral obliquity," and all students had to be of "sound health, good mental capacity, good moral character [and] free from spasmodic and eruptive diseases" (p. 2).

During the early 1900s, some innovative public school programs began to serve students who were blind and visually impaired. Chicago began a public school program in 1900 at the urging of Frank H. Hall (Roberts, 1986), and a few large cities developed and operated their own public school programs from the early 1900s. However, as a result of the births of large numbers of children who were visually impaired from retinopathy of prematurity, then called retrolental fibroplasia, the focus shifted to individual learning characteristics of the children themselves and to new and more creative ways for those children to acquire the same information available to children with better vision.

Educators have since come to realize that there is no single answer that prescribes the way all children should be taught. The setting and educational needs of children with visual impairments vary, and a continuum of services and settings must be available to meet the needs of the students optimally. This recognition has been the primary impetus for innovative educational planning and programming during recent years.

LEGISLATIVE INFLUENCES

In more recent years, federal legislation has provided the mandate for educational opportunities that in the past existed only in some areas. The Education for All Handicapped Children Act (P. L. 94-142) was passed in 1975; as a result, children with visual impairments were served in a wider variety of settings than they had been previously. This act was retitled in 1990 as the Individuals with Disabilities Education Act (IDEA), and additional requirements were added in 1997. By mandate, public schools are required to make available an appropriate educational program for all children. If the schools are unable to offer such a program, they must secure and pay for that program to be delivered in another setting.

Although the federal laws dictate the requirements for states in providing appropriate educational programming, it is the states' responsibility to identify eligible students; to establish, implement, and monitor programs; and to interpret the federal mandates with regard to each state's educational system. Therefore, questions of student eligibility, teacher qualification, and alternative settings might vary greatly from state to state according to interpretation.

Under the original law, services were to be provided to children with disabilities 3 years of age or older, unless this was contrary to state law. In 1986, the original law was amended through P. L. 99-457, the Disabled Infants and Toddlers Act, to require that all states provide services to children ages 3 to 5 years of age. States that chose to apply for special funding to serve children from birth through 2 years of age could also serve that group's students who were disabled or at-risk, and most states that were not already doing so chose to provide these services.

These new amendments require that an individual program be written for the families of children in the birth to 2 age range. This plan, known as the Individualized

Family Service Plan (IFSP), recognizes that family members are the primary teachers during the early years and that professionals support the family's interaction with children in helping them to respond to the environment.

The value of complete parental involvement in any early education program cannot be overemphasized. According to IDEA, parents must be included as part of the educational team in designing experiences, being a part of the instruction, and evaluating the child's progress. Teachers and counselors provide information, guidance, and support to parents. In addition, interaction and participation with other parents of children with visual impairments can have many benefits for some parents. These can take place through informal local groups or through branches of national groups such as the National Association for Parents of Children with Visual Impairments (NAPVI).

The passage of legislation requiring an appropriate education for children with disabilities and the extension of that education to all children from birth to age 21 have guaranteed an appropriate education for all children, regardless of disabling conditions. To qualify a student for specialized services because of a visual impairment, medical and educational professionals must collaborate to determine the extent and implications of an identified visual difference.

The 1997 revisions of IDEA include some added requirements that ensure appropriate education for students with visual impairments. Under these amendments, orientation and mobility is a related service that should be included on the IEP when the need has been identified during assessment. These amendments also require that parents be informed of the availability of a continuum of placement options for students with visual impairments.

In addition, braille must be considered for each student with legal blindness, and an assessment must be conducted to determine whether braille is appropriate. In cases where braille is not recommended, the reasons must be identified in the IEP. Many states also have laws that enforce the importance of assessment of reading media and ensure that braille is considered for each student with a visual impairment (Pugh & Erin, 1999).

Recent laws have been enacted to ensure the continuation of the rights of the adult with a visual impairment beyond the educational years. Among the most important of these is Section 504 of the Rehabilitation Act of 1986, which ensures that people with disabilities have building accessibility and job opportunities in government-supported agencies. The Americans with Disabilities Act of 1990 provides a legal foundation for the rights of people with disabilities in regard to equal access to public facilities, including transportation and job opportunities. The legal mandate for equal opportunity now extends throughout life for people with disabilities.

IDENTIFICATION AND ELIGIBILITY

When an infant has a severe visual impairment, this fact usually is recognized by his or her parents, caregivers, or medical personnel early in the first year. A child's father might notice that his son does not smile and turn toward him when the father quietly enters the room; a grandmother might notice that her granddaughter does not try to reach for her shiny earrings as her other grandchildren did at that age. Such observations might not be confirmed for some time by medical evaluation, and this can result in delays in diagnosis and in important early intervention services. For example, if Lucy's parents had not been concerned by her erratic visual behavior and sought a specialist's opinion, she might never have received the early visual stimulation so vital for maximum development of the vision she was able to use.

Children with less severe visual impairments might remain undiagnosed for years, sometimes until they reach school age. Many infants and preschoolers have never been examined to determine their clarity of vision at near and far distances or whether they see equally well with both eyes. A promising trend in recent years has been to stress the need for screening of all young children in order to detect visual problems much earlier.

A few states have passed mandatory vision and hearing screening for all children. Trained regional teams make preschool screening available in shopping centers, daycare centers, private schools, and community centers. Often the state health services are involved, sometimes a ladies' medical auxiliary, and frequently the Society for the Prevention of Blindness (SPB). SPB has developed a home kit with instructions for parents to check their children's vision. Such techniques as visually evoked responses and preferential looking (a technique in which the child turns toward a patterned stimulus) can be used by clinicians to screen high-risk infants and children with severe disabilities who are unable to respond to symbol charts such as the widely used Snellen chart.

SPB sponsors screening programs throughout the country for children with less severe visual impairments, including those with nearsightedness, the majority of whom can be identified easily during the preschool years by using the standard Snellen eye chart with E symbols printed in various sizes and arranged in different positions. Strabismus (a muscle imbalance that results in eyes that are turned outward or inward) often can be recognized easily and should receive immediate attention from a specialist. If it is not treated before the age of 3 or 4 years by patching of the better eye or the prescription of glasses, the child may develop amblyopia or lazy eye, in which one eye loses its sharpness of vision because of disuse.

Other problems, such as farsightedness (hypermetropia) and astigmatism (irregularity of the cornea), are less easily detected and may not interfere with visual function until the child begins close work in school. Although observation of the use of vision for every type of activity may be one means of recognizing minor visual limitations, it is not necessarily the most critical, because observation may not give evidence of clarity of vision at various distances. Cellular changes in general growth patterns may alter visual function. The eyeball and its internal structures grow rapidly until about age 7, and they continue their physiological growth of a slower rate into adolescence. This growth process alters the refractive components as well as the accommodative mechanisms; therefore, a child may experience visual problems for the first time in the midelementary school or even the teen years.

Without well-planned and regularly conducted visual screening programs during the preschool and the early school years, many children and youth with limited vision are never identified. The tragedy is that they may be labeled academic failures or even mentally retarded because their learning and achievement have been limited by undetected visual problems.

Occasionally, it is difficult to determine when a child requires special educational services because of a visual impairment. IDEA describes a child with a visual disability as one who cannot benefit fully from education because of the visual difference (Office of Special Education, 1981). Each state sets its own criterion for determining whether a child qualifies for services as a child with a visual impairment. Although a few states still rely on a clinical criterion, such as legal blindness (20/200 acuity or less in the better eye or a field of less than 20 degrees), for deciding whether a child is eligible for special educational services, many now consider the functional use of vision as a primary criterion for providing services. Along with the eye specialist's report indicating a serious vision loss, many states also require a written observation by a teacher of children who are visually impaired or by an orientation and mobility instructor. This document, a functional vision assessment, is considered by the team that determines whether a child experiences disadvantages in learning due to a visual impairment.

Once a child is identified as needing specialized services because of the visual impairment, a team—the child's family, teacher, the child when appropriate, an administrative representative, and other professionals as needed—determines what services are desirable and how often they should be provided. This team might be known as an IEP team; an ARD team (Admissions, Review, and Dismissal), or a multidisciplinary or transdisciplinary team. The team is responsible for determining the specialized program goals for each child, as well as identifying the least restrictive environmental setting in which these goals can be met appropriately plus the related services that are needed to facilitate a child's attainment of the specified goals. For the child with a visual impairment, effective decisions about the appropriate organizational plan and setting are based on the assumption that a continuum of placement options is available.

ORGANIZATIONAL PLANS AND EDUCATIONAL SERVICES

Organizational programs and services may differ in nature from community to com munity and from state to state. Ideally, program patterns should be determined by the needs of the children to be served, but that is not always possible and, unfortunately, often is not the primary consideration. Organizational patterns may be based on availability of personnel, the attitudes of individual school districts, financial resources, administrative expediency, or all of these factors, rather than on an objective appraisal of the needs of the children to be served.

Service delivery options in public schools have not changed dramatically since a survey by Jones and Collins (1966), who identified five basic types of organizational patterns: itinerant, resource room, special class, cooperative special class, and teacher consultant. The major differences are in services to preschool children, in those at the postsecondary level, and in those in rural areas. Generally, organizational plans in public schools include some variation of those mentioned in the next few pages.

Infants ages birth to 3 years are usually served in home programs under the supervision of transdisciplinary specialists with periodic evaluations and parent instruction in the school setting. Preschoolers ages 3 to 5 years are in school programs, either in self-contained classrooms or with other children with disabilities or in regular preschool or kindergarten.

Under P. L. 99-457, many infants and preschoolers with visual impairments have expanded options for intervention. Community nursery schools continue to serve children with visual impairments who are able to function with little or no assistance in a group of sighted children. Children with moderate and severe low vision might adapt well to such a setting, although fewer children who are totally blind will be ready for this experience. Socialization, and development of the many emotional characteristics that contribute to a child's personal and social development, can be gained through association with normally seeing children, especially when teachers and children include them in all the regular activities.

Special nursery schools, either private or sponsored by community agencies, may be more desirable for children with severe visual and other disabilities who seem to be slower in their development. Most children who are totally blind need highly specialized attention and can learn to function more easily in a group of children who function primarily through the senses of touch and hearing. Some children who are severely visually impaired or totally blind develop rapidly and may be included in nursery programs with sighted children, when their movement skills and self-directed learning strategies permit them to participate with the total group. Very few residential programs are available to children under the age of 4 or 5 years, although many specialized schools operate outreach programs that provide home-based services or parent training for families of infants and preschoolers.

The current emphasis on kindergarten and early childhood education for all children, and especially the legislative provisions for early childhood education programs for the disabled, have opened the way for many children and their families to participate in preschool activities that would not previously have been available because of geographic location or lack of funds for establishing such programs. Preschool programs for children with disabilities are found in community agencies and more often as part of public school programs (Felix & Spungin, 1978). Outreach programs are being developed by state regional centers and some specialized schools to serve children and parents in rural areas. When specialized or residential schools are too far from the child's home, parents are reluctant to even consider such programs, even though no specialized services are available to them nearby. Some states have developed outreach teams to serve parents and children within a radius of approximately 100 miles.

Mainly rural states in the United States and rural provinces in Canada have been very successful in giving support to parents and in guiding home teaching until the children are old enough for public schools or until specialized services can be made available.

The objectives for most of these programs are to provide information and support to parents and to evaluate consistently the development and learning in infants and young children. Parents do most of the teaching, with suggestions from specially qualified personnel in visual impairment as well as support personnel in other disciplines. Some programs are located in hospital settings where qualified persons from many disciplines are available to assess both clinical and educational needs. Other programs, which utilize the services of trained personnel from related disciplines, emanate from regional education service centers or intermediate units within certain states in combination with various state agencies serving children. Children with visual impairments and multiple disabilities, whose progress might be slow or who have extensive medical and developmental problems, may require total care facilities when families are unable to assume the responsibility and no other program is designed to meet their numerous needs. The objective of many programs is to assist children in developing learning readiness to enter either public school academic programs or modified academic and vocational programs.

Children like Carlos and Lucy will probably develop the necessary learning skills to move into regular school programs with little difficulty. Some studies (Hull & McCarthy, 1973) have indicated that when children with low vision are given special instruction in visual development at nursery and kindergarten levels, they are able to move into regular school programs and to perform as competently as their normally seeing peers. Although this might not be true for all children with low vision, the idea is worth considering. It also will not be true for all children who are totally blind, such as Carlos, but because of his parents and preschool teachers, he is learning and developing similarly to other 4-year-old children, and can function within a group with only minor modifications. All children with severe visual impairments need to be given the opportunity to experience the specialized learning experiences available through early childhood educational programs designed for their specific needs.

For children who make steady progress in development and learning during the preschool years, the options for services expand during school years. Hazekamp and Huebner (1989) described five minimum options that should be included among the range available to students with visual impairments: (1) specialized instruction provided by an itinerant teacher, who may travel among several schools to serve students individually; (2) a resource room, in which students spend some portion of their day in a separate classroom equipped with needed equipment and materials, and with a teacher specially trained in visual impairment; (3) a self-contained classroom, in which students spend the majority of their school day in a separate classroom; (4) a special school, in which only students with disabilities such as visual impairments or developmental delays are in attendance; and (5) a non–public-school setting, an option when there is no publicly funded agency that can provide appropriate services for the child.

The question should be not which plan is best for any school district to adopt but, instead, through which programming patterns can children in the area be served most appropriately and effectively. Some districts have formed cooperative plans with one or more nearby districts where only small numbers of children with visual impairments live in each district. It is imperative that children who are totally blind or who have low vision have the assistance of an individual specially trained to teach children with visual impairments. These specialists must be familiar with special materials, basic learning concepts, difficulties that are related or unrelated to the visual impairment, and the difference in learning-to-read and learning-to-write processes for children with visual difficulties. The decision regarding where to place a child needs to take these factors into consideration and not rely solely on the concept of the least restrictive environment (Curry & Hatlen, 1988).

For many years, the general policy in local schools and in a few specialized schools was to separate for instructional purposes children who were blind from those who were then called "partially seeing." This practice might have originated when there were very few teacher education programs, and the majority of them focused on the concept of sightsaving, or sight conservation, for partially seeing children. All the teacher education programs that were available had separate training programs for teachers of the blind and teachers of the partially seeing. At present, teachers are educated as specialists to serve all children and youth with visual impairments. There is no longer a controversy about integrating children who are blind with those who have low vision, regardless of whether the delivery system is a special class, a resource room, or itinerant consultation (Jones & Collins, 1966). Terms such as partially seeing and legally blind are used infrequently in the professional literature because clinical measurements are no longer the criterion for determining need for educational services in most states. Professionals in special education have moved from the medical model to the functional model, at least for children and youth with visual impairments.

Although no data on the achievement of readers who use braille or print, when instructed together, have been reported in the United States, one study done in England (McLaughlin, 1974) recorded no differences between braille readers and print readers in integrated instruction programs. The similarity in learning ability is a more important factor than the nature or extent of the visual impairment. Children who find achievement difficult or who are not yet ready to develop such academic skills as reading, writing, or computation may need a special class placement for a long time. In fact, the current population of children with visual impairments, many of whom have other problems interfering with their development, has required local school districts to create or reinstate self-contained classes, resource room programs, or both, to serve these children more effectively and to try to prevent the almost inevitable cumulative lag in educational progress that occurs when the regular teacher tries to assume responsibilities for which he or she has received no training.

As a result of IDEA—the mandate for public schools to provide services to all children—and the cost of materials and specialist teachers (even when available) to small districts, more and more children are being served on an itinerant basis with limited visits by the specialists in the region. In many cases, very young children, especially those who are totally blind, are being placed in regular classrooms long before they have their basic learning skills. Some are placed in generic special education classrooms with other children with disabilities whose learning needs are quite different, and with a teacher who may not have any coursework related to visual impairment. Only time will enable us to determine the appropriateness or inappropriateness of this approach. We may regret the overwhelming stress on inclusion if we discover in a few years that children and youth with visual impairments have been cheated educationally because of our needs for expediency and efforts to save money. There is nothing cost-effective about such service delivery if children pay the price by being unable to take their rightful places as independent, tax-paying citizens.

In a few local school settings, the majority of children at the elementary level are served through the resource plan. This plan involves selection of a particular school to which all children with visual disabilities within that district are transported; it is more often available in densely populated areas where there might be groups of visually impaired children of similar ages and functional abilities. This school contains a specially equipped classroom with a teacher who is specifically trained for work with these children. Integration into regular classes within that school for varying amounts of time during the day or week is desirable, according to each child's needs as determined by the educational team. Although this plan requires that some children be placed in settings other than their neighborhood schools, it does offer the children a readily available constellation of materials and support services. In such a situation, a child who needs more intensive assistance can spend several hours a day with the resource teacher in practicing and refining social and academic skills, while other children can spend the majority of their time in regular classes with their peers, receiving only minimal help and consultative services from the resource teacher.

Itinerant services afford the opportunity for children with visual impairments to remain in their neighborhood schools and in regular classrooms with peers, while still being served on a periodic basis by a specially qualified teacher in visual impairments. In this model, the education of children with visual impairments is the primary responsibility of the classroom teacher, with the consultative services of the special teacher and the provision of special equipment and materials adapted to the children's learning needs. For children and youth who have reached the level of self-direction and independence in learning skills, these itinerant services provide them with sufficient assistance. For children or youth who have not yet developed their academic learning skills or who are not as socially aware as their sighted peers, this plan may offer less than the necessary range and intensity of services actually needed.

The number of children to be served on an itinerant basis should be determined by the characteristics of each child rather than by a specific number determined by some formula. This plan also requires a great deal of teacher time spent traveling from school to school. The decision to establish such a procedure must be made on the basis of the effectiveness and efficiency of the plan for the child to be served, in addition to considering the appropriate use of the time of highly trained specialists.

Many school districts, especially large ones or those in strategic population centers, find that a combination of resource and itinerant programs best meets the needs of their districts. Ideally, when students with visual impairments reach the academic level of junior and senior high school, they have acquired sufficient independent learning and other skills, which allow them to progress consistently with minimal help from itinerant special services. Many elementary level students actually need the resource plan. A few of the very young or slowly developing children need self-contained situations for some time. Therefore, in large cities or heavily populated areas, probably the most effective plan would be to provide early childhood education programs, self-contained classes, resource rooms, and itinerant programs.

Traditionally, many states have established specialized schools to provide educational experiences for children with severe visual impairments. A few states have combined their specialized programs with programs for children who are deaf, creating what have been known as dual schools. Formerly, most children with visual impairments within some states were sent to the residential school established specifically for them. Since the 1950s, the general trend has been to increase the percentage of students with visual disabilities attending local public schools, and the passage of P. L. 94-142 not only lowered the percentage of students attending specialized schools but also caused a reevaluation of the role of residential schools for the future. Spungin (1982) and others suggested that specialized schools develop cooperative relationships with state and local education agencies and place capable students in local schools, which some have done with good success.

The role of the residential school is becoming increasingly specialized, according to state and regional needs. Some specialized schools serve children with visual impairments and multiple disabilities who need a round-the-clock consistency in programming. Some provide statewide services in the areas of diagnosing and assessing; case finding, counseling, and parent training; teaching skills of daily living, leisure time, and vocational pursuits; in-service training and continuing educational programs for all teachers; developing curricula; managing and distributing materials; serving as research centers; and providing respite care to relieve parents. Harley and English (1989) reported that residential schools are moving in the direction of providing more support services for children who are in public school programs; frequently these services include summer school programs in recreational activities and daily living skills, as well as in-service seminars for public school teachers.

A recent study by McMahon (2000) provided demographic information on 1,962 students who were enrolled in specialized schools for the blind and visually impaired. These data represented 23 of 44 specialized schools for the blind and visually impaired in the United States. It reflected an ethnically diverse population, more than half of whom were students in the 12 to 18-year age range. A high percentage of the students (70.5%) were eligible for food subsidy, suggesting a disproportionate number of students from lower socioeconomic levels. Almost 60% of the students were totally blind, which is a much larger group than in the national population of students with visual impairments. These data suggest that the responding schools are serving stulents with more intensive educational needs than the general population of learners vith visual impairments.

There is no overall policy for specialized schools or states. In some cases, the esidential school serves primarily children from remote, less populated areas of the tate, those whose families for various reasons prefer to have them attend a residential rogram, or children who cannot, for whatever reason, fit into the local school program in their community. Despite the mandatory legislation for public schools, some tates have been slow to enforce the legislation and develop quality public school rograms. The small number of students and their sparse geographic distribution ave influenced the delay in some areas. Professionals hold different views on appropriate placements, and these perspectives can influence recommendations about the ighest quality education setting for a student with a visual impairment (Kim & Corn, 1998). In a few states, the residential school has ceased to serve children who an progress normally in academic learning and serves only those children who, because of their multiple disabling conditions, require a special curriculum and highly dapted program.

The variability of the nature and role of the residential school has made it difficult or policy to be established concerning the legal requirement for this option under the uidelines of P. L. 94-142. Silverstein (1985), who reviewed court cases regarding resilential school placement, suggested that three issues have influenced policy decisions: he broad definition of the term *education* to include nonacademic skills, the fact that rogram issues must be addressed before the least restrictive requirement is followed, nd the determination that some children require programming beyond the normal chool day.

Many states are reevaluating their total special education program for children vith visual impairments in an effort to provide a range or continuum of educational ervices through a variety of educational plans. For example, some states are planning o bring all programs and services together under one agency, thereby creating a coninuum of services for students with visual disabilities from birth to vocational independence. Still other states are expanding their residential programs to maintain their cademic nature, while providing a broader spectrum of programs for children with nultiple disabilities in diagnostic services, daily living skills, and vocational programs. This expanded arrangement places an almost impossible task on administration and is ar more costly, to say nothing of the difficulties encountered in maintaining quality nd diversity in the academic area.

There are no clear guidelines for placement decisions regarding children with visual impairments. Hatlen (1990) emphasized that placement decisions should be ased on each child's program needs, and placement should not be a "goal in itself but means for meeting goals" (p. 81). In selecting appropriate placement, the team hould consider what is known about the characteristics that contribute to successful tudents who are included in the regular classroom. In a national survey of teachers, dministrators, students, and parents, Bishop (1986) identified the characteristics asociated with a successful public school experience. The five factors ranked highest were an accepting classroom teacher, acceptance by peers, appropriate social skills high academic achievement, and a good self-image. Ashcroft and Zambone-Ashle (1980) stated that higher academic achievement was characteristic of children in pub lic schools with resource or itinerant support, and they emphasized the importance c student social skills and the availability of educational resources and specialized teach ers as requirements for successful public school education.

The beliefs that no one educational setting is the most appropriate for all childre with visual disabilities and that a diversity of educational settings is desirable to mee the needs of children and their families (Abel, 1959) are still valid. The decision abou placement must be based on student needs, including such factors as alternative learn ing media, enlarged visual images, independent living skills, orientation and mobility and use of assistive technology (Pugh & Erin, 1999). The acceptance of this idea ha resulted in the expansion of programs into a variety of settings during the preschool elementary, and secondary school years (Felix & Spungin, 1978). At the present time it is estimated that approximately 90% or more of school-age children with visual im pairments receive services within their communities and, in most cases, within publi school settings.

TEAM APPROACHES AND SUPPORT SERVICES

Until recently, little attention has been given to the quality of programs in the publi schools. The concerns of professional organizations such as the Council for Excep tional Children Division on Visual Impairments, the National Accreditation fc Agencies Serving the Blind and Visually Handicapped, and the American Foundatio for the Blind, have led to a group of suggested guidelines and standards from birth to 2 years of age (Scholl, 1981; Spungin, 1980; Stager, 1978). In 1989, Hazekamp an Huebner published their guidelines for excellence in programming for children wit visual impairments; this document provides essential information to public school prc grams that serve children, including a self-review guide that can be used by profession als to evaluate local programs.

The National Association of State Directors of Special Education has recentl published a policy manual that provides guidelines for quality educational services fc learners who are visually impaired. This document addresses the standards for suppo services, preparation of personnel, appropriate assessment, placement options, and th importance of an expanded curriculum for students who are visually impaired that al lows for instruction in areas that are specifically related to their disabilities, such as dail living skills and social skills (Pugh & Erin, 1999). These guidelines provide essenti information for public school personnel, including administrators, who are unfamilia with the educational needs of learners who are visually impaired.

The major responsibility for assessment and programming for children with visu impairments rests with the educational or IEP team. In all cases, the parent should be a active and involved member of the team and, in many cases, the child should be an ac tive participant. An administrator from the child's school district and the child's primary teacher are important members of the team. A psychologist is usually involved in the evaluation of the child, according to state requirements, and may also contribute to the team process. In addition, support staff such as physical therapists or speech–language therapists may participate as appropriate.

The child with a visual disability usually requires the services of several professionals who work with the family to support educational progress. Decisions about who will participate in the planning and implementation of the child's program can be difficult ones; unnecessary additional services can waste valuable learning time and fragment the child's whole educational experience, whereas insufficient involvement by specialized team members can deprive the child of necessary learning opportunities and skills.

Several professional roles are critical in effective educational programming for a child with a visual impairment. One is the role of the regular classroom teacher, who is responsible primarily for the academic curriculum of the child in a public school setting. An accepting and flexible classroom teacher was one of the most frequently named of 70 factors cited by respondents to Bishop's 1986 study of the factors that influence success in the mainstream. Hazekamp and Huebner (1989) described the role of the classroom teacher as including direct instruction and cooperative work with the teacher of children with visual impairments; among the cooperative tasks they identified are providing classroom materials to the specialist teacher in a timely manner, providing times for the student to work with the specialist teacher, and modifying classroom procedures as needed for the student with a visual impairment.

Another essential member of the educational team is the teacher trained to teach students with visual disabilities. In most states, this teacher must be certified through the state education agency to teach children with visual impairments (Huebner & Strumwasser, 1987). These teachers are required to complete a college undergraduate or graduate program in teaching these children. The recent trend toward noncategorical preparation of special education teachers has influenced schools in some states to employ teachers of special education to serve children with visual impairments; this trend toward general services has raised concern among professionals about the adequacy of services provided by those who are not specifically prepared to work with people having visual impairments (Gallagher, 1988; Harrell & Curry, 1987).

The role of the specialist teacher for students with visual disabilities includes a wide range of activities that varies according to the ages, numbers, functional levels, educational settings, support services available (such as transcribers), and extent of visual impairment of the children served. Spungin (1984) described activities that might be included in this teacher's role as they relate to six major areas: assessment, learning environment, unique curriculum, guidance and counseling, administration and supervision, and school community relations. In the area of assessment, the teacher of students with visual impairments performs functional vision assessments and participates in evaluation and placement decisions, among other activities. Within the learning environment, the specialist teacher promotes understanding of vision loss among the student's general education teacher and classmates; the specialized teacher also assists in the preparation and adaptation of materials and instructional methods. Spungin listed 16 areas of unique curricula, such as braille instruction, typing, visual development and efficiency, and techniques of daily living.

The teacher of students with visual disabilities also may have varying levels of direct contact with each student, depending on each student's educational needs. Many teachers serve as consultants, supporting the child's program through work with the classroom teacher and staff, rather than through regularly scheduled direct contact with the student (Erin, 1988). Others work individually with the child in the regular classroom to teach skills that support the child's ability to function in the primary educational environment.

Suvak (1999) described the use of time by teachers of visually impaired students in Colorado. In that state, teachers spent most of their direct service time teaching skills and activities related to braille reading. They also spent a significant amount of time on adaptation of materials for their students. Although 45% of the students needed less than a half hour of direct service each week, 11% required more than 5 hours a week of direct service, and 42% required consultative services rather than direct services. This study reflects the wide variations in activities performed by specially trained teachers of students with visual impairments, as well as the range of educational needs of these students.

The unique role of the teacher of students with visual disabilities can result in a different level of morale in some situations. Teacher isolation and the acceptance of children with visual impairments in the regular classroom are among the factors that have an impact on teacher morale. Bina (1982) surveyed 238 teachers of students with visual impairments in 10 western states, and found higher morale among those from smaller cities (populations ranging from 10,000 to 50,000) than among those in larger cities. However, the most critical factors influencing morale were lack of supervision and democratic leadership. Teachers reported that they often had no one with whom to discuss problems or brainstorm strategies. They also were frustrated with the type of service delivery, often feeling that itinerant services did not provide appropriately for some of their students. In addition, the continuing shortage of teachers of students with visual disabilities has an impact on the workload of teachers who are serving those with highly individualized needs. Many geographic areas, particularly rural locations, are unable to secure or retain teachers with knowledge of visual impairment; children are often unserved or underserved in these areas and may be placed in more restrictive environments than necessary because districts are unable to adequately staff their programs for learners with visual impairments.

Fewer than 20 colleges and universities prepare teachers of students with visual impairments, and decreased funding for low incidence areas is causing some of these programs to close. The fact that teachers from geographically remote areas often must travel far from their homes to acquire preparation in teaching children with visual impairments makes the shortage problem even more acute. All these factors make it difficult to maintain a strong pool of well-prepared professionals in rural or economically disadvantaged areas, where salaries are often quite low.

Another critical member of the team for some students is the orientation and mo-ility specialist. This individual evaluates the child's orientation within the immediate nvironment and works with the team to set goals to improve the child's awareness of ody image and space as well as to teach skills that lead to independence in movement nd travel activities (Uslan, Hill, & Peck, 1989). For children who require the use of ravel devices, such as low vision devices, the long cane, or even wheelchairs, the ori-ntation and mobility instructor works individually with the child to teach the use of his specialized equipment during movement. In some areas, rehabilitation teachers of ndividuals who are blind or visually impaired are working as members of the educa-ional team. These individuals might work with students at home or at school, teaching ndependent living skills, career and transition activities, or other skills that are not ypically addressed in the regular school classroom.

Other professionals might be involved in programming for the child as consultants r as direct service providers. These individuals provide related services, which are eeded to permit the child to benefit from the educational program. These professionals night include physical therapists, who are responsible for programming to facilitate ef-ective motor development; occupational therapists, who monitor activities to promote unctional use of the child's fine motor skills; speech–language therapists, who focus on he child's communication abilities for most effective interaction; counselors and thera-ists, who work with the child and family to resolve emotional and behavioral concerns.

Parents and professionals meet at least annually, and sometimes more often, to de-ide on the best educational plan for the child. The decision-making process may be nformal, or it may follow a more systematic model (Hupp & Rosen, 1985). However, he ultimate goal is to provide a program that will meet the child's learning and educa-ional needs at a level that will foster maximum potential. Many districts and special-zed schools employ paraprofessionals who work directly with the learner who is visu-lly impaired. It is important that these individuals have some understanding of how isual impairment affects a student's development and learning and that they have earned the basic skills and techniques related to instruction. A manual published by exas School for the Blind and Visually Impaired (Miller & Levak, 1997) describes asic techniques and strategies for paraprofessionals who are working with learners vho are visually impaired.

Paraprofessionals should have regular contact with a teacher of students who are isually impaired in order to ensure that their instructional approaches address the stu-ent's educational program. There should be a clear distinction between their role, vhich includes providing reinforcement and practice opportunities, and that of the rofessional, who carries out initial instruction in specialized skills such as braille or ori-ntation and mobility. A paraprofessional might provide too much assistance to learn-rs with disabilities, and this can discourage the student from taking the initiative that an include him or her in the regular classroom environment (Giangreco, Edelman, uiselli, & MacFarland, 1997). Paraprofessionals should participate in team decision naking whenever possible because they are responsible for implementation of the stu-ent's educational goals.

Educational teams vary in composition and structure. Their membership varies over time (Giangreco, Edelman, Nelson, Young, & Kiefer-O'Donnell, 1999), and this fact reinforces the importance of developing consistent and clear educational programs that can be communicated among members of the team. Team members must approach educational planning as an individual process in which placement decisions follow the establishment of educational goals.

SUMMARY

Education for children with visual disabilities started in the United States within residential settings; however, it has evolved to provide a continuum of options for students, depending on each child's individual needs. The special educational process must begin with identification of the child's eligibility as a child with a visual impairment. The identification of an appropriate program depends on the needs of the child, parental preference, and the geographic location. Whereas some children can be educated in their neighborhood schools, others require the more comprehensive services of a specialized setting. The multidisciplinary team may include a number of professionals, such as the teacher specially trained in visual impairments, the orientation and mobility instructor, the occupational and physical therapists, or all these professionals. The availability of a continuum of services and the flexibility to develop a program that meets the changing needs of each child are critical to an effective education for all children with visual disabilities.

Assessment and Evaluation of Individual Functioning

Assessment is a process, not a test or an event. This is even more true when a child has an unusual characteristic, such as a visual impairment, which makes it important to explore abilities and behaviors individually. For a student with a visual impairment, the comprehensive assessment process reaches beyond typical academic performance to address skill areas that might be affected by the visual impairment. Included among these areas are compensatory or functional academic skills, orientation and mobility, social interaction skills, independent living skills, recreation and leisure skills, career-vocational skills, technology, and visual efficiency skills (Hatlen, 1996; Lewis & Russo, 1998).

Assessment and evaluation of all students are challenging for several reasons: Not all states have the same policies and requirements for identification and assessment; the school population is constantly changing; and there is a paucity of valid instruments and reliable procedures. These concerns are especially challenging when evaluating students with visual disabilities for predictive purposes. Because most educators who work with these children are not psychologists, and because most psychologists have had limited contact with the development and behavior of students who are visually impaired, coordinated approaches to individual functioning are even more difficult to achieve.

The use of instruments designed for and standardized with sighted students to assess children with visual impairments has been questioned through the years. The trend to compare these students' educational and psychological development and functioning with sighted peers on the basis of scores also has been controversial. In gathering such information and reporting results, very little distinction has been made between those students who were totally blind and those who had usable vision. The use of contaminated samples, along with the lack of desirability of the instruments, has called into question the validity of the findings and negated the possibility of generalizing to a total population with only one characteristic in common—visual impairment.

Although children and youth with visual impairments as a group function psychologically and educationally at levels below those of sighted peers, many of these children seem to achieve just as well or better in academic work and are able to perform a comparable or higher levels in real-life situations. Contradictory observations of thi nature have led psychologists and educators not only to examine the procedures use in evaluation, but also to call into question the entire approach toward assessment an evaluation as applied to students with visual disabilities. Moore and McLaughli (1992) conclude that "special expertise in nonstandard evaluation and clinical judg ment as well as an interdisciplinary approach are necessary to yield valid and relevan conclusions from assessment" (p. 1).

Some of the provisions in IDEA specify that assessments are to be done by pec ple who are qualified to assess each individual. Thus, the American Foundation fc the Blind sponsored a series of workshops for psychologists and psychometrists over 3-year period. Subsequently, a manual with a model for such workshops was mad available (Jastrzembska, 1982).

Critical issues and questions raised by Bateman (1965), Weiner (1967), Chas (1972, 1975), and Morse (1975) indicated that more careful consideration should b given to a wide variety of variables and approaches. Chase (1986a) suggested that eac examiner might wish to evaluate personal attitudes toward visual impairment an blindness in order to have the fair and open-minded approach necessary, citing the ex aminer's lack of ease as a primary impediment to effective evaluation of students wit visual disabilities. Prior to any testing or assessment, the following questions deserv careful consideration:

1. For what purpose is the assessment being made? Is it to exclude the child from som program or service, or is it to prove eligibility? Is assessment for the purpose of prediction, c is it an attempt to determine present level of functioning in many areas as specified by law Is the primary purpose to have the information necessary to plan a more realistic learnin program?

2. When, if ever, are definitive norms or age-level equivalents desirable? Should asses ment tools and measures designed for sighted children be utilized, or should specific measure and tools be designed for children with visual impairments—separate ones for children wit low vision and for those who are totally blind? Should items be adapted from those alread available, or should criterion-referenced items be individualized across the dimensions of be havior to be evaluated?

3. In evaluating functioning, how does one determine whether the level of functionin below that which is anticipated is related to the visual impairment resulting in a lack of ex perience or opportunity to learn? Conversely, is a high level of functioning a result of an en riched background of experience, or does the person have a greater learning capacity?

4. How can the examiner determine whether an inappropriate response or behavior the result of the visual problem, a neurological problem, or a learning problem, or whether is a manifestation of an interaction between all these variables?

5. Can the instrument be adapted appropriately, are accommodations in testir needed, or both? ("Adaptations" refers to making changes in the content, whereas "ac commodations" refers to changes in timing or other procedures.)

6. Are the questions based on concepts the child has been able to acquire through vision or other senses, or are concepts visually based that the child has not yet had an opportunity to observe?

Substantial information about whether tactual and auditory experiences are analogous to visual experiences is lacking. Possible differences in how various sensory systems process the data received could influence learning styles and patterns; however, these differences in information processing have eluded assessment through present instruments and procedures. Despite the perplexing questions, assessing functional behavior can be valuable to the students, the teachers attempting to work with these students, and the parents. Thus, instead of rejecting the idea of evaluating children with visual impairments because we do not agree on a process or a cadre of tools or instruments, a better approach would seem to be to suggest how procedures could be improved and which measures and approaches are most valuable to individual children.

BEHAVIORS TO BE EVALUATED

Intelligence or Mental Development

Although attempts have been made to develop and standardize instruments specifically for assessment of cognitive development in students with visual impairments, none has been published to date that has shown the degree of reliability desired. The *Interim Hayes-Binet* was used for years but is now out of use; the *Perkins-Binet Test of Intelligence for the Blind,* which followed, was recalled because of unreliability probably related to inadequate sampling, especially at the younger ages (Chase, 1986a). The most widely used scales for estimates of mental development are the Wechsler intelligence scales: the *Wechsler Preschool and Primary Scale of Intelligence–Revised* (WPPSI–R) (Wechsler, 1989), the *Wechsler Intelligence Scale for Children–Third Edition* (WISC–III) (Wechsler, 1991), and the *Wechsler Adult Intelligence Scale–Revised* (WAIS–R) (Wechsler, 1981). Although only the verbal portion is appropriate for students who are totally blind, Chase (1986b) recommended giving the performance subtests to people with usable vision without regard for time restraints; in this case, no score would be given, but the amount of time required would be recorded. The purpose would be to evaluate whether the task could be completed and, if so, the amount of time it required. Some studies have shown a positive correlation between scores on the verbal measures and future academic success in school, possibly because of the nature of classroom learning situations.

Despite efforts through the years to develop an instrument for evaluating functional intelligence on performance tasks by students who are blind, none has yet been produced that is comparable to the Wechsler scales. The lengthy time required to develop such projects, the great expense, and the difficulty in finding sufficient numbers for standardization samples of students who are totally blind are some of the problems limiting these endeavors. A group in the Netherlands (Dekker, Drenth, Zaal, & Koole, 1991) designed an intelligence test series for children who are blind or have low vision purported to be comparable to the Wechsler scales, but at the present time, the series needs further cross-validation and longitudinal studies to establish their validity and reliability on larger numbers of students.

Although not widely publicized in the psychological or psychometric disciplines, *The Blind Learning Aptitude Test* (BLAT) (Newland, 1961, 1979), based on abstract symbol discrimination, recognition, seriation, and association, uses culturally neutral items to sample the psychological operations by which learning takes place. The entire procedure is process oriented, not product oriented, in that it seeks to determine how the child goes about learning. Memory and verbal adequacy are not required. The items are constructed of embossed dots presented in bas-relief on heavy plastic paper. Total configurations are larger than the traditional braille cell. Minimal emphasis is placed on what the child has learned previously, so that the predictive potential for future learning by touch is uncontaminated. Unfortunately, the age range for use is limited to that approximating the WISC–R, and no other such measures are available for younger or older students. The BLAT is recommended as a supplement to the verbal portion of the WISC–R for children without any vision who have good tactual learning skills.

The need for assessment of psychological functioning in even younger children has been precipitated by the increasing number of programs beginning at birth, particularly from 3 years of age. Portions of widely used preschool instruments may be valuable if used with discretion by a psychologist, psychometrist, or diagnostician with specialized training or knowledge of visual impairments. Uzgiris and Hunt's (1975) *Ordinal Scales of Psychological Development*, the *Bayley Scales for Infant Development–Second Edition* (Bayley, 1993), and the *Battelle Developmental Inventory* (Newborg, Stock, Wnek, Guidabaldi, & Svinicki, 1984) all have some items that might be useful even for children who are totally blind (Bradley-Johnson, 1986; Ferrell, 1998). The *Reynell-Zinkin Developmental Scales for Young Visually Handicapped Children* (Reynell & Zinkin, 1980) were developed in response to the clinical need for professionals to be able to work more effectively with parents (Wilhelm, 1989). These scales have the unique characteristic of being appropriate for use with children who have multiple disabilities. They include assessment on six subscales: social adaptation; sensorimotor understanding; exploration of environment; response to sound and verbal comprehension; vocalization and expressive language, vocabulary, and content; and communication. Many of these areas are not assessed on previously mentioned scales. The examiner needs to have a thorough understanding of early intellectual development and how that development is different in children with visual disabilities because the focus is on intellectual processes rather than on skills or specific knowledge that has been obtained. Experienced examiners might be able to make adaptations of many items from other measures as well. Caution must be exercised in assigning global developmental ages to young children on the basis of selected or adapted items or in overinterpreting the results of the responses. These various measures of intellectual and mental evaluation can provide valuable clinical data and some pertinent information for educational planning; however, to assign intelligence test scores and use them as reliable indicators of learning potential or future academic achievement could do a great disservice to some children.

Nevertheless, teachers would like to use information from psychological or psychometric reports of mental functioning to help them plan realistically for children, and to identify critical needs to be included in the IEP as required by IDEA. They want to know each child's strengths and weaknesses in specific learning areas, and they may be unable to make such inferences based only on test or subtest scores. Diagnosticians, psychometrists, and psychologists would provide a real service to teachers and students if they would specify the mental processes evaluated in certain tasks and highlight the areas of present intellectual deficits.

In addition to, or instead of, using single measures to obtain IQ scores, selected subtests from several measures could provide useful information for educational planning. Bullard and Barraga (1971) analyzed the subtests of numerous evaluative instruments and organized them according to the type of mental tasks required in each. The following categories were identified: immediate recall, association, logical thinking, discrimination, spatial relations, deductive reasoning, inductive reasoning, imitation, generalization, attention span, and language development. Sampling intellectual functions in such a manner would not yield scores but could result in a profile of functional abilities and deficits useful for prescriptive planning of learning experiences. Chase (1986a) reported the use of a similar approach, adding the *McCarthy Scales of Children's Abilities* (McCarthy, 1972), the *Peabody Picture Vocabulary Test* (Dunn, 1965; revised in 1981 by Dunn & Dunn), and the *Goodenough-Harris Drawing Test* (Goodenough & Harris, 1963) as valuable supplements to those already mentioned. Others have suggested that, with careful modifications, some subtests of the *Kaufman Assessment Battery for Children* (Kaufman & Kaufman, 1983) may be appropriate for children with low vision (Moore & McLaughlin, 1992).

Affective and Social Development

For younger children, the revised *Vineland Adaptive Behavior Scale–Expanded Form* (Sparrow, Balla, & Cicchetti, 1984) and the *Maxfield-Bucholz Social Maturity Scale for Blind Preschool Children* (Maxfield & Bucholz, 1957), adapted from the original Vineland and standardized on preschool children who are blind, can be quite useful. The items give some indication of personal, social, and functional development, including physical control of the body, eating, dressing, and finally communication and self-direction. Also included are items that indicate response patterns; interactive styles; relationships with family, peers, and others; frustration tolerance; and the ability to enjoy social pleasures, friendships, and intimacy. Observational scales, such as the *Callier-Azusa Scale* (Stillman, 1979) and Langley's (1980) *Functional Vision Screening Inventory for the Severely and Multiply Handicapped*, have been reported as applicable, especially for preschool and multidisabled children. The ISAVE (Langley, 2000) may also be useful in screening for a variety of behaviors. Portions of other scales or instruments may also be helpful in evaluating the above-mentioned factors.

Achievement

Achievement testing of students with visual impairments began in the early 1900s, and the American Printing House for the Blind (APH) has been publishing a variety of such tests, both in braille and in large print, for many years. The *Stanford Achievement Test–9th Edition* (Harcourt Brace Educational Measurement, 1996) has been adapted specifically for students with visual impairments and permits them to be ranked in relation to their sighted counterparts. This is especially important now that approximately 92% of students with visual disabilities attend public school programs and only 8% are in specialized schools (APH, 1997). Many states require mandatory achievement testing for all students at several grade levels. In addition, more and more states are requiring competency testing for high school graduation. Appropriate modifications in content and format permit students with visual impairments to take tests in a reading medium they prefer, such as braille or large print, or with an optical device, a listening machine, or a reading machine.

Special Skills

The increasing number of infants and preschool children receiving services and the growing percentage of children with visual impairments and multiple disabilities have created a need for more functional approaches to assessment of various abilities. Some of the more basic skills needed by children with visual impairments include assessment of the use of sensory abilities, especially vision, hearing, and touch; gross motor development and freedom of movement in the environment; the performance of tasks of daily living; and prevocational and occupational skills. Many, if not all, of these are best accomplished by the teacher in cooperation with the child's parents using planned observation, checklists, and selected criterion-referenced measures, especially with preschool and elementary-age students, and with some older students for transitional purposes or for further habilitation and occupational preparation.

Assessment of Vision and Reading Medium

The specially trained teacher of students who are visually impaired is responsible for the primary assessment of the student's use of functional vision as well as the assessment of information related to the student's reading medium. The functional vision assessment is the primary method of assessing and describing the student's use of vision. This involves gathering information about the student's vision through observation, informal interactions, and formal activities. The report typically includes background information, a description of the physical structures of the eye, description of the use of near and distance vision, visual fields, color and perceptual abilities, eye movements, and any other visual skills observed during routines and activities. The assessment should include a variety of activities in several environments, and it should provide clear recommendations for adaptations related to the child's visual functioning (Erin & Paul, 1996).

The functional assessment can be supplemented with the *Visual Efficiency Scale* (VES) (Barraga, 1970), which was designed to assess the level of visual functioning through a series of increasingly less visible and smaller items sequenced in complexity from gross form to visual detail and finally to sentences and words. The scale was planned primarily for use with students having low vision, who previously might have been considered unable to use their low vision for learning purposes; it might be useful also for those with less severe visual problems who have difficulty discriminating specific types of detailed material or whose difficulties are related to perceptual problems. Many teachers now use it as a screening measure that can be administered in 10 to 15 minutes, before a more comprehensive assessment of visual potential. Many states now require that a functional vision assessment be a part of the battery for all students who have light perception or more extensive visual responses; a variety of checklists and criterion-referenced measures may be used for this purpose and the recommendation generally is that this be done by the teacher of students with visual impairments or a clinical vision specialist.

The revision and expansion of the VES resulted in publication of a *Program to Develop Efficiency in Visual Functioning*, suitable for developmental ages 3 to adult (Barraga & Morris, 1980). This program, which is the most comprehensive functional vision assessment procedure available for children in this mental age range, includes a complete instructional guide for teachers, observation checklists, and a book. Criterion-referenced assessment tasks are used to evaluate a wide variety of functional vision skills, from the beginning stage of visual development to the visual reading stage. Field testing indicated a high reliability coefficient (.94) and established the sequential nature of the items in eight broad categories (Berla et al., 1980; Collins & Barraga, 1980). The instructional program provides 150 lesson plans to use as guides in planning individual learning programs. The revised source book (Barraga & Morris, 1998) contains general knowledge needed by people working with low vision learners, as well as suggested handmade and commercial materials necessary for use in the instructional tasks. The program was designed for use by direct service personnel, such as teachers and therapists, as well as psychologists and psychometrists, orientation and mobility instructors, and other eye specialists. It is used extensively worldwide and has been translated into numerous languages.

The teacher of learners with visual impairments is responsible also for evaluating the most efficient learning medium for each student. This is typically achieved through administration of the *Learning Media Assessment* (Koenig & Holbrook, 1995). This procedure involves conducting a series of observations to determine the sensory channel that a student uses most frequently. This information, in combination with the functional vision evaluation, is used to determine the initial literacy medium. Koenig and Holbrook provide a detailed process for the continuing evaluation of learning media, including assessment of reading efficiency through reading rate and grade level, assessment of handwriting skills, and academic assessment of literacy tools. This assessment tool has made an important contribution in the assessment and decision making related to literacy skills of learners who are visually impaired. The authors emphasize that some students will read in both print and braille and that the assessment must be ongoing and precise in order to enable the team to make appropriate decisions about a child's learning medium. Regular assessment of reading skills, with respect to miscue analysis and general efficiency, is especially critical in ensuring that the student is using the most effective literacy tools.

The role of clinical low vision evaluation and instruction in the use of optical devices is critical when reading media is being determined. Consideration must also be given to whether large print or standard print with optical devices, or standard print alone should be used with readers having low vision. Distance reading is a factor in assessment to determine the effectiveness of a distance device (monocular) for overheads, dry-erase boards, street signs, and so forth.

Although the learning media assessment is an important tool in moving students toward literacy, it is effective also for students with multiple disabilities. It can provide the team with direction in planning for communication and learning media using materials such as drawings, symbols, and photographs. The development of this assessment tool has provided teachers of learners with visual impairments with a valuable source of data on which to base decisions about how a child can learn most effectively, so the ability to use this assessment is a vital skill for teachers of learners with visual impairments.

Tactile Assessment

For children who are totally blind and those with severe low vision, evaluation of their use of the tactual sense is of paramount importance. The *Roughness Discrimination Test* (RDT) was designed to measure the development of the ability to make coordinated tactual discriminations with the hands and fingers, which is important in learning to use braille (Nolan & Morris, 1965). The measure was validated with groups of first-grade children and showed that children who did well on the RDT at the beginning of the first grade tended to be successful in learning to read braille, whereas those who did poorly were less likely to be successful (Nolan & Morris, 1965). The American Printing House for the Blind (APH) has made available tactual discrimination worksheets, which can be used to assess skill in discriminating geometric forms, lines, angles, and braille characters, all of which are indicators of readiness to perceive and understand braille symbols. The RDT and the worksheets assess the tactual discrimination ability of young children accurately and are designed to be administered by teachers in the classroom. The advantages to this method are that no special training is required for administration and no clinical interpretation is necessary. However, because the stimuli are made from different gradations of sandpaper, some children might not wish to touch specific items.

Because braille reading involves far more than simply discriminating tactile characters, Caton (1977) concluded that there was a need for a means of identifying specific deficits in the knowledge of concepts acquired by children who were blind. Obviously, mastery of basic concepts—learning to learn and learning to read—is necessary for success in first grade and second grade. Caton developed and evaluated tactile analogs to the *Boehm Test of Basic Concepts* (Boehm, 1971) called *The Tactile Test of Basic Concepts* (1980). The tactile analogs are simple geometric shapes in raised forms for tactual perception. The format and arrangement of the shapes are comparable to the visual pictures on the original test. Use of these two measures, the RDT, and the *Boehm Test of Basic Concepts* will provide information regarding the readiness of young children for using braille in reading, and teachers may find them useful prior to the introduction of braille-reading material (Caton, 1980).

Other Assessments

Children's knowledge of body image and spatial concepts is of critical concern to teachers and to orientation and mobility instructors. Cratty and Sams (1968) developed a screening test to determine knowledge of body parts, planes, and movements. This test, the *Body Image of Blind Children*, is available from the American Foundation for the Blind. Hill and Hill (1980) have validated and revised a test for assessing the spatial–conceptual abilities of children 6 to 10 years of age.

Other special skills assessment measures and tools are available, although many lack specific standardization or reliability criteria. The *Revised Children's Manifest Anxiety Scale* (Reynolds & Richmond, 1985) is considered useful in identifying global anxiety and was the basis of a study by Wilhelm (1989) with children who had low vision and those who were blind. Another measure, designed for a doctoral dissertation, *Children's Fear Survey Schedule–Revised* (Ramirez, 1986), is a self-report survey that purports to identify specific fears evidenced by children with visual impairments. Hackney (1986) found the *Piers-Harris Children's Self-Concept Scale* (Piers & Harris, 1984) useful with gifted children in determining the attitudes and concerns they had about themselves as individuals. Several measures are designed to assess the speed and efficiency of manipulation with tools and materials, and may be quite helpful as prevocational evaluations.

SPECIAL CONSIDERATIONS IN EVALUATION AND ASSESSMENT

Regardless of the qualifications of the professional doing the evaluation and the purpose for which the child is being assessed, several critical variables affect whether or not the evaluation provides meaningful information. If a child is totally blind, then it is important to know whether the vision was lost through a deteriorating condition (as in the case of Ching Lan) or whether the blindness was present from birth (as in the case of Carlos). If the loss of vision occurred after the child had learned to function visually, the age of onset of blindness is an important factor. For students who are totally blind to feel at ease and to understand the nature of the task and the examiner's expectations of them, there needs to be a special method of presentation. Standard instructions used with sighted people are often inappropriate and confusing, leaving the child to wonder what to do as well as how to do it. Instructions should be clear and concise, permitting only one interpretation of the task to be performed. If the task is to be timed, the child should be told this so that it is clear that work is to be done with the greatest possible speed and efficiency. If various objects are to be used, the child should have time to examine them tactually and determine their location as well as the space in which they are displayed before the timing begins.

The information gathered from children who have some vision and are performing a primarily tactual task may be less easily interpreted because it is difficult to know to what degree low vision has enhanced their performance. An effective procedure might be to ask the student to close his or her eyes so as to obtain more valid results. However, this may be a disadvantage to children who have not relied solely on tactual learning in the past. In contrast, when the task is primarily visual and the person has limited visual capability, it is hard to determine whether the inability to perform a task is related to the visual impairment or whether there is lack of understanding of what is to be done. This poses another dilemma related to using evaluative materials designed for sighted individuals, especially if the performance of those who are visually limited is compared with that of their sighted peers, which would be highly inappropriate. Those with visual impairments may be perfectly capable of performing the same task, but are likely to require more time.

Psychologists and diagnosticians who are evaluating students with visual impairments should consider the following adaptations:

Students with Low Vision

- Lighting is based on needs: Some people prefer clear, bright light; others may need low light with absorptive lenses; and some may prefer to use an illuminated magnifier.
- Testing materials should be free of glare and offer high contrast.
- Printed materials should be in the form and print size used by the student for classroom activities. The student's typical optical devices and eyeglasses should be available.
- If the student prefers to hold materials closer than 14 inches, a bookstand or tiltboard should be offered.
- Students who use print adaptations are typically offered full testing time plus half. This additional testing time should be noted in the report.
- If the student has difficulty with materials and pictures that contain fine detail, magnification and enlargement should be available. Difficulties resolving detailed pictures should be noted in the report.

Students Who Are Blind

- Students should have the opportunity to be oriented to the testing room and to the assessment material if these are not familiar.
- If prompting is needed, verbal description is preferred to guiding or placing the student's hands. If it is necessary to use physical guidance, tell the student that this will occur.
- Real objects should be used in preference to models or raised line drawings, especially if the child is in preschool or early elementary school.
- Testing materials should be available in braille in preference to auditory media if the student is a braille reader.
- Students who use braille are typically offered twice the regular testing time. This additional testing time should be noted in the report.

Although any adaptation to a standardized instrument or procedure violates the normative data, this point is moot because the test already is being administered to a student who is not represented by the normative group. It is inevitable that instruments normed with sighted students will be administered to learners who are visually impaired, and psychologists or educators should note this in their reports. In addition, they should identify any error patterns that may be directly related to the visual impairment (e.g., a student who misses definitions of visual terms on the WISC–R).

COMPREHENSIVE ASSESSMENT PLAN FOR USE IN EDUCATIONAL SETTINGS

An extensive plan of behavioral evaluation includes information from many disciplines, representative samples of behavior in numerous situations, and both observational and objective data from parents, social workers, teachers, educational diagnosticians, psychometrists or psychologists, and medical specialists. The objective of assessment and evaluation at any age is to make practical judgments and decisions regarding appropriate interventions to increase performance and to determine the effectiveness of previously used strategies.

Weiner (1967) suggested that behavioral responses might be considered in the following contexts:

1. *Level of performance* indicates how much development has taken place in any dimension and the point from which to design future learning tasks. The length of time required to achieve a certain stage of development or learning is indicative of the rate at which gains may be expected.
2. *Range of behavior* suggests the array of learning opportunities provided for functioning in a broad spectrum of activities. Accuracy or behavioral adequacy in

relation to speed of performance characterizes the efficiency of achievement to be anticipated.

3. *Autonomy* can be perceived as independence when self-initiated and self-directed tasks are approached and executed without instruction. Approach and completion of assigned tasks also give insight into the ability to work toward a specific goal.

ASSESSMENT THROUGH OBSERVATION

Skills such as speed, independence, and accuracy may be evaluated through observing and recording general and specific behavioral patterns. This process can be a valuable procedure at the beginning of assessment, especially with young children or with those who have numerous problems or disabilities. For teachers, observing students on a one-to-one basis and in groups is probably the simplest means of gathering information about present levels of functioning. Teachers of students with visual impairments may use observation freely and consistently as a supplement to more structured procedures or information from objective measures. To become a sophisticated observer requires time to learn to select appropriate situations for observation, significant behaviors and responses, and practical means for recording what is seen. Observation permits the immediate assessment of the task or objective by use of a rating scale or by evaluating mastery or nonmastery of a response criterion (Silberman, 1981). Some writers use the term *ecological assessment* to describe the gathering of information under different conditions and in various environments.

For example, children may be observed in free play in a multitude of totally unstructured settings; or the environment and the materials available for use may be semistructured to limit, to some extent, the behaviors possible or to encourage certain desired responses; or the situation may be structured to require a specific type of task performance or interaction. Children who have disabilities often undergo numerous medical examinations and educational assessments. It is important for them to enjoy a sense of anonymity at times, so that they do not feel as though they are continually being assessed. Older students should have all assessments explained to them at their level of understanding.

Whatever the setting or situation, knowing what to observe is the key. Each observer might be interested in assessing particular behaviors, and consequently focus exclusively on those. Observing the following behaviors can provide pertinent information about children with visual limitations: awareness of and attention to the surrounding environment and those within it; seeking and exploratory patterns of movement; use of senses (especially vision and touch) in acquiring information and moving; use of language to elicit contact or to respond to encounters; the nature and variety of cues used for self-directed and independent actions; and the extent to which the child originates behavior or adapts to materials or to people. These few suggestions may stimulate teachers and others to develop their own ideas about what to observe.

Carefully recording the observations on checklists or scales can help estimate the functional status of children across all developmental dimensions including sensory (especially visual development); motor; language; cognitive; social, emotional, or self-help; and academic skills (Chase, 1986a, 1986b; Moore & McLaughlin, 1992). A chart or profile plotted or drawn across all behavioral domains might give the teacher a basis for determining some reasonable short-term objectives, for planning appropriate tasks or interactions, and for beginning instruction pending more comprehensive and ongoing assessments.

For some children, observational evaluations might be the most desirable procedure for quite some time, whereas others might be ready for more extensive or other types of assessment techniques using carefully selected criterion-referenced or standardized measures, or both. The following section provides a sequential summary of procedures and instruments mentioned earlier, which may provide a guide for gathering assessment information about children with visual impairments from the time of identification (as soon after birth as possible) until they leave school and are part of the larger society. The assessment and evaluation procedure is followed by a period of instruction, after which additional assessment and evaluation on an ongoing basis are conducted as required by present legislation.

The guidelines for assessment and evaluation outlined in this chapter are to be considered as options from which professionals and parents may choose when designing the most feasible plan for each child. The choices reflect the quality of information considered to be most helpful to teachers in planning the instructional program.

Preschool Assessment

Eligibility requirements for service delivery to infants and toddlers specified in P. L. 99-457 necessitate the establishment of developmental delay in one or more of the following areas: physical, cognitive, speech–language, psychosocial, and self-help; children at risk due to environmental or biological factors are also eligible. Careful assessment of each dimension is required before any delay can be documented. The ideal is for a team of specialists in all these areas to work with the parents in making the determination and evaluation. The approach to assessment in the infant and preschool–age child might include information gathered from the following sources:

- *Medical information*. The nature and severity of the visual impairment and the prognosis as to whether the condition is stable, treatable, or deteriorating can be acquired from diagnostic files, consultation with the eye specialist, or both, along with the uses for prescribed lenses or optical devices.

- *Family history and experience*. A home visit by a case worker, social worker, or teacher can assess family attitudes and parenting skills of family members. A complete analysis of these findings may give an idea of the general patterns and expectations to include in future evaluations.

• *Checklists or developmental scales*. These can be initiated during a home visit and completed on subsequent visits or through other contacts. A wide variety of these are available to evaluate physical, personal, social–emotional, and language development.

• *Selected instruments*. The *Vineland Adaptive Behavior Scales–Expanded Form* (Sparrow, Balla, & Cicchetti, 1984) and the *Maxfield-Bucholz Social Maturity Scale for Blind Pre-school Children* (Maxfield & Bucholz, 1957) can be administered during a home visit, but verification is suggested to take place through future observations in other environments. The *Reynell-Zinkin Developmental Scales for Young Visually Handicapped Children* (Reynell & Zinkin, 1980), *Functional Vision Screening Inventory for the Severely and Multiply Handicapped* (Langley, 1980), and the *Diagnostic Assessment Procedure* (Barraga, 1980b) all were designed specifically for children with low vision. The *Callier-Azusa Scale* (Stillman, 1979) has been validated for use with children who are deaf-blind, as well as others with multiple disabilities. Portions of the following standardized (on sighted populations) instruments may be selected for use with specific children as appropriate: *Bayley Scales for Infant Development* (Bayley, 1993); *Battelle Developmental Inventory* (Newborg et al., 1984); Ordinal Scales of Psychological Development (Uzgiris & Hunt, 1975); *Kaufman Assessment Battery for Children* (Kaufman & Kaufman, 1983); and the *Wechsler Preschool and Primary Scale of Intelligence–Revised* (Wechsler, 1989).

Primary and Elementary Assessment

The following materials are recommended for assessing primary and elementary students with visual impairments:

• *Teacher observation and checklists:* Teachers often find it valuable to record information derived from both informal and formal observation of movement behavior, use of hands in exploration, use of low vision, and responses to sound and auditory stimuli. Teacher-made or selected checklists might be useful also for documenting personal and social skills observed and other functional behaviors considered desirable. The *Reynell-Zinkin Developmental Scales* (Reynell & Zinkin, 1980) and the *Callier-Azusa Scale* (Stillman, 1979) can be used with children who have multiple disabilities. Other recommended instruments include the *Peabody Model Vision Project Scales* (Harley, DuBose, & Bourgeault, 1980), the *Peabody Mobility Scales* (Harley et al.,1981), and the *Developmental Activities Screening Inventory* (Fewell & Langley, 1984).

• Available and appropriate instruments (all or portions):

Mental Development

Wechsler scales (WPPSI–R or WISC–III; Wechsler, 1989, 1991)—Verbal and Performance subtests as desired

The Blind Learning Aptitude Test (BLAT; Newland, 1961, 1979)—for students who are blind or near blind

An Intelligence Test for Visually Impaired Children (ITVIC) (Dekker et al., 1991)

An Intelligence Test Series for Blind and Low Vision Children (Dekker et al., 1991)

McCarthy Scales of Children's Abilities (McCarthy, 1972)—selected subtests as appropriate

Readiness and Achievement

Boehm Test of Basic Concepts (Boehm, 1971)—for students with low vision

The Tactile Test of Basic Concepts (Caton, 1980)—for students who are blind or near blind

Peabody Picture Vocabulary Test–Revised (Dunn & Dunn, 1981)—screening measure for word meanings

Stanford Achievement Test–9th Edition (Harcourt Brace Educational Measurement, 1996)—in braille or large print

Visual Functioning

Visual Efficiency Scale (Barraga, 1970)—screening measure

Diagnostic Assessment Procedure (Barraga, 1980b)

Tactile Discrimination

Roughness Discrimination Test (Nolan & Morris, 1965)

Body Image and Orientation

Body Image of Blind Children (Cratty & Sams, 1968)—screening test

Hill Performance Test of Selected Positional Concepts (Hill & Hill, 1980)

Other Assessments

Piers-Harris Children's Self-Concept Scale (Piers & Harris, 1984)

Revised Children's Manifest Anxiety Scale (Reynolds & Richmond, 1985)

High School and Young Adult Assessment

The following instruments are useful for assessing high school students and young adults who are visually disabled:

- *Haptic Intelligence Scale for Adult Blind* (Shurrager, 1961)
- *Wechsler Adult Intelligence Scale* (Wechsler, 1981)

- *Scholastic Achievement Test* in braille and large print
- Selected special skills tests or criterion-referenced measures

Assessment and evaluation at the secondary level are valuable for counseling the student on his or her potential for advanced academic work or for specific vocational goals. Determining attitudes and interests in specific vocations is important as a basis for selecting training, and can minimize the tendency to try to fit a student into a vocation rather than helping a student identify vocations for which he or she is best suited. Continued assessment should be made of family attitudes, personal management skills, and the competencies necessary for independent living. The more information given to young people, the greater the likelihood of their success in the future.

Excellent guidelines for assessment can be found in Chase's chapters (1986a, 1986b), Bradley-Johnson (1986), and VanderKolk (1981). Valuable suggestions for educational and psychological assessment (Glenshaft, Dare, & O'Malley, 1980) stress the factors that should concern the professionals doing the assessments. The summary of listings presented is not intended to include all of the possible instruments or approaches to assessment, but is a beginning, and it may be helpful to teachers and less experienced examiners in choosing measures from which selections can be made.

SUMMARY

Even though federal legislation specifies that the use of appropriate instruments and procedures of assessment be administered by qualified people, tremendous discrepancies exist across and within states regarding interpretation of the guidelines. The types of behaviors to be assessed and the measures to be used vary from school to school, even within states or provinces. These facts indicate that there is little consistency in assessment and evaluation of students with visual disabilities. This may not be entirely negative, but some minimal universal standards would certainly be useful. Nevertheless, many positive trends have been observed, including expansion of the range of behaviors assessed, a greater role for teachers in the process, and more measures included in assessments.

The suggestions for assessment and evaluation outlined in this chapter are to be considered options from which professionals and parents can choose when designing the most feasible plan for each child. The choices may reflect the quality of information considered most helpful to teachers in planning children's instructional programs and to parents in understanding the strengths and weaknesses of their children.

Core Curriculum and Adaptations

As Ching Lan, who is rapidly losing her vision, continues her education in public school, she will meet teachers who will react in different ways to their responsibility to instruct a student with a visual impairment. If they have never taught such a student before, they may have many questions about whether Ching Lan can learn effectively in their classrooms: Will she be able to get all her books in braille in time for her classes? How can she participate in classes such as physical education or art, which involve special activities and materials? Can she continue to read printed material even after she has started to use braille as her major reading medium?

In the education of students with visual impairments, two key questions must be addressed: What should be taught, and how should that content be presented? This chapter addresses the core curriculum, which focuses on what should be taught. The following chapter deals with educational materials used in presenting the curriculum. In both chapters, instructional decisions are highly individualized and require the IEP team to balance the importance of minimizing adaptations for greater normalization with the need to present learning in a form that can be best interpreted by a child with a visual limitation.

SPECIALIZED CURRICULUM

The general practice in educational programming for students with visual impairments, especially in public schools, has been to parallel the academic curriculum of sighted students but to provide different materials, equipment, and teaching devices. The underlying assumption is that this practice enables students to learn the same academic subjects as sighted peers; however, this assumption is not always based on an objective appraisal of the student's functional achievement.

In specialized schools, this tendency has been less prevalent. Although residential schools offer the same or similar academic subjects as public schools, they usually include many other subjects not considered necessary or appropriate for students with visual disabilities who attend some public schools (e.g., homemaking, vocational education, computer skills). After federal legislation provided funds to establish teacher education programs across the entire field of special education and to expand educational research through colleges and universities as well as through the American Printing House for the Blind, increasing evidence indicated that greater attention should be given to selecting a specialized curriculum regardless of the type or location of the program.

In 1994, a national initiative was planned by a group of parents, professionals, and other stakeholders with interest in the education of students with visual impairments. A consortium of individuals met at the Josephine Taylor Institute in Washington, D.C., to develop goal statements that set priorities for the field. Guided by a steering committee that included Anne Corn, Phil Hatlen, Kathleen Huebner, Frank Ryan, and Mary Ann Siller, participants in the conference set eight goals that would have a significant impact on education over the next 10 years.

All of the following goal statements apply to infants, children and youth who are blind or visually impaired, including those with multiple disabilities (Corn & Huebner, 1998):

1. Students and their families will be referred to an appropriate education program within 30 days of identification of a suspected visual impairment.
2. Policies and procedures will be implemented to ensure the rights of all parents to fully participate and equal partnership in the education process.
3. Universities, with a minimum of one full-time faculty member in the area of visual impairment, will prepare a sufficient number of educators of students with visual impairments to meet personnel needs throughout the country.
4. Service providers will determine caseloads based on the needs of students and will require ongoing professional development for all teachers and orientation and mobility instructors.
5. Local education programs will ensure that all students have access to a full array of placement options.
6. Assessment of students will be conducted, in collaboration with parents, by personnel having expertise in the education of students with visual impairments.
7. Access to developmental and educational services will include an assurance that instructional materials are available to students in the appropriate media and at the same time as their sighted peers.
8. Educational and developmental goals, including instruction, will reflect the assessed needs of each student in all areas of academic and disability-specific core curricula. (pp. 9–10)

The implementation of these goals is underway at the state and national levels. Individual states have made progress in informing legislators about the needs of learners who are visually impaired, determining needs of these students in their states, and obtaining funding to address the *National Agenda* goals. The ability of families and pro fessionals to address these goals on a national basis is an indication of the collaboration that is critical in advocating for students with low incidence educational needs.

In the following sections, seven broad classes of content are discussed: communication, orientation and mobility, social interaction, independent living, recreation and leisure, visual efficiency, and career–vocational preparation. Specific issues in each area are described.

Communication

The more efficient an individual is in communicating with other people, acquiring information, and functioning in all aspects of learning and living, the more his or her confidence and feelings of self-worth will grow.

For most students with visual impairments, spoken language will be the primary form of communication with others; however, for some children with additional disabilities, oral communication through speech may not be an option. These children will be taught to express themselves through the use of natural gestures, augmentative communication systems such as communication boards, or a formal manual language such as American Sign Language (ASL). Regardless of the system, communication methods should be adapted to make them accessible to each child with a visual impairment; one child might require the use of symbols with high contrast on a communication board, whereas another might need instruction in receiving signs and gestures tactilely.

For the student who uses speech as a primary form of communication, development of skills in the effective use of spoken language will contribute to success in the academic environment as well as in the workplace during later years. Because students with severe visual impairments are usually unable to see a speaker or an audience to perceive their nonverbal cues, skills such as eye contact, organized expression of thoughts, and changing topics appropriately, may need to be developed using planned strategies. A course in spoken communication for junior or senior high school students is essential. It could include the following topics, as suggested by Simon (1974): interviewing, conversation, small-group communication, listening and receiving information and responding, appropriate language and expression, and nonverbal communication. For older students, planning, organizing, and presenting a public speech for communicating an idea is a useful project.

Listening is another critical area of specialized knowledge for the student with a visual impairment. Exercises in listening skills should begin in the early school years and receive increased emphasis as children with visual impairments progress through school. Even though junior high and high school students continue to use braille or print reading for most of their school learning, data on efficiency in acquiring information suggest that these students should begin to rely more on listening as a primary source of information. The process of listening actively for learning, which is called "auding," can be taught through the use of gradually more complex and independent tasks.

At the early levels, students develop readiness for formal listening experiences. Harley, Truan, and Sanford (1987) and Heinze (1986) described the readiness skills that may develop a foundation of listening abilities: awareness, identification, and discrimination of sound; ability to detect similarities and differences in words; development of a listening vocabulary; aptitude in following directions; and ability to follow a sequence and associate meaning with sound.

Later, students develop critical listening skills, learn note-taking skills, and develop the ability to summarize information and identify the most important points. Heinze (1986) emphasized the importance of "active" listening to increase comprehension. This approach encourages the student to react to the material being heard through the use of note taking, review, or problem solving. Well-developed listening skills are even more important now that speech access is available through technology. Optical scanners can translate speech into sound, and synthetic speech is available to provide spoken output from computers. Students who are visually impaired must be skilled in scanning auditory material and identifying important ideas in order to use spoken language as a means of learning.

Students may want to try several forms of rapid speech and evaluate their comprehension when information is provided at a faster rate. This can be done by simply accelerating the speed of standard recording devices; however, with increased speed, the pitch also accelerates and creates a chipmunk-voice effect. Devices to produce compressed speech are available; through this variation, pitch is not raised, although speed is increased. The pitch-down effect is included in the recorders provided for auditory readers by the American Printing House for the Blind and the National Library Service. Some students can manage increased speed produced on a standard tape recorder and can maintain comprehension up to 275 to 300 words per minute (Harley, et al., 1987; Swallow & Conner, 1982).

Nolan (1966) compared braille reading with listening and found that listening to recorded materials required only about one third of the time required for tactual reading of the same material, and that no loss in comprehension was experienced. Several studies have indicated that there is no difference in comprehension of material presented at a normal rate of speed, material presented at a compressed rate, and material read in braille. Studies do show, nevertheless, that "reading" by listening to compressed speech is more efficient, from the standpoint of both speed and comprehension, than either reading through braille or reading by listening to a recording at a normal rate of speech.

Study skills are also an important part of a curriculum in communication skills within an academic environment. A student's ability to set priorities by outlining material, taking notes, and summarizing important points is critical both when listening and reading. In addition, a student's ability to schedule study time efficiently and to manage assignment deadlines play a part in academic success. As a child grows older, responsibilities such as locating and scheduling readers and maintaining equipment will also influence the efficiency of learning.

Written language forms pose some special challenges to students with visual impairments because of either the need for adaptations in writing standard print or the need to learn a separate writing system through braille. Students with severe visual impairments almost always require specialized instruction in written language during the elementary years. This is universally true for students to become braille readers because instruction in the mechanics of the braille code, skills in proper reading and writing techniques, and the rules for appropriate usage of braille symbols are not taught in the regular classroom. New technology, described later in the chapter on educational materials, has made braille materials more widely available and has made the process of braille translation possible for anyone who has a knowledge of keyboard skills; therefore, it is likely that braille will become an even more important medium for those students who do not have sufficient vision to manage print efficiently.

During the first few years when children are learning to read print, braille, or both, there is little difference in reading speed between braille and print reading (Nolan & Kederis, 1969); however, after the midelementary years, even the best braille readers are unable to achieve the same reading speed as the sighted reader. Efficiency in braille reading requires thorough knowledge and recognition of the symbols; therefore, training in recognizing braille symbols as a means of increasing reading speed should be emphasized very strongly by teachers. Several professionals have explored the importance of efficient mechanical and motor training in developing the movements that are important for braille reading (Mangold, 1978; Wormsley, 1981). Mangold created a set of materials designed to train students in the efficient use of hand movements and knowledge of concepts necessary for successful braille reading.

There have been recent concerns about the process of deciding whether a child is to be a braille reader or a print reader. These concerns might be influenced in part by the emphasis on visual development skills over the past 20 years, as described by Rex (1989); she underscored the importance of a balanced perspective in encouraging literacy in the most efficient media. Jones (1961) found a wide variation in the reading medium (braille or print) in children with varying degrees of visual acuity. Some children with very low acuity were found to be print readers, whereas other children with much higher visual acuity were found to be braille readers. Children who have limited visual functioning, and whose visual reading is slow and requires specifically prepared materials and optimal lighting conditions, may learn to read in both print and braille; while print can serve them for brief, functional tasks such as reading labels on food packages or short notes or assignments, braille may remain their primary reading medium for larger quantities of information such as novels or textbooks.

The decision about which media are appropriate for a child cannot be based on visual acuity alone; a variety of factors must be considered. Mangold and Mangold (1989) identified five major considerations in the selection of reading media, including working distance, portability, reading rate, visual fatigue, and assessment results. These authors recommended consideration of braille for students who are not reading print faster than 60 words per minute by late elementary school. Koenig and Holbrook (1995) have described a detailed procedure for use in identifying the primary reading medium for students. In some cases, a secondary medium will be appropriate also. This procedure identifies a variety of factors that will influence the decision about what medium a student should use, including stability of the eye condition, intactness of central visual field, reliance on visual or tactile means of gathering information, presence of additional disabilities, and general readiness for reading instruction.

Visual media are preferred for children who can develop sufficient speed and endurance while reading print. Studies (Ashcroft, Halliday, & Barraga, 1965; Barraga, 1964, 1980b) have indicated that, when given an appropriate program in visual perceptual development and use of vision, many children with low vision can be effective visual learners. This can be a long process for some children, depending on their other characteristics, such as motivation, intelligence, and the readiness to learn visually. Although children used to be blindfolded, or in some other way prevented from looking at braille so as not to read with their eyes, it is now generally accepted that, if a child can read braille with the eyes, then something easier to read visually than braille should be provided. The provision of optical devices probably would permit such a child to do some visual reading and satisfy the innate desire to use whatever vision is available.

Writing skills are another aspect of communication that require particular emphasis. For children who are totally blind, braille writing usually begins after the child has been exposed to the braille reading system, understands that the symbols produced through writing can carry meaning, and follows basic instructions and attends well enough to operate a braille writer. It is not necessary to delay braille writing until the child can read letters and words; in fact, there has been some tendency to teach reading and writing of braille simultaneously. The student who is blind will also use the slate and stylus, usually beginning in midelementary school. This tool provides a more portable writing method as content demands increase in school and the need for making notes in other settings becomes more necessary. Two advantages of the braille writer for the younger child are that less fine motor coordination is required to use the writer and the child's braille productions are immediately available in an upright position for examination and feedback. In contrast, paper must be turned over and the slate removed to read what is written by the stylus because the dots are depressed. Using the slate and stylus also requires that the student understand the process of reversal with respect to the braille cell because each letter is written as a mirror image of the readable cell. For this reason, learning the braille symbols by dot numbers might make writing much easier. Writing with the slate and stylus is done from right to left because the braille dots are punched down instead of up, unlike the dots made with the braille writer. Developing efficiency in braille writing is necessary for all students who are totally blind; this efficiency gives them the ability to monitor sentence structure for academic work and also to communicate among themselves.

Handwriting can pose special challenges for the student with low vision, and the teaching techniques used may vary. Rather than teaching manuscript letters from the beginning, it is often more appropriate to begin with cursive or a modified method of cursive such as the D'Nealian script. This precludes the child from having to lift the pen or pencil from the paper each time a letter is completed. Harley et al. (1987) identified the cursive letters *b*, *v*, *w*, and *o* as particularly difficult because they terminate at midline rather than on the baseline. In addition, because spacing is hard to estimate when vision is poor, learning from the start to connect letters in cursive writing is easier and more logical. However, learning to form the letters and to join them may take longer than it would for normally sighted children and will require more assistance. Some teachers have found that beginning the writing process at the chalkboard makes it easier for the student with low vision to see at eye level and to use larger (gross motor) movements when forming the letters. Legibility rather than perfection is the goal. Heinze (1986) cautioned that although cursive writing may be easier for a child with a visual impairment to produce, it may be less easily read; therefore, decisions about the most appropriate method needs to be made based on an individual child's visual and motor ability. Some teachers have found the closed-circuit television screen to be helpful to the student with low vision in learning to write script because the size of the product can be adjusted for self-evaluation.

For the student who is blind, handwriting should be taught in order to produce a legible signature. This can begin when the child has an interest in the use of the pencil and motivation to produce a readable signature. Some teachers advocate teaching handwriting along with braille writing to acquaint children with both braille and print symbols as a means of facilitating the association between them. From the standpoint of motor development, it would be appropriate to teach students who are blind (as suggested for those with low vision) to write on the chalkboard first, because gross movements are easier than the finer movements required by pencil and paper. Once they have learned the letter formations, they can transfer the skills to pencil and paper. Some materials are designed specifically to produce raised lines that are tactually distinguishable. Some children without any vision learn to write script well and can thereby communicate with their sighted classmates through writing. Students with very low vision or those with additional motor problems may write script only for personal reasons and do most of their schoolwork using the typewriter for the sake of legibility and efficiency.

For most students with visual impairments, keyboarding, or typing, is also an essential part of the curriculum. It can be introduced as early as third grade, when the child has learned a basic writing vocabulary. Introducing typing as early as seems appropriate for the individual may prove valuable for strengthening spelling skills and perhaps also for fostering mental memory because the typist with a visual impairment must remember not only what has been typed, but also what is to follow in order to become aware of location within the paragraph and on the page. As soon as children in public schools become efficient in typing, they can prepare their own work much more independently. This ability can influence the extent to which they can be integrated with sighted peers and achieve success in the classroom. It is the responsibility of the teacher of the visually impaired to teach touch-typing to the child who is ready for this skill.

With the increasing early use of computers in the elementary school, a variety of technological options are available for keyboard instruction and practice that provide immediate feedback to the students. Speech synthesizers and screen review programs allow the child to hear the computer speak the name of the letter just pressed or read the sentence just written. In addition, the lighter touch required on computer keyboards might allow children to master keyboarding skills at an earlier age. The variety of highly motivating software and the opportunity for immediate feedback through computer instruction make typing a skill that may be more readily attainable at a younger age for the learner with a visual impairment.

Academic skills related to concepts, experiences, and ideas also will need to be adapted for many learners with visual impairments. Social studies, science, and mathematics all encompass abstract ideas that involve space, distance, visual features, or large or small objects that might not be understandable to a child who learns through touch. Representation of ideas through the use of real objects, tactile models and diagrams, and meaningful verbal description will ensure that the learner has understood the concept and perceives the relationship of elements in a larger idea. The recent development of new ways of producing tactile graphics through technology offers options for complex processes such as creating graphs or charts by translating printed lines into raised lines. In using such methods, professionals should be sure that the tactile representation is simple and does not reduce a three-dimensional drawing to a raised line drawing that is not meaningful to blind individuals.

In all areas of academic learning, students with visual impairments may require alternative approaches to learning. With appropriate materials and the opportunity for practice, students can master academic concepts and skills.

Orientation and Mobility

A second aspect of the specialized curriculum is instruction in basic skills and concepts related to orientation within the environment, and independent travel. All students with visual impairments should be assessed by an orientation and mobility specialist to determine whether instruction in these areas should be part of the student's educational program. The orientation and mobility specialist is trained to work with students on the development of skills in body and environmental concepts, interpretation of maps, maintaining orientation in space, use of travel devices including the long cane, and route travel.

As students acquire basic knowledge of the body and its relationship to environmental space, mobility instructors can teach them to move within that environment without assistance. Individuals with visual impairments can travel using a cane, guide dog, independent skills, human guide, or with the assistance of travel devices. Acquiring efficient travel skills requires long and intensive attention to the physical activities and skills of each student from a qualified orientation and mobility instructor.

Instruction in orientation and mobility is important also for the student with low vision. Awareness of one's own near and distance vision, visual fields, and ability to recognize contrast in the environment are skills that can be applied during travel. Many people with low vision benefit from the use of optical devices during travel, and the orientation and mobility instructor can teach skills related to scanning, locating targets, tracking, and tracing to locate targets. The student with low vision should be aware of the advantages of the long cane during travel. Some students will use canes to travel only in specific situations such as poorly lighted environments (Smith & Geruschat, 1996).

For young students, orientation and mobility instruction will focus on understanding body parts and spatial relationships as well as early use of devices that will provide protection and information about the environment. Cane travel is now introduced to preschoolers, in contrast to past practice that recommended waiting until children had developed basic concepts. Sometimes younger students or those with multiple disabilities are taught to use adaptive mobility devices, which are custom-designed devices that can be moved in front of the children to provide wider coverage or ease of handling, without the need for the firm manual control required for use of a cane (Skellenger & Hill, 1997).

As students become older, they will learn skills to travel independently within their neighborhood and later, in the community and beyond. Use of the long cane and low vision devices, skills for requesting assistance and information, the ability to plan and negotiate a route, and the ability to use public transportation will need to be learned through a process of specific planning and feedback. Because most students with visual impairments will not drive a car, they should also learn the skills associated with being a nondriver. Instructional responsibilities in this area go beyond the responsibilities of the orientation and mobility specialist and include other team members who can address social skills related to requesting rides, choosing transportation options, and planning trips. A recent publication, *Finding Wheels: A Curriculum for Nondrivers with Visual Impairments for Getting Control of Transportation Needs* (Corn & Rosenblum, 2000), provides a variety of goals and activities to assist nondriving students in making choices and becoming more independent travelers.

Students with multiple disabilities also can benefit from specific instruction in orientation and mobility, even though their ability to travel independently may be limited. Bailey and Head (1993) described the importance of teaching functional skills in real-life environments for these students. These authors emphasize the use of discrepancy analysis, which involves conparing the student's performance to that of a typical individual and identifying steps that need to be taught. By breaking the route or activity into small steps, the orientation and mobility instructor can teach one step at a time, providing specific feedback and instruction.

Social Interaction Skills

The area of social–emotional adjustment has received increasing attention over the last few years, and there is mounting evidence that many students with visual impairments in mainstream settings need special instruction to acquire the skills that will enable them to interact appropriately with peers and adults in the school setting. A study by Hoben and Lindstrom (1980) reported significantly fewer interactions by students with visual impairments in a regular school classroom, based on detailed observations of 22 students whose vision ranged from total blindness to acuities better than 20/100. In this study, 61% of classroom teachers saw these students as spending more time alone than other students in the class. Corn and Bishop (1984) reported lower than normal scores for students who were visually disabled on the *Test of Practical Knowledge*, which includes social knowledge among its subtests. In her 1986 study of factors that influence success in the mainstream, Bishop found that respondents rated peer acceptance and social skills as the second and third most important variables in determining success, outranked only by the role of an accepting classroom teacher.

Recent research in social skills has targeted some areas in which social experiences may be different for students with visual impairments. Wolffe and Sacks (1997) reported that students with low vision engaged in more passive activities during their leisure time, and that students who are blind or have low vision spent more time alone. However, in studying the friendships of adolescents with visual impairments, Rosenblum (1997) found that these students had numbers of close friends similar to sighted adolescents, and reported satisfying and mutually supportive friendships. MacCuspie (1992), though, found that participation in group activities decreased with age for students with visual impairments. These studies suggest not only that there may be differences in the extent and frequency of social interactions for some learners who are visually impaired, but also that many students with visual impairments have shaped their social experiences to accommodate their interests and abilities.

The role of parents in supporting the social development of young people with visual impairments is an important one. Chang and Schaller (2000) described the importance of parental support for students who are visually impaired, emphasizing the significance of values and sense of safety within the home environment. Students in their study who did not feel supported by families cited overprotectiveness or negativity as barriers to support. Professional support might be helpful to families who are working to cope with their own feelings about their child's visual impairment as they attempt also to support the student.

For children with visual disabilities, both with and without multiple impairments, acquiring functional skills related to socialization might take precedence over academic learning in the beginning, especially if the children are expected to spend time in the regular classroom. Social amenities of how to respond to others and how to behave in certain social situations might be unknown to children who are unable to monitor the environment or to see the social behavior they are expected to imitate. Such social skills must be practiced with understanding teachers.

The curricular goals in social skills for students who are visually impaired have received increasing attention in the literature. Corn (1985) proposed an independence matrix for learners, which promotes decision-making strategies for students in the areas of resources, problem solving, self-advocacy, and social skills. Corn stressed the importance of student initiative and independence in managing problems as they arise. Read (1989) presented an observational checklist for preschoolers with visual impairments, which specifies behaviors in the areas of participating in actions with others, maintaining relationships, assertiveness skills, classroom skills, and cafeteria skills

Huebner (1986) identified major areas of concern in social skills for students with visual disabilities as the following: stereotypical behaviors and nonverbal communications, including body motion, physical characteristics, touching behavior, voice qualities, proxemics, artifacts or objects that provide nonverbal cues, and the environment.

In these and other areas, students may require specific instruction and feedback in generalizing what they have learned into a natural setting. With respect to nonverbal communication, for example, students may work with their teacher on the appropriate use of the hands to express excitement or conviction while speaking. The instruction might begin with the student touching the adult's hands and modeling the gestures until they can be produced with appropriate timing and fluency; then the student can begin to use those gestures with friends and family who can provide feedback about the appropriateness of the gestures; finally, the student can begin to use them with unfamiliar people and in formal speaking situations until they look quite natural.

Other areas in which students with visual impairments might need additional feedback and practice include the establishment of eye contact (or apparent eye contact); entering and exiting from conversations because spatial and nonverbal cues might not be read easily; communication through space decisions (e.g., in an empty theater, one does not select a seat right next to the only other person); and voice control according to the size of the room and the group receiving the information. Awareness of social routines in these areas will help a student appear more like schoolmates and will make others feel comfortable during informal interactions.

For the student who experiences unusual difficulties related to socialization, the educational program should provide support services to help in dealing with short- and long-term needs. These might include counseling for the student and, in some cases, referrals for families to assist them in working with difficulties or crises within the family structure. Ching Lan's family, for example, might want some support during the time that their daughter is experiencing an unpredictable loss of vision. Family referral to genetic counseling can be of assistance when there is a question about the origin of the child's visual disability; the provision of additional information or options in this area can contribute to the well-being of the entire family.

Human sexuality is also an area of social skills that requires special attention in the curriculum of the child with a visual impairment; Huebner (1986), Spungin (1984), E. Scott (1982), and Neff (1982) all emphasized the importance of sexuality education in the unique curriculum. An awareness of oneself as a sexual being begins early for all children; attitudes and understanding related to normal sexual development are formed according to whether, and in what ways, questions arising from a child's normal curiosity are answered or ignored (Dickman, 1975; Knappett & Wagner, 1976; Neff, 1982; Tait & Kessler, 1976). The nature of these attitudes emerges through the interplay of three factors: the child's own impression of a sexual self; the visible, audible, and tangible expressions of all those around the child; and the child's own desire for sex education. Typical experiences of the sighted child, such as seeing a young baby bathed, brothers or sisters unclothed, and men and women in pictures and in television and movies, cannot be experienced by children who are blind.

By the time children with visual disabilities reach high school and begin to thin about relationships (and marriage), they might have incomplete or erroneous ideas o even be totally ignorant of the basic facts regarding body parts and functions. Distorte ideas or lack of information about the consequences associated with sexual relation ships could have unfortunate results. Courses in sex education and preparation fo marriage and family life are absolutely necessary for children and youth with visual im pairments. Suggestions and guidelines for planning courses can be found in the entir May 1974 issue of *The New Outlook for the Blind* as well as in Neff (1982).

Many concepts related to sexuality can be presented in alternative ways for stu dents with visual impairments. Differences in clothing and hairstyles of males and fe males, for example, might need to be explained to a young child with a visual impair ment and can be confirmed through touch and conversation. Other concepts particularly those related to anatomy and reproduction, are more difficult to presen concretely because of society's taboos on touch as it relates to gathering information in these areas. Anatomical models are available from a number of companies as well as from local Planned Parenthood organizations; these can be helpful in presenting con cepts such as reproduction and birth control, when a student is ready to learn abou these processes.

Sexuality and social skills are a necessary part of the curriculum for the child with visual limitations. Because these students often miss information about the world that others gain incidentally, it takes careful planning to provide them with the skills needed to interact appropriately with others. Even for children as young as Carl and Lucy, parents and teachers should begin to include information about social events beyond the children's immediate scope and to provide opportunities in which the children can actively participate and monitor interactions with other children their age as well as with adults.

Independent Living Skills

Many of the concepts a sighted child learns incidentally about managing daily routines might not be learned incidentally by a child with a visual impairment. For example, children who are blind cannot watch others tie their shoes before they begin to try it. They might not be aware of how to open a milk carton or prepare a sandwich unless others call attention to these activities through verbal description or actual participation. Instruction in such areas as dressing and clothing care, eating, grooming, food preparation, housecleaning, safety skills, and home maintenance may be necessary as part of an educational program that moves students with visual disabilities toward independence.

Attention to daily living skills should begin during the preschool years. At this age, children should learn mealtime, toileting, and dressing routines. They should be able to use eating utensils at stages similar to those of sighted children, and they should be able to dress themselves fully by school age, with the possible exception of difficult fasteners and shoe tying. Also by school age, a child with a visual impairment and no additional disabilities should be able to manage toileting routines independently.

During the elementary school years, children should take increasing responsibility for managing their own care and their own possessions. Activities that an elementary school child can learn include selecting clothing according to preferences and weather conditions; washing and caring for his or her own hair; participating in household routines such as laundering clothing and shopping for food; and handling small amounts of personal money. Frequent communication between home and school about self-care responsibilities is important at this time to ensure consistency in instructional approaches and program priorities.

By high school, students should be taking primary responsibility for their own grooming, care, and organization of personal possessions. This includes ordering and maintaining special devices and equipment, such as braille writers. In addition, the older student should be able to apply social skills appropriate for different settings (e.g., be aware of the differences between behaviors expected at a fast-food restaurant and those expected at a formal restaurant).

Instruction of specific skills related to daily living often can be accomplished by breaking the task into its component substeps, a process called *task analysis*. The sighted instructor might be able to distinguish the components of the task that require adaptation by personally attempting the task while wearing occluders. It is surprising to discover that many familiar tasks (e.g., opening a jar or tying a shoe) provide tactile feedback that is sufficient to accomplish the task without the use of vision. Other tasks (e.g., threading a needle or putting on makeup) might require use of alternative strategies or equipment to accomplish the tasks without the feedback normally provided by vision.

In teaching daily living skills, some adaptations are common across tasks and should be considered when planning instruction. Ponchillia and Ponchillia (1997) describe safety, orientation and mobility, organization, identification, and monitoring as principles that may require adjustments when teaching daily living skills. These areas can be addressed by instructing the student in managing them or by using adapted materials, such as a knife guide, when doing specific tasks.

In some public school settings, students with visual impairments are discouraged from participating in subject areas such as home economics and industrial arts, in which these students would have the opportunity to learn practical skills to help them become independent. McConnell (1984) described some approaches for integrating children with visual impairments into industrial arts classes, and suggested resources to facilitate this integration. He stressed the importance of teacher and classmate attitudes, availability of a special teacher, limitation of class size, and use of special devices, as factors that could enhance the student's ability to gain from participation in such specialized classes.

Students with visual impairments in public schools usually have busy schedules that must encompass regular curricula as well as disability-specific skills. Frequently, instructional activities in daily living skills are set aside, and emphasis is placed on keeping up with peers in academic subjects. It is the responsibility of the teacher o students with visual impairments, along with the child and the family, to advocate fo instruction in daily living skills and to convince the greater school community of th importance of these skills, which contribute to the long-term success and independence of the student.

Recreation and Leisure Skills

Students with visual impairments should have the opportunity to explore a wide variety of leisure and recreational activities, just as their sighted peers do. Awareness o opportunities for physical and recreational activities can be attained through forma instruction, such as physical education classes, and through informal opportunities t join friends and family members who are engaging in recreational pursuits.

Physical activities might not be motivating to students with visual impairments fo several reasons. Because of the lack of visual feedback and confidence in movin through space, children with visual disabilities frequently are less physically active an develop poor tone, physical posture, and stamina. Literature in this area reflects the poo physical development of many students with visual impairments (DePauw, 1981). Eve students with visual disabilities who participated in a quality program of physical education demonstrated a poor general quality of physical development and problems such a being overweight, having poor muscle tone and stamina, and lacking motivation t participate in physical exercise, according to a study by Jankowski and Evans (1981).

Appropriate programming in physical skills may be an area of special concern i the educational program of children with visual impairments. Because of the large size of many public school physical education classes and the frequent emphasis on tean sports with strong visual components, students with visual impairments may be involved only to a limited degree, and lack opportunities to become active participants Teachers may assume that these students are incapable of participation or that the have no need to acquire certain skills. Students may be reluctant to participate in activities that are physically challenging, and the teacher may not encourag participation.

Although IDEA requires participation in physical education or the provision of a adapted program for students who are visually impaired, many students do not receiv quality opportunities to improve physical skills and to participate in regular physica activity (Craft, 1986). Many physical activities and most competitive sports need to b modified or adapted for some students with visual limitations, but their participation i beneficial, providing social interaction as well as contributing to a positive body imag for the development of a stronger self-concept. The use of environmental connecto (e.g., ropes or railings), the location of consistent auditory cues for orientation, and th establishment of tactile boundaries can provide sufficient information to allow a student who is totally blind to function in a gymnasium. No adaptation other than modeling or verbal description is required for such activities as calisthenics, tumbling swimming, or the standing broad jump. Minor adaptations are required for wrestling, so that contestants maintain body contact. Considerable adaptations must be made in competitive running or games requiring visual accuracy. As long as the specialist teacher instructs the students on basic body movements and skills, and explains how to follow verbal directions, there is no reason why the majority of students who are visually impaired cannot participate in regular physical education activities and, in some cases, competitive events.

Physical education is also important for children who have multiple disabilities, including those who may not have independent locomotion. Activities can be modified to permit them to use their physical skills in satisfying leisure activities, such as modified bowling, in which a student throws and rolls balls toward an auditory target; tug-of-war; wheelchair or scooter board races; and relays involving several children performing different tasks. Despite physical differences, the child with multiple disabling conditions should not be relegated to being a spectator or a scorekeeper; physical participation at an appropriate level is important.

A wide variety of other leisure activities are also possible for students with visual impairments. Playing a musical instrument or vocal music can be accomplished with relatively little adaptation. Instruction in these areas depends more heavily on oral and aural methods, although many braille readers become accomplished in the use of braille music as a means of learning new musical scores. High school students who are blind are often active participants in marching bands, high school vocal groups, and informal musical groups. For a few students with visual impairments, these musical abilities develop into career goals. It is important that students with this goal are aware that professional music is a highly competitive field that requires skill in business matters and communication as well as musical ability.

The fine arts, including sculpture, drawing, photography, weaving, drama, and writing, all are possible for learners with visual impairments, with some modifications. Activities with a strong visual component, such as drawing or visiting an art museum, might not appeal to some people who are blind because they do not receive direct feedback about the product. Some people who are blind, especially those who have had vision in the past, do enjoy the experience of visiting an art gallery with an acquaintance and hearing accurate descriptions of the paintings or drawings on display. For young students with congenital blindness, two-dimensional art will be meaningful primarily through description, use of representative objects and materials, and association with personal experience. Such representations should be simple and concrete, and extensive detail should be provided only if there is evidence of interest on the part of the student.

Drawing, painting, and photography are often of interest to the person with low vision. They may adapt the materials and environment to enhance contrast effects and lighting in order to increase visibility. For many people with low vision, photography offers a way of seeing increased detail in objects that are normally viewed from a distance.

Dramatics are enjoyed by many people with visual impairments, and dramatic activities offer a way for students with visual impairments to learn about the importance of gestures and movement in the processes of communication and personal expression. With specific feedback about the movements of characters in a production, an individual who is visually impaired can participate in the production of plays and presentations. Creative writing also requires very little adaptation for the individual with a visual impairment, as long as that person has an efficient reading medium.

For students with multiple disabilities, recreational activities begin with others recognizing their likes and dislikes and arranging ways for the individual to make choices. The process of future planning for people with severe disabilities should include a personal profile that identifies preferences, including leisure activities (Silberman & Brown, 1998). Although some of these preferences might not be conventional, they can often be integrated into an appropriate activity. For example, a student who enjoys tearing paper might help prepare materials for recycling, and for him this might represent a leisure activity.

A person with a visual impairment can participate in almost any leisure activity with varying levels of adaptation. People with visual impairments arrange flowers, weave fabric, jog, volunteer at local food banks, swim, and make pottery, just as their sighted neighbors do. In order to pursue enjoyable activities such as these, they must be aware of opportunities for leisure activities and must have the knowledge to adapt the activity as desired.

Family and friends can play a critical role in encouraging students to pursue physical leisure activities such as dancing, hiking, swimming, and bicycling. Parents who participate in active recreation with their children provide effective models of physical activity and communicate satisfaction with physically challenging pursuits. The importance of physical and recreational activities for the child who is visually disabled cannot be overemphasized because of its importance to the health and life adjustment of adults. Unfortunately, too little attention is given to these activities, and many students with visual impairments do not pursue physical skills beyond the structured environment presented in their school setting.

Visual Efficiency Skills

Recognition that the use of vision is not automatic but must be learned requires that attention be given to "learning to see." If the visual system is not used by looking, storing visual images, and coordinating vision with movement, there is no activity in the occipital area of the brain (the portion that receives visual information), and no visual perceptions are formed. Although most children with low vision gather their major information through vision, their perceptions may not be organized or consistently accurate. Therefore, a planned program of visual perceptual development and visual learning should be part of the specialized curriculum for all those with visual potential regardless of whether they will become visual readers. Functional vision for use when traveling, moving, performing daily living skills, and relating to others and the world is one of the most important personal characteristics to be developed (Barraga, 1980c).

Instruction in the use of low vision can either be infused in the general program or presented as a separate instructional area by the teacher of children with visual impairments. For students who need specific instruction in visual or perceptual skills, such as discrimination, separate instruction may be the most efficient approach. For the child with multiple disabilities or the child who needs to apply vision in functional situations such as travel or self-care activities, coordination between the classroom teacher and the specialist is necessary for the most effective learning. The process for learning to use vision is described in Chapter 6.

Career–Vocational Preparation

The process of preparation for an adult role begins early in life. Information about what people do, how they do it, and what is required of an individual to perform a certain job is not commonly available to children with visual disabilities. In providing a student with the skills to pursue a satisfying career as an adult, schools need to teach the relationship of academic subjects to job preparation.

It is important that students be encouraged to be involved in work experiences during secondary school. Wolffe and Sacks (1997), in a study of the lifestyles of adolescents, found that most of the students with visual impairments had worked for pay; however, in contrast to the sighted students, most students who were visually impaired had not found their own employment. These students usually had different types of jobs than sighted students, and they were more likely to be employed in office or clerical positions than the sighted students, who were more likely to work in fast-food jobs or outdoor positions. Although this level of support might be appropriate when a student is exploring the job market, she or he must develop initiative in locating and maintaining a job as an adult. Nationally, students with visual impairments often pursue academic skills at the postsecondary level, but these skills do not always translate into employment (Wolffe, 1999).

Four steps that are necessary for the student with a visual impairment to attain a career goal are awareness of career opportunities and requirements, exploration of possible work roles, preparation through the development of competencies, and placement in a preferred career role (Simpson, 1986). The process of career development is described in detail in Chapter 11. Career development should be infused at every level of the educational program, both within the regular classroom and with support from specialists, such as vocational counselors and work experience coordinators.

The integration of early work skills for learners who are visually impaired goes well beyond the boundaries of task accomplishment. Socialization, concept development, direct contact with jobs (including volunteer experiences), organization, and time management are areas that must be addressed for a student to be successful in obtaining and keeping a job. In her book *Skills for Success*, Wolffe (1999) provides a complete curriculum for the instruction of students in the skills needed to promote career development.

Students' visual limitations may require specialized approaches or curricula in the areas described in this section. In many instances, the success and efficiency of the learning process may depend on the use and availability of specialized equipment, materials or techniques. The next section of this chapter describes techniques and equipment commonly needed during the instructional process by students with visual impairments.

USE OF ASSISTIVE TECHNOLOGY

In the past 20 years, technology has revolutionized the ways in which we learn and receive information. Scadden (2000) describes technology as "either instruments or knowledge" (p. 907). For students who are visually impaired, both components must be realized for full access to the world. Students with visual impairments use technological tools and skills to gain access to new information and to enhance efficiency in orientation and mobility (Scadden, 2000).

Technology has provided opportunities for students with visual impairments to readily access information far more rapidly than in the past. Computers can now provide a means for instantaneous braille translation, with output printed on paper by a printer or produced on a refreshable braille display, a device that produces braille cells that allow the reader to perceive what is on the screen. Screen readers allow spoken output and editing of material for users who are blind and who prefer speech access. Printed material can be scanned directly into the computer and translated to speech or braille. The individual can choose the combination of devices that will best meet his or her needs in a given situation.

Imagine the options that will be available to a student like Ching Lan at the college level. If Ching Lan prefers to use braille, she can take a portable note-taker to class with her and record her notes in braille. If she is using printed material, a note-taker with a typewriter keyboard might be her choice. She may read some of her assignments using a closed-circuit television, a large screen attached to a camera that enlarges materials to be viewed. She can load material on a computer disk into her computer and access it in speech, print of varying sizes, and braille.

Although technology has opened many doors for individuals who are visually impaired, it also has posed challenges. The use of graphics and icons that are difficult to translate into text has made some computer functions inaccessible for the user who is blind. The rapid evolution of technology also has increased employer expectations of work speed and quality, and the individual who is blind or visually impaired must become proficient quickly. The individual who is visually impaired and successful in using technology must not only have mastered the basic processes, but must also know how to obtain assistance when equipment does not operate properly. In addition, the availability of appropriate training for both students and their teachers can be challenging in a rapidly changing school environment. It is important that educators keep in mind that technology is a means to an end, and not an end in itself. If it does not facilitate the accomplishment of a task, then it is not useful for the learner who is visually impaired.

SUMMARY

In addition to the regular subject matter curriculum required of all students, many other aspects of learning need to be available to students with visual impairments. In order to achieve the goals of the academic work, adaptive skills related to reading and writing are necessary for optimum communication. Students who are visually impaired must learn how to move inside and outside efficiently; care for their own personal needs; use leisure time wisely; prepare for future vocations or careers; operate a variety of useful technological devices; and refine their visual skills for greatest efficiency in functioning.

Educational Materials

Itinerant teachers of children with visual impairments often comment that they can be identified best by their personal vehicles, because the backseats and trunks are full of the bags, boxes, and kits of equipment that enable them to meet the needs of students of various ages and educational needs. Because the limitations imposed by a visual impairment often are manifested in the child's inability to use standard educational materials, the choice of appropriate equipment and the use of efficient instructional methodology can make a critical difference to success in learning for the child with visual disabilities.

For many years, students who were blind or visually impaired were the only group in special education that had materials manufactured and distributed exclusively for their use. Presently, federal funds are being provided for other groups of students with special needs in a similar manner.

In 1879, the federal government designated the American Printing House for the Blind (APH) in Louisville, Kentucky, as the producer of books for blind students (Koestler, 1976). APH has continued to be the major worldwide producer of materials for students with visual limitations. It is supported in part by federal funds, which are allotted to states under a quota system on a per student basis. Other countries can purchase materials from APH as desired. Materials produced by APH include books in large type, instructional computer materials, materials and equipment for low-performing students with low vision, and manipulatives for preschoolers and students with multiple disabilities.

The recent expansion of technology has encouraged private enterprise in the production of materials for students with visual impairments. Independent efforts funded through federal and private grants and by the private sector have become more common; some have focused on the production of one particular device, whereas others have expanded to produce a variety of technological products. In the areas of technology and in the distribution of optical devices, the potential for the development of a competitive market has just begun to be tapped.

Providing educational materials for children with visual impairments that are comparable to the wide variety of materials available for all students has posed problems throughout the years, and many of these have yet to be solved. The educational materials explosion has motivated increased research into the learning processes of students with visual limitations and has created an impetus for greater experimentation and adaptation of media and materials.

MATERIALS FOR STUDENTS WHO ARE BLIND

Braille Codes

After years of controversy, the basic braille cell of six dots, designed by Louis Braille, has been accepted internationally as the one graphic symbol for use by readers who are blind. The 63 possible dot combinations form the basis for a literary braille code, a musical code, a mathematical code, and a scientific code. The variety of codes developed from this basic six-dot braille cell and all the possible combinations thereof have been likened to a series of foreign languages. The multiple arrangement of symbols, the use of the same symbols with a variety of meanings depending on their relation to other symbols or their spatial position, and the many arbitrary rules for using these symbols, make all braille codes complex language systems for interpretation. An abbreviated braille code known as Grade 2 includes contractions, letter combinations, and shortened forms of words that save space in reading material. Although it increases efficiency in reading more familiar material, such extensive abbreviation might increase the time required for interpretation and recognition of new words in unfamiliar contexts (Henderson, 1973; Lowenfeld, 1973; Nolan & Kederis, 1969). There recently has been consideration of the possibility that uncontracted braille might be more efficient than the contracted form for some readers (D'Andrea, 1997).

The importance of early exposure to braille as a reading system has been emphasized in recent literature related to braille learning. During the preschool years, before a child is ready to decode or understand the construction and pronunciation of words, the opportunity to experience braille in the immediate environment, such as in a book being read by a parent, on labels of favorite objects, or on name tags placed on personal possessions, is a valuable precursor to braille reading. Miller (1985) described activities that encouraged her daughter to become a motivated braille reader, namely, use of objects related to stories being read, tactile books, and experiential stories.

An important factor in the development of successful reading skills appears to be the early introduction to the mechanics of braille reading. Mangold (1978) designed a reading program that suggested precision teaching of braille through a graduated sequence of activities; she emphasized the importance of accompanying the traditional program in word recognition and decoding with a foundation program in the mechanics of braille reading. Wormsley (1981) examined the effects of motor training on braille reading speed among elementary-age students; although her training program in hand movements did not result in gains in reading efficiency among the children involved, she noted a decrease in inefficient hand movements among her younger students and suggested that strong association of motor and perceptual training at the early levels is important for later efficiency in reading.

Direct translations into braille of printed books used in the early school years present a problem because words easily recognized by sight may be difficult when transcribed into braille. The difficulty level of reading materials in the first few school years may suggest the use of controlling symbols, or special reading materials, for those children who will use braille, in order to introduce gradually the perplexing word symbols of the braille literary code (Rex, 1970). Long-term research projects should be designed and conducted to evaluate the efficiency of various braille literary code abbreviations in facilitating learning to read. *Patterns*, the braille reading series produced by APH, includes controlled vocabulary and introduction to braille symbols and contractions.

Regardless of the process of learning or the methodologies used, the braille reader will be required throughout the school years to refine recognition skills and knowledge of the various aspects of the code and its multiple uses. Those young people who intend to continue in academic and literary pursuits beyond high school will find even greater challenges in the use of Grade 3 braille, an even more abbreviated but more efficient and space-saving form for adult use.

Tangible Materials

Until the recent development of extensive recorded materials, the most lasting products of the work of students who were blind have been tangible ones. Therefore, materials and devices that provide feedback through touch are an essential part of learning for students without vision.

Recent research has provided some enlightenment on the ability to discriminate tactile information by learners with visual impairments. With a greater variety of options for creating tactile displays, such as the *Tactile Graphics Kit* distributed by APH (Barth, 1982), teachers can now prepare many graphs, charts, and diagrams for students without vision to use in the regular classroom.

With the increase in technological innovations, there are new alternatives for providing tactile displays of materials, which are presented two-dimensionally for the sighted student. Graphs and diagrams are still reproduced manually by the teacher in some cases. This can be done with a tracing wheel and stiff paper or with an applied substance, such as a white glue or Puff Paints, which leave a raised line when dry. The use of a fluid pen that creates a raised line on a special paper has also been explored but not finalized.

Durable and complex versions of charts and diagrams can be produced using the *Tactile Graphics Kit*, which provides aluminum sheets and a variety of tools for creating tactile lines and spaces. Such materials are most often copied using the thermoform machine, which reproduces tangible reproductions using a heat press and a plastic paper to create multiple copies. A recent innovation known as the stereocopier can reproduce printed material in raised format on a special paper; although it provides an exact reproduction of the printed copy, the cost of this device is still well beyond the reach of individuals and of many agencies. Computer programs can now translate graphics into raised line or raised dot configurations, a more rapid form of presenting graphics.

The challenge of performing mathematical computations has been facilitated by a number of devices designed for use by students who are blind. Early approaches included the Taylor slate, which involved the placement of tiny six-sided pegs in rows to indicate numbers, and the cubarithm, which required the positioning of cubes with raised dots on them in a plastic grid to represent numbers. The adapted abacus was developed by Cranmer, of APH, in 1962; this abacus is used widely in the instruction of mathematics for students who are blind and provides a method of examining each step of the calculation process as a problem is solved. M. Lewis (1979) found that 66% of school programs were using the abacus; however, more recently, Rossi (1986) noted that "the brailler is still the most popular device for working out computations" (p. 370). Brothers (1972) noted that arithmetic computation continued to be a critical concern among educators. He suggested that there seemed to be several possible alternatives:

> (1) the use of the numberaid or other concrete manipulative devices at the third and fourth grade level; (2) providing an opportunity for all students to become proficient with the abacus by the completion of grade six; and (3) placing much less emphasis on the braille writer as a computational aid. (p. 7)

More recently, the talking calculator has assumed a role in the process of mathematical calculation. Although it provides a rapid method of solving problems that allows many students without vision to keep pace with their classmates in complex computational activities, the calculator does not teach the process of problem solving, and it allows the student to attain an answer without being aware of the process. Most teachers of students with visual impairments prefer to introduce calculators at the same time that sighted classmates are allowed to use them in the classroom; however, they plan the mathematics curriculum to include instruction on the abacus and with brailled numerals to ensure the student's understanding of the calculation process.

Although the problems in computation for students who are blind have not yet been resolved, it is clear that easy-to-handle computational devices, as well as sets of real objects and manipulatives, must be widely available during the child's early school years for arithmetic concepts to be understood. These tools also might be useful for children with low vision; for example, numberaid and the abacus might supplement paper-and-pencil computational skills to increase efficiency. No single process or device has been identified as the most appropriate for all children. Thus, teachers should continue to experiment with various approaches to permit children with severe visual limitations to acquire computational skills and to achieve in arithmetic a level comparable to that of their sighted peers.

Concrete objects and materials known as realia play an important part in the learning process for the student who is blind. These may be purchased commercially or gathered from environmental sources; they are valuable in providing experience with basic concepts to students who are blind, and they should be a part of every classroom, especially during the early educational years. Carlos can never know the form and texture of a bird unless he has the opportunity to touch a live bird or to examine a taxidermist's model. He cannot observe a picture of a starfish or compare photographs of seeds in his science book; he can understand these organisms well only if he can handle and examine them himself.

In the first few grades, models and three-dimensional representations of objects appear to have little use because of the discrepancy in size and texture between the model and the real object. The child with a visual impairment, whose ability to generalize is not well developed, might only be confused by a small, solid representation of an animal that is actually large, furry, and warm. As students grow older and are able to make the association and transfer through abstract thinking, models might come to have some use, especially for representing large or inaccessible objects. Harley et al. (1987) presented a hierarchy of abstraction that can be helpful in selecting the appropriate materials for the instruction of a student; the levels range from the child's own body as the most concrete through the use of the object itself, various models and representations, and verbal descriptions as the most abstract.

Basic geographic concepts (Miller, 1982) and adaptations of science activities (DeLucchi & Malone, 1982) have been welcome additions to the curricula for students with visual impairments. Provision of tapes for teaching concepts and kits of hands-on materials may make it easier to teach social studies and science activities to these students within the regular classroom setting, especially at the junior and senior high school levels (Davis & Hawke, 1978). Curricula such as *Science Activities for the Visually Impaired* (DeLucchi & Malone, 1982) and *Laboratory Science and Art Curriculum for the Blind* (Hadary, 1977) have been developed to promote the use of the inquiry method of science instruction for students with visual limitations. These activity-based approaches can enhance the understanding of science for all children, not only those who have special learning needs.

In art, as in science and social studies, direct experience with objects and materials is vital to the learning process. A study by Rubin (1975) emphasized that the aesthetic experience of the blind student is different from that of sighted students because it depends on a tactile reference system. Rubin found that young children who are blind preferred the sculptures of other blind students, whereas students with low vision preferred sculptures created by others with similar vision. Swenson (1987) suggested the inclusion in curricula of simple, familiar materials that encourage creativity, particularly at the early stages when the purpose of art activities is to provide experiences in manipulation and control of materials rather than to produce a product.

Availability of simple, durable materials that offer children without vision the opportunity to participate in and control experiences will encourage greater enthusiasm for tactile activities. Although some materials are made commercially, others might be simple, ordinary household materials, such as styrofoam packing worms or ice-cream sticks, which can be counted, sorted, and arranged in original and pleasing ways. The use of manipulable materials is most critical at the early level, but the practice should continue at all levels for students who are blind, particularly when new concepts are being introduced, or when participation and motivation are crucial to the understanding of an idea.

Auditory Materials

The increase in production of auditory materials for students with visual impairments and other disabilities has facilitated information availability, particularly at the secondary and postsecondary educational levels. Since the Pratt-Smoot Act in 1931, the National Library Service, a federally funded branch of the Library of Congress, has provided recreational listening materials for individuals with visual impairments (Koestler, 1976). Recently, most books loaned by the library are on cassette tapes, and each individual who qualifies receives on loan a cassette player for use with these tapes. Students can receive tape-recorded versions of textbooks through application to Recording for the Blind, a privately funded agency in Princeton, New Jersey, or from numerous regional studios that provide educational materials in recorded form to people who are visually impaired.

Auditory materials in other forms have expanded options to students with visual disabilities. Audio-card readers, speech synthesizers that translate computer programs into speech, and reading machines can provide increased independence to the student in the classroom. With such equipment, teachers can prepare individual instructions for students or provide their work on a computer disk. The benefits of using prepared instructional materials with students having visual impairments have been explored only minimally; however, the continued interest of engineers and other specialists in developing technological alternatives for standard learning materials will ensure further refinements of materials and processes to enhance the learning and functioning of students with severe visual limitations.

Technology

The world of communication through braille has broadened with the introduction of many technological options that increase the speed of braille production and the ease of translation. Braille can now be produced by a typist who does not know the braille code; print can be translated into braille using a personal computer and the appropriate software; and braille can be mechanically printed at speeds up to 100 characters per second. Technology has made the braille system more universally available and has offered more options for braille use in educational and professional settings.

Technology for individuals who are blind began to emerge with the development of the optacon in 1965 (Linville & Bliss, 1966). The refinement of the optical-to-tactile conversion instrument, originally manufactured by Telesensory Systems, Inc., provided the first method by which a person who was blind could access the printed word without a sighted intermediary. In the optacon, a tiny camera passes over printed symbols, and the image is converted to a tactual representation of the letter shape through vibrating pins, which are perceived on the forefinger of the person. It represented the first innovation in an explosion of technological options that are now available for the person who is blind.

For the student in school, this explosion of technology provides a greater number of options for learning. For taking notes, students without vision can consider a laptop computer with speech capabilities or a portable braille note-taker. The student can prepare papers for class using a preferred computer or a paperless brailler, and then can edit using a refreshable braille display or a screen review program that provides spoken output. The student can produce a brailled or printed copy of classwork and can access print materials independently through the use of an optical scanner.

Despite the array of technological options for students who are visually disabled, some issues must be considered in applying these options with a particular student. The cost of the equipment that would allow students to function most efficiently is often prohibitive; teachers and other professionals may find that they must make time to seek out funding sources to provide equipment for their students. The choice of technology must be made with each student's needs in mind, and the need for instructional and practice time on the devices must be available for students to become proficient in using them.

Scadden (1984) has presented a perceptive analysis of the implications that technology may have for the individual who is blind. For this individual to benefit from advancing technology, according to Scadden, it is critical that attention be given to preparing professionals to instruct students and clients in the use of technology, the increased development of software and personal computers that are accessible to readers who are blind, and the expansion of standard microcomputers that can be used by them. For the student who is visually impaired, the right choices in technology and training could make the difference between success and failure in school and in the job market.

MATERIALS FOR STUDENTS WITH LOW VISION

Students with low vision rely mainly on visual information during the learning process, even though the visual environment might vary from that of normally sighted students. If students with low vision learn to use vision efficiently, they will need to interpret incomplete or unclear images, draw conclusions about the identity and relationship of objects in the environment, increase individual visual advantage through the use of positioning as well as optical and nonoptical devices, and make decisions about the use of vision in conjunction with other senses. Students must develop a sense of themselves as individuals with unique reference systems that are not mainly tactile and auditory, and as people who are blind. They must also develop a sense of a world that is not a damaged version of the world that is seen by others. Instead, it is a separate reference system that combines broad configurations and images with the knowledge and awareness of detail that can be learned through experience.

The environment can be made more accessible to the individual with low vision in three ways: by increasing the size of the material itself, by bringing the image or the material closer to the eye, or by using a device or projection to magnify the size of the material. When selecting an approach to facilitate the visual environment, the student and the team should consider a number of factors such as cost, versatility, social acceptability, physical strength and endurance, visual needs, and convenience, all of which may play a part in the choice of an adaptation to enhance the visual environment.

Adaptations for children with low vision may be either optical or nonoptical. Nonoptical adaptations generally are less expensive and involve the adjustment or alteration of the environment to make it more accessible. Corn (1983) identified environmental cues that can be altered to create differences in the visual environment. Increasing color differences in material to be viewed, altering viewing distances, or intensifying lighting to increase contrast are methods that Corn suggested to provide a more visually accessible environment.

For younger children, these adaptations might involve controlling materials presented to emphasize the use of simple patterns and high-contrast materials. Consistent presentation of certain familiar patterns and forms enables children to begin to generalize these to more complex, poorly contrasted configurations that are natural parts of the environment (Harrell & Akeson, 1987).

Holding material closer to the eyes to reduce viewing distance enlarges the size of the image. Contrary to popular notions, holding materials even a few inches from the eyes is not harmful and can enhance the clarity of material for the reader. Decreasing the reading distance enlarges and clarifies the image without requiring the use of specialized materials or devices. The use of an easel to hold the book at an angle or varying the reading position to reduce neck strain can enable children to maintain a reduced distance comfortably while doing close work.

The assumption often is made that the student with low vision requires enlarged materials for most efficient functioning in school. For a number of reasons, this may not be true. Enlargement of materials automatically imposes spatial inconvenience; materials occupy more space and become heavier; more head movement and adaptive positioning is required of the large-print reader; large-print readers look so different from standard books that some children are embarrassed to use them; and, particularly for the student with a major field loss, less material can be presented at once. Producing large-type books is expensive, and the pictures in these textbooks are more difficult for children with limited vision to use than the color pictures in regular textbooks. Because of the expense, the number of titles available in large print is limited (Goldish, 1968).

The use of enlarged materials, such as books with large type, is now considered a last resort, less desirable than either the reduction of reading distance or the use of optical devices. For a number of years, it was assumed that the child with low vision would find it easier to see large-type materials; however, studies have reported inconclusive and often contradictory evidence regarding the size of print most easily read (Eakin, Pratt, & McFarland, 1961; Nolan, 1959). Further studies relating to school achievement and the effect of type size on reading and achievement (Bateman & Weatherall, 1967; Birch, Tisdall, Peabody, & Sterrett, 1966) have suggested that type size has little to do with the reading speed or comprehension of students with low vision.

Two ophthalmologists, Faye (1970) and Fonda (1966), wrote that many children have been encouraged or even forced to read large-type materials when they could have more easily read materials in regular print size, either with or without magnification. Sykes (1971, 1972) found that high school students, when provided with magnifying devices and special lamps or lighting arrangements, were just as efficient with regular-size print materials as they were with large-print materials. Reading standard print was found to be no more tiring than reading large print, implying that the concern should not be with the size of the type but with the quality of the print and the illumination.

Use of optical magnifying devices is frequently the most efficient approach to enlarging or enhancing an image for the individual with low vision. The refinement in the quality of nonprescription magnifiers and the development of low vision clinics that prescribe devices for children have resulted in a trend toward the increased use of magnifying devices. Neither visual acuity measurements nor the nature of the visual impairment seems to have any relationship to the student's preference and efficiency with low vision optical devices or large print. However, the teacher's training in the knowledge and use of optical devices might be a critical factor (Corn, 1980).

For many reasons, magnification devices are preferable to the use of large-type books for the student with low vision. Not only do they provide access to a larger selection of material and eliminate the expense of enlarging every piece separately, but they also are less obtrusive and easier to carry and store. Corn and Ryser (1989) surveyed the teachers of 351 children with visual impairments in Texas with respect to the use of optical devices and large type. They found that students who used optical devices increased their reading levels and speeds with age, that there were no differences in fatigue between users of large type and optical devices, and that magnifying devices appeared to be more cost-effective over time.

When children cannot be fitted with spectacle lenses that enable them to function efficiently, hand-held magnifiers, stand magnifiers, or both, are the most feasible solution. There is still worldwide controversy regarding large-print and visual devices. It is more logical to consider both devices for children to function more efficiently visually than to take an either-or position. The decision should be based on the individual child, the visual condition, and the motivation to function with either large type or magnification of regular-size materials and still maintain speed and comprehension.

The style, spacing, and density of print are significant variables to consider. Teachers need to provide many varieties of print sizes and styles to enable children to choose what is best for them. Because the letters appear to run together, large, bold type with letters spaced close together is more difficult to read than smaller type with letters spaced farther apart. Letters with low density are difficult to discriminate. The most visible print is simple in style, moderately bold, and well spaced. Lighting also is a critical factor; some children need more light or light directed onto the material, while others can function more efficiently with less direct or intense light. Again, teachers should let children try many different lighting conditions to determine those that are optimal.

All optical devices and many magnifiers require considerable practice for children to use them effectively. Proper use of optical devices, including magnifiers, cannot be left to chance. Such tools should be prescribed after a thorough examination by a low vision specialist who explores the practical requirements of the user. It is not the role of the teacher of the students with visual impairments to prescribe visual devices. Once these have been prescribed by the low vision specialist, the educator can provide the training the child needs to use the device.

It is important that this training to use visual devices begin with high-interest, motivating materials, particularly with younger children, to ensure acceptance of whatever device is prescribed. Introduction of distance devices can begin as young as 5 years of age to provide the child with a means of identifying objects at a distance and, later, to provide the child with a method of copying material from the chalkboard at school. Generally, training begins with practice in handling, focusing, and storing the device. The child then experiments with scanning and locating (spotting) a stationary object, tracking a moving object, and finally using the monocular for complex tasks such as reading a bus sign or scanning the faces of performers at a concert.

Technological innovations have provided more opportunities for the individual with low vision to access printed material, as well as to read and edit his or her own material. Some technology that is most useful in learning settings is described in the remainder of this section.

Closed-circuit television (CCTV) is among the most common technological devices in use. Through the use of a camera, the CCTV device enlarges printed material on a monitor similar to a television screen. A source of light illuminates the material, which is presented on a viewing table. The viewer can alter the size and contrast of the material, and specialized devices allow the CCTV to be connected with a typewriter or a computer, allowing an individual to read and edit materials being written. Recently, some companies have developed a camera that can project an enlarged image from a distance onto the monitor.

DeWitt, Schreier, and Leventhal (1988) recommended that a closed-circuit television be purchased only after an individual has a thorough low vision evaluation. They described five major design features that should be considered in the purchase of this equipment: image, reliability, cost, versatility, and portability.

The development of computer options for the user with low vision has expanded over the last 10 years. An individual who wishes to vary print size might choose a computer with built-in enlargement capabilities, a software program that enlarges the type size on a conventional computer, or a magnifying device that is placed over the screen to enlarge the image (Goodrich, 1984; Harley et al., 1987; Todd, 1986).

Most students with low vision use various combinations of optical and nonoptical devices at different times during their school years. In working with such a student, educators should stress the importance of regular low vision evaluations, the options the student has in gathering information, and the student's responsibility for selecting the most appropriate environmental adaptation.

For children with visual impairments, the selection of appropriate instructional approaches and materials can facilitate the learning process and increase motivation and independence in learning. The opportunities that have become available through technology not only have multiplied the choices in learning media, but also have presented additional challenges. Ultimately, the most important skill that students with visual impairments can acquire is to take responsibility for the selection of approaches and methods that facilitate personal learning.

SUMMARY

For children with visual impairments, an individualized curriculum and specialized materials are often necessary to facilitate learning. Unique curricular areas include content related to communication, movement and physical skills, social skills, daily living skills, skills in the use of vision, and career–vocational skills. For students who are blind, appropriate learning materials include classroom and supplementary materials in braille, as well as tangible objects that enhance the understanding of concepts. In addition, auditory materials and technological equipment can facilitate the learning process. For students with low vision, the availability of optical and nonoptical devices is critical; technology such as closed-circuit television has also been developed to make printed information more readily accessible. For any child with a visual disability, the combination of identifying priorities in the curriculum with acquiring practical materials is important to efficiency in learning.

Paths Toward Independence

Education should provide a feeling of success early in childhood and throughout the years, as well as ultimately preparing the student for an adult life that includes a satisfying occupation and lifestyle. For students with visual impairments, this preparation may involve not only the development of skills in a chosen career field, but also the development of skills in life management and in communicating effectively with others.

In the lives of most children and youth, and some adults, with visual impairments, conflicts may seem to exist between the goals of education and those of rehabilitation. Each sector, at different times, may seem to give too little consideration to the individual's personal desires and needs. The prevailing assumption of most school programs is that their primary role is to ensure that all students with visual impairments are included in regular class programs, and that they succeed academically to the maximum extent of their abilities, a role that sometimes overlooks personal and vocational development. Some programs invest a great deal of time and effort in repetitive academic activities, even when a student's potential for independent living and functioning may be quite limited.

Premature decisions to prepare a student for one occupational skill or vocation may pose an equally perplexing dilemma, especially for the competent youth who leaves school and finds that few opportunities are available to practice limited skills. Service delivery systems in rehabilitation for people who are losing or have lost some or all of their vision have been geared traditionally toward adults who have already become part of the workforce or who previously have established vocational or professional goals. Only recently have rehabilitation systems begun to expand their services to meet the needs of individuals who are congenitally visually impaired and whose awareness and experience related to the work world may be limited, and the needs of people with additional disabling conditions for whom competitive employment may or may not be an option.

In the past, community and state agencies have tended to provide a set of undifferentiated services defined by the agency itself and not necessarily related to the client's needs. Also, educational programs and specialized schools have had their own traditional, although not necessarily realistic, objectives for individual students or for career possibilities (Scott, 1969). Services now increasingly reflect that education, as well as rehabilitation, begins at birth and continues until death, making conflicts between the two both artificial and detrimental.

This fact is recognized increasingly in building transitional programming to pave the way from primary school through elementary, junior high, and high school, and on into the adult world. Program features such as summer work programs at specialized schools and rehabilitation centers, supported work experiences, written Individualized Transition Plans (ITPs), and mentoring programs encourage students to develop skills to prepare them for adulthood during the time that their academic preparation is still taking place.

As suggested by Simpson (1986), career development requires a holistic process, which uses a collaborative planning approach. Students should ask what they can do at school to prepare for their futures as adults. Teachers can explore the potential of individuals, their interests, and their possible contributions as members of society. There must be awareness of possible careers, exploration of various career options, planning of activities, decision-making strategies, career preparation, and career progression from apprentice to supervisor or superintendent. All of this must be infused with the teaching–learning process from the beginning of schooling through graduation. This process enables the student to begin to establish control of learning and actions; to make choices at any point in time; to progress from the general to the specific in terms of skills; and to gain a sense of responsibility for self and decision making.

Educators must learn a great deal more about the occupational, vocational, and career world in which the rehabilitation counselor functions. Counselors in agencies must learn more about educational and school philosophies, curriculum offerings, social and recreational opportunities, vocational programs, and the scope of mobility programs. The present gap between education and rehabilitation might be bridged if both sectors were to consider a broader range of variables affecting all children and youth with visual impairments. This chapter will examine some of those variables within the context of occupational, personal, and social skills.

OCCUPATIONAL AND ECONOMIC CONSIDERATIONS

Career and vocational preparation is related closely to economic factors. If federal and state governments were to invest funds for acquainting people who are visually disabled with careers and vocations in which they would have a high probability of success, not only would society need to spend less for habilitation after the school years, but also these people would produce a greater volume of goods, services, and taxes. Independence, or even partial independence, at earlier ages would reduce the need for many of the economic expenditures associated with caring for these people in later years. In fact, according to the latest federal statistics, only 26% of people with visual impairments between the ages of 21 and 64 were employed. In contrast, 80% of working-age people with no disabilities were employed (Kirchner & Schmeidler, 1997).

In addition to the economic benefits, the human considerations are important. Tuttle (1984) described the importance of appropriate employment in maintaining the self-esteem of people with visual impairments: "The degree to which a blind individual has attained or regained a status equal to his peers with comparable abilities is the degree to which he is likely to achieve self-acceptance and self-esteem" (p. 261). Knowing that one has economically valuable skills and that using those skills provides personal satisfaction can be motivation for increasing independence.

Developing realistic attitudes about the facts of a visual disability is as much a part of vocational preparation for independence as acquiring skills and knowledge. Medical costs may be substantial in some cases because of eye conditions; living expenses may be proportionately higher for personal services and travel expenses in some careers; reduced income is a regrettable but real possibility. Young adults need not only to understand these facts, but also to gain confidence in their ability to make the decisions that will best enhance their personal success. Because young people who are visually disabled are often naive about the responsibilities, the demands, and the stresses experienced in many occupations, counseling courses, as well as frequent contacts with adults who are visually impaired as friends or mentors, can be very informative. Indeed, these young people may even be so uninformed about the real world of work that their first actual experience might be traumatic. This doesn't need to happen if a school program has introduced them to work, given them realistic feedback, and suggested better ways of functioning or using their materials or skills more effectively.

Simpson (1986) emphasized that the process of career development should begin during the early school years and the Individualized Education Program (IEP) should include objectives related to career awareness and planning from the earliest stages by exposing students to a wide variety of career possibilities. Students with visual impairments might not learn incidentally about the working world, so it is important to involve workers within and outside the school, and to plan field trips to encourage awareness of various occupational fields. The occupations observed should reflect a range of skills and income levels, so that students are able to develop respect for every occupation that allows a worker to be employed actively at an appropriate skill level. Wolffe (1999) has developed a complete curriculum for teachers who are working to prepare students of all ages who are visually impaired for future careers. Her text addresses the development of social skills, compensatory skills, expectations for responsibility, and opportunities for work as areas that should receive attention early in the educational years. It presents specific activities that will encourage development of work-related skills.

These opportunities will help students learn that dependability means working hard, staying at a task until it is complete, being at work on time, and being willing to stay after work if necessary to complete a project. They can observe that flexibility and versatility will help them to keep a job, even when there are cutbacks, and that in the workplace, it is necessary sometimes to pick up another task when a colleague is absent or ill (Wolffe, 1998).

Some studies have indicated a difference in occupational expectations among students who are visually impaired. A 1988 study by Bush-LaFrance indicated that adolescents who are legally blind may have lower occupational expectations as a whole; however, in this study, the expectations were lower among students with more vision, such as those having low vision. A 1985 study by Corn and Bishop noted a high interest in artistic expression but a dislike of selling, performing, and nature-related occupations among 8th to 12th graders. More extensive investigation is needed into the ways in which a visual impairment affects a student's perception of possible and desirable occupations, as well as how realistic those expectations are.

There is a paucity of studies of adults with visual limitations, but Luxton (1980–1981) surveyed graduates from both local and residential school programs. The information indicated that a high percentage are either overeducated and underemployed or show an inconsistency in job stability far greater than that of the general population. It may be that some youth with visual impairments have no philosophical understanding of work as an integral part of a full life. Work can be viewed in two ways: as a goal and as a process. Perhaps education should also be viewed as a goal and as a process. Any process is a continuum of skill, training, experience, evaluation, and reevaluation directed toward both general and specific goals. To the present time, most school programs have been concerned with the narrow goal of teaching academic subject matter and little else when students have visual impairments. Certainly the time may have come to consider an array of options within education, including specialized programs within cities or states that allow students to pursue a chosen field of study according to their life goals.

The first step in effective career development is the implementation of specific and detailed assessment processes in the area. Use of specific instruments such as the *Occupational Aptitude Survey and Interest Schedule* (Parker, 1983) provides the student with the opportunity to evaluate the suitability of a particular work situation in relation to individual skills and interests. In addition, assessments that lead to skill development and mastery, such as the *Vocational Readiness Curriculum* (McCarron & Hurst, 1985), are being applied more frequently to identify specific areas of strength and weakness.

A proactive approach, in which the student takes initiative in seeking out resources and information about prospective careers, should be encouraged from the beginning. The student should consider options for careers based on personal interests and skills, and not rely on stereotyped notions of what others think people with visual impairments can do. Too many adolescents leave high school with a nebulous dream of being a musician or a disk jockey, without a realistic concept of the competition in those occupational fields. Their repertoire of vocational–career knowledge is limited, and they can picture themselves only in the roles of well-known adults with visual limitations, even though they may not possess the abilities and skills to succeed. Professionals and parents are responsible for making students aware of the wide array of jobs that are now available, as well as for emphasizing the dignity of work of any kind, regardless of whether it is in a glamorous or high-status profession.

Current studies of what is available and what is desirable in preparing students who are visually disabled for careers indicate that there still is a wide gap between needs and opportunities. In a study of career needs and resources for visually impaired individuals, Bagley (1985) surveyed students, parents, teachers, rehabilitation personnel, and adults with visual impairments. She noted the high perceived need for resources in career development, along with the inaccessibility of many of these resources. Likewise, Graves and Lyon (1985) noted in a study of the perceptions of ninth graders with visual impairments that most of these students did not feel that schools were meeting their needs in the career discovery process. Clearly, there is agreement that career development is important; in recent years, more careful planning for life after school has emerged in many programs.

In response to this concern, specialized programs that focus on career development skills are becoming more widely available, particularly at the secondary level. Alternatives such as independent living programs based at specialized schools (Stewart, Van Hasselt, Simon, & Thompson, 1985; Venn & Wadler, 1988) or weekend programs that involve families in the career planning process (Houser, Moses, & Kay, 1987) recognize the importance of combining career and life skills preparation with the development of formal education for secondary students. Community-based alternative programs can supplement or intensify the career development experience, providing specialized skills that are not a regular part of the high school curriculum, and assist students to view career development as an ongoing long-term process rather than only a means of getting a job for the sake of immediate income.

As alternative approaches for preparing students for careers evolve, it is critical that professionals evaluate the success of these programs with respect to employment and life satisfaction. Heiden (1989) presented follow-up information on one program, which indicated a 44% employment rate for graduates of the Wisconsin School for the Blind, a higher percentage than the national average of 31%. According to this study, graduates found classes in adaptive living, orientation and mobility, and word processing to be most useful in their preparation for adulthood; most reported satisfaction with their quality of life. This type of follow-up is critical to the planning of appropriate programs that will lead students to effective career choices.

When students are planning to attend college after high school, a precollege program can be quite useful. A college campus (even a small one) is quite different from a specialized school or a local high school, not only in terms of relationships but also in academic and social demands. The personal responsibilities might be overwhelming for those who are not prepared to handle such responsibilities as laundry, money management, and communication of needs to professors and others. Some programs use a career caravan approach, which includes an intensive period to refine job-seeking strategies, learn specific skills for different situations, acquire transportation skills, and develop reading, writing, and computer skills. Realistic feedback in relation to needed skills is provided. Visits to a variety of job sites and eating out in restaurants (not fast-food places) offer opportunities for social interactions.

People with visual impairments plus additional disabling conditions present a challenge for teachers and job placement specialists. For teachers, the need is to simulate actual work stations, each station requiring a specific skill or skills, and have the students work at a station until that skill is sufficient to accomplish the task. They then move on to the next station with a different skill requirement, and so on until all the tasks in the various work stations have been achieved. This process has the potential to prepare the student to move to a selected job site in the community.

The supported employment model has met with some success. In this model, a job is identified in a setting with nondisabled employees, and a job coach supports the disabled individual until the skills needed to accomplish the tasks have been mastered. Students may be apprentices at first, then receive some compensation as their job readiness increases, until they can be considered as regular employees. Others prefer a sheltered workshop setting, which employs only those with disabilities. In such a setting, adaptations for visual and other differences are available quite readily. Some adults with severe disabilities attend day activity centers, in which they are involved in recreational, occupational, and life skills activities appropriate to their functional level. Having an opportunity to explore a variety of settings and job requirements gives the student more choices and makes a successful placement more likely.

For an appropriate placement to be available by adulthood for those with severe disabilities (school programs conclude by age 21), work must begin during early adolescence. Vocational counselors from involved agencies should be invited to the annual IEP meeting, and care should be taken to make the student's program functional and focused on realistic adult goals commensurate with individual limitations. Family involvement will broaden to include long-term concerns such as guardianship and estate planning; it is important that families seek legal counsel in making decisions about these issues. Only with this type of careful planning can an individual be assured of the placements and opportunities that will provide a satisfying adult lifestyle.

LIFE SKILLS

Parents and professionals often stress the importance of career planning in preparing a student for a viable career. In the planning process, the importance of general life skills training can become secondary to the goal of attaining a job. However, skills in personal and life management are equally important; they may determine whether a student is able to live independently or with minimal assistance, or they may ensure that a student is a contributing member of the family unit.

The student with visual impairment should be an integral part of all planning in order to understand the need to develop the skills that will allow maximum independence and quality of life as an adult. These include personal care and management routines such as choosing and caring for clothing, styling one's own hair, personal hygiene, preparing and storing food, and cleaning and caring for the home. Several resources are available that provide practical ideas for the acquisition of daily living skills (Swallow & Huebner, 1987; Wehrum, 1977; Willoughby & Duffy, 1989).

Skills related to personal care and home management also must involve those that require problem solving and complex choices: When is it more practical to grocery shop with sighted assistance rather than to order groceries to be delivered? How should a resident respond when a smoke alarm buzzes in an apartment? How should spilled liquid be wiped from different surfaces? An individual must be able to anticipate and manage unexpected events and must perceive the choices implicit in every situation as well as to know how to follow routines.

In addition, financial management is an important factor in preparation for maximum independence. The skills of maintaining a checking account, making long-term financial plans, paying bills, and building financial security are important for any young adult. For the student who has a visual impairment or is blind, specific concerns must be addressed: What procedures will be used for signing checks and maintaining account records? When sighted assistance is needed, who can provide trusted and reliable help? From elementary school, the student who is visually impaired, like all students, should have the opportunity to manage money and experience the decisions that go along with spending and saving. The ability to make financial decisions and to be aware of their consequences is critical for financial responsibility.

For the individual with severe additional disabilities, life skills are equally important, although priorities might be different. The emphasis is on teaching those skills that represent tasks that otherwise would have to be performed by others; where independent performance or adapted independence is not an option, partial participation, cooperation, or both, become the goals. The presence of a visual impairment makes it even more critical to establish routines, provide cues for future events, and make symbols for choices available so that the individual can control some aspects of daily living. Even relatively small increments of learning can enable an individual to be perceived more positively by caregivers and to maintain some control over routine activities.

SOCIAL AND ADVOCACY SKILLS

The final element of a satisfactory adult life is the acquisition of skills that allow the student both to act and interact with ease and confidence. Not only must a young adult with a visual impairment develop general social skills that might not be learned incidentally, but the individual also must learn to manage the specialized social decisions that result from a visual impairment; these disability specific skills might include understanding the sighted world's reaction to an individual with a visual impairment and using devices or materials that enhance visual efficiency or travel skills (A. Corn, 1989). The individual with a visual impairment must be comfortable in responding to strangers who are oversolicitous or who offer too much help, as well as in dealing with aspects of a visual impairment that are unfamiliar to others. For example, a person losing vision might need to explain how vision fluctuates according to the environment, and the adaptations necessary to manage the change from one situation to another.

The ability to advocate effectively to fulfill one's needs in the larger community is a skill necessary for interactive communication. A young adult with a visual impairment must be assertive in stating changes that would be helpful to functioning more efficiently. Harrell and Strauss (1980) described techniques for a person who is visually impaired to apply in entering conversations, making requests for services or assistance, and handling anger in an interaction.

Along with the assertiveness to advocate for oneself, an individual must have the skills to acquire information necessary for self-advocacy, which involves establishing a network system. This includes knowledge of the organizations and agencies that provide services or information, as well as the ability to use the telephone, library, and Internet to locate information about important resources. To be a self-advocate, one needs an understanding of governmental agency support that is available for those with visual impairments; many states have a service unit for individuals who are blind or visually impaired that provides frequently needed vocational counseling and guidance, home teaching, family support, and other public services. Of particular importance are the social skills that enable a young adult to seek a job successfully. Problems posed by the interview process can be overcome by careful planning and practice; specific preparation in such skills as asking appropriate questions and using positive "I" statements can contribute to an individual's effectiveness in a job interview (Howze, 1987). The individual with a visual impairment must decide how and at what point to disclose the fact of a visual impairment and how it affects functioning, in order to emphasize strengths and overcome the initial apprehension of prospective employers.

Many people with visual impairments choose to join an organization of other individuals with visual impairments in order to share experiences and knowledge about services, gain emotional support, and collaborate on issues of mutual concern. The two largest of these consumer organizations, the American Council of the Blind and the National Federation of the Blind, each publish a newsletter or journal for their members and hold regular meetings and conferences on topics of common interest. They are active in advocacy for the rights of people who are blind or visually impaired as well as in the initiation of new services, such as radio reading and Internet access.

For individuals with functional delays or additional disabilities, social skill instruction is critical in order for them to be considered for any type of remunerative employment. The ability to turn toward a speaker, to use voice or sign to indicate needs, or to enter into reciprocal interactions with others creates a social support system and enables individuals to be even more functional and accepted by others.

SUMMARY

The young person with a visual impairment faces new challenges after leaving the more protected environment of the school setting and entering the adult world. A strong network of support between educational and rehabilitative systems will facilitate movement into adulthood for the young person with a visual impairment. These systems need to establish a collaborative relationship that provides early exposure to career awareness and an educational plan that has as its goal successful employment in a chosen field. With a solid foundation in career awareness and experience, support from transitional service systems, and appropriate preparation in life skills and social skills, there is no reason why each young person should not have a satisfying life that includes a variety of choices and opportunities. Professionals have an obligation to ensure that school experiences are planned to provide a clear pathway to the future.

Looking to the Future

What is actually known about learning and behavior in children and youth with visual impairments remains a controversial issue among psychologists, medical and optical specialists, and educators. The hope of reaching agreement is an illusion that often inhibits understanding of the present and clouds visions of the future. However, this should neither deter attempts to identify issues that are of paramount importance at the present time nor minimize efforts to anticipate topics that, inevitably, will need attention early in this new century.

Previous chapters presented facts about present knowledge and practices; however, not all the information available is being utilized fully, and numerous unresolved issues remain. Some concerns that have not yet achieved consensus among professionals and parents can be summarized under the following general topics: low vision, braille literacy, early intervention, multiple disabilities, orientation and mobility, placement and service delivery, and classroom technology such as computers. As indicated in the following sections, critical questions being asked in each of these areas may call attention to the need for resolution of controversy, despite the empirical and research evidence.

CRITICAL QUESTIONS

Because there is no single definition of low vision that is applicable to every individual, it is difficult for teachers and parents to determine just how much vision is needed for performance of specific tasks. Not all blind children develop at the same rate, and some children have multiple impairments. These facts present a challenge for parents and teachers to determine the most effective strategies for planning educational programs relating to the nature and types of services needed at certain ages, and how to deliver them most efficiently. Consideration of the following critical questions in numerous categories might be helpful.

Low Vision

- When there is indecision about whether children with low vision should use print or braille materials, is it appropriate to think in terms of either/or? Could it be that the selection of a medium takes precedence over exploring the most efficien means for the child to learn as much as possible by acquiring available informatio through a variety of media, depending on the environmental conditions?

• Why do so many professionals recommend large print, when a multitude of research evidence indicates that most learners with low vision can read as comfortabl and efficiently by using regular print with or without magnification?

• Are teachers and parents being fair to children with severe low vision by insisting only on print (even when closed-circuit television is required), and depriving then of learning braille as either a primary or a supplementary medium?

• Conversely, why do some professionals and parents require many students wit moderate low vision to learn braille when they are just as efficient (if not more so) in prin reading, especially when print materials are far more accessible than braille materials?

• With the widespread availability of low vision clinicians and optical devices, wh isn't every child with any potential visual disability regularly evaluated by a low visio specialist?

Braille Literacy

• What factors have contributed to the concern about braille literacy? Has th widespread inclusion concept deprived some children with visual impairments of th specialized services necessary in acquiring basic learning skills?

• Should regular class teachers who have braille-reading children in their classrooms be required to learn the braille code? Or should educational regulations mandat that all children who need braille have a specially trained teacher available to them o a regular basis?

Early Intervention

• Is legislation (federal or state) needed to mandate services to all children wit visual impairments from birth as an extension or supplement to IDEA, which only provides the option from birth to 3 years? Some states are serving children from 3 to years, and are giving no consideration to providing services from birth. Evidence acquired from neonatal nurseries using evoked response techniques, along with studies c children with visual impairments in the first 2 years of life, validate the effectiveness c early intervention in preventing many lags in the various dimensions of development

• What types of early intervention need to be available, and which professionals should be responsible for intervention, education, medicine, health, or possibly combination of all of these disciplines? What can be expected of parents (or other caregivers), especially when the number of working mothers and single parents continue to increase? Can intervention services be a part of day-care centers which serve children with impairments? Can the public be convinced of the cost effectiveness of such programs and provide public moneys?

Multiple Disabilities

• Who should be involved in the identification and diagnosis of children with multiple disabilities? Should one condition (e.g., mental retardation, visual impairment, cerebral palsy, deafness) take precedence over others as primary, and other conditions be ignored in terms of reporting and provision of services?

• Are there legal and moral issues that are influencing decisions about children with multiple impairments? Are children being labeled prematurely in order to secure services? Should all children be maintained for long years on life support systems simply because the technology is available? Whether to sustain the lives of some damaged infants is becoming a decision of the courts, often against the wishes of the parents. Has the medical community made any strides in coming to terms with the ethical issues surrounding infants who are severely damaged at birth?

• Should there be some guidelines for the appropriate use of specialized schools and public schools where children with multiple disabilities are involved? Who makes the decisions? Are the decisions based on best care and education of the children, or on what is least expensive or administratively expedient?

Orientation and Mobility

• At what age should mobility devices be utilized by orientation and mobility specialists?

• With what children and at what ages can electronic travel devices be useful?

• Are there identifiable personal characteristics that can be associated with success in the use of particular devices?

• Are electronic devices, in fact, useful enough to warrant the time, expense, and effort required to learn to use them efficiently?

• At what age should children learn to use a cane for travel? Are there individual characteristics that override the age issue?

• At what age should guide dogs be considered for travel?

• Should people with visual impairments be certified as mobility instructors, and can they teach outdoor travel safely? Many more related issues have been discussed by Hill and Jacobson (1985), but not all can be addressed in this overview.

Placement and Service Delivery

- What process determines the appropriate placement and the nature of the services to be delivered to children with visual impairments? Are specially trained people involved in the decisions and the development of IEPs?

- Are some children being deprived of needed skills because the school administration does not make the effort to find trained specialists or refuses to expend the funds to secure them?

- Is placement in a regular classroom (least restrictive environment) taking precedence over the most appropriate setting for some children with visual impairments? How can these two concepts be considered equally in the best interests of children?

- How can specialized personnel be prepared to support the needs of children in a wide variety of geographic locations that include rural and remote areas?

- What is the most appropriate role(s) for specialized schools in the future?

Many more questions could be raised, some of which might be more important in some local areas and less important in others. The preceding questions are being debated in the literature and in professional meetings, but as yet have not achieved universal consensus, although empirical evidence is becoming available that should assist in resolution in the very near future.

Unfortunately, only a few institutions of higher education have professors engaged regularly in research that can be applied to improvement in classroom instruction. Even fewer researchers are investigating basic human attributes that influence learning and functional behavior. Valuable contributions have been made by these researchers, but much more needs to be done.

The American Printing House for the Blind maintains a research division that studies the usefulness of certain academic and tangible materials and methods of instruction as a precursor to the issuance of educational materials. Other research activities are conducted by private nonprofit and for-profit agencies, relating primarily to devices and equipment that can be marketed to individuals, schools, and agencies with the funds to purchase them.

Technology

- How can people who are visually impaired keep pace with changing technology, especially graphically based programs?

- How can universal access to technology and information be achieved in educational and employment settings?

- How can students with visual impairments develop the skills to make choices in technology that will enable them to be most efficient as adults?

FORCES OF THE FUTURE

The twenty-first century is here. Are we ready to accept the challenges and understand the realities that indicate a very different world? Huebner (1989) has addressed some of the forces that will be shaping the educational needs and interventions indicated in response to social changes. The survival rates of high-risk infants is likely to increase significantly the number of children with visual impairments. This may result in more students with more complex multiple disabilities that require individualized educational planning. Students who are visually impaired come from increasingly diverse backgrounds, and their varying languages, family experiences, and family expectations influence their educational needs.

The decrease in people choosing teaching as a career is likely to cause an even greater shortage of trained teachers. One suggestion (although it fails to address the teacher shortage) is that teachers should have multiple certifications to better serve children with visual impairments, most of whom are being placed in regular school settings. Perhaps the *National Agenda*, which is discussed in the next section, will more clearly identify some of the changes that will address these problems.

Barraga (1989) painted a broad picture of possible dreams to be realized in the twenty-first century. She emphasized the need to expand communication linkages with colleagues locally, nationally, and internationally, as machines and telecommunications continue to become more sophisticated; to exchange research and literature with professionals in related disciplines so that the best of all knowledge can be applied to people with visual impairments; to learn, share, and participate in exchange programs with teachers around the world in order to experience a variety of cultural and political settings; and to find ways to determine how to ensure that children with multiple impairments develop and use all their capacities to promote the highest possible quality of life.

In 1990, Bishop completed a survey of active medical, educational, and rehabilitation personnel and parents in the field of visual impairment throughout the United States and internationally, requesting that they predict future events in the field. The following five major statements emerged:

1. An increased understanding of brain and neurological functioning as it relates to sight would improve methods of teaching those with visual impairments.
2. Due to increased litigation and bureaucratic constraints, teachers would have less contact with families during the educational program planning process.
3. Childcare and early intervention programs for children with visual impairments would be required to have specially certified teachers.
4. Disability labels would no longer exist relative to education; therefore, individualized assessment of specific disabilities would no longer be required.

5. State schools and other specialized institutions exclusively for people with visual impairments would serve only children with the most severe visual disabilities.

THE *NATIONAL AGENDA*

In 1994, a national initiative was planned by a group of parents, professionals, an other stakeholders with interest in the education of students with visual impairment A consortium of individuals met at the Josephine Taylor Institute in Washington, D.C to develop goal statements that set priorities for the field. Guided by a steerin committee of Anne Corn, Phil Hatlen, Kathleen Huebner, Frank Ryan, and Mar Ann Siller, participants in the conference set eight goals that would have a significar impact on the education of children with visual impairments.

The following goal statements apply to infants, toddlers, children, and youth wit visual impairments, including those with multiple disabilities:

1. Students and their families will be referred to an appropriate education program within 30 days of identification of a suspected visual impairment.
2. Policies and procedures will be implemented to ensure the rights of all parents to fully participate in the education process.
3. Universities, with a minimum of one full-time faculty member in the area of visual impairment, will prepare a sufficient number of educators of students with visual impairments to meet personnel needs throughout the country.
4. Service providers will determine caseloads based on the needs of students and will require ongoing professional development for all teachers and orientation and mobility instructors.
5. Local education programs will ensure that all students have access to a full array of placement options.
6. Assessment of students will be conducted, in collaboration with parents, by personnel having expertise in the education of students with visual impairments.
7. Access to developmental and educational services will include an assurance that instructional materials are available to students in the appropriate media and at the same time as their sighted peers.
8. Educational and developmental goals, including instruction, will reflect the assessed needs of each student in all areas of academic and disability-specific core curricula.

The implementation of these goals is underway at the state and national levels. ndividual states have made progress in informing legislators about the needs of learn-rs who are visually impaired, determining needs of students with visual impairments n their states, and obtaining funding to address the *National Agenda* goals. About half he states have reported on their progress to date and their state plans for the future. he ability of families and professionals to address these goals on a national basis is an ndication of the collaboration that is critical in advocating for students with low inci-ence educational needs (Corn & Huebner, 1998).

THE CHALLENGE

lew discoveries about the development and learning of children with visual impair-nents will be influencing programs and services far into the new century. Unfortu-ately, educational practitioners do not always keep abreast of or utilize all available nowledge. Some teachers who do not attend in-service sessions or workshops on crit-cal topics or read professional literature may not have ready access to new ideas, or nay have difficulty translating them into practice, without help and encouragement. lore probably, the lag in putting new knowledge into practice arises from a reluctance o question traditional attitudes and methods (complacency) or from a lack of courage o take the risks implied in making dynamic and innovative changes. Even though here continues to be a shortage of specially trained teachers for children and youth ith visual impairments, those entering the profession in the next century are likely to e bright and capable, acquainted with new information about the learning and func-oning potential of human beings, and qualified to provide the leadership needed to nove beyond traditional strategies to those more appropriate for the future. The chil-ren and youth in our educational programs deserve educational services appropriate o their present level of functioning that are also designed to help them move, step by ep, up the ladder of independence to a life of freedom and dignity. Only through col-aboration of families and professionals can quality education be achieved and main-ained. The key to the future is in the hands of families, teachers, and their communi-es as they seek to implement the goals set forth in the *National Agenda*.

References

Abel, G. L. (1959). Problems and trends in the education of blind children and youth. In G. L. Abel (Ed.), *Concerning the education of blind children* (pp. 79–81). New York: American Foundation for the Blind.

American Printing House for the Blind. (1997). *Annual report*. Louisville, KY: Author.

Americans with Disabilities Act of 1990, 42 U.S.C. §12101 *et seq*.

Amerson, M. J. (1999). Helping children with visual and motor impairments make the most of their visual abilities. *RE:view, 31*, 21–28.

Anater, P. F. (1980). Effect of auditory interference on memory of haptic perceptions. *Journal of Visual Impairment and Blindness, 74*, 305–309.

Anderson, D. W. (1984). Mental imagery in congenitally blind children. *Journal of Visual Impairment and Blindness, 78*(2), 206–210.

Anderson, D. W., & Fisher, K. P. (1986). Nominal realism in congenitally blind children. *Journal of Visual Impairment and Blindness, 80*, 896–900.

Arnheim, R. (1969). *Visual Thinking*. London: Faber & Faber.

Ashcroft, S., Halliday, C., & Barraga, N. (1965). *Study II. Effects of experimental teaching on the visual behavior of children educated as though they had no vision*. Nashville, TN: George Peabody College for Teachers.

Ashcroft, S. C., & Zambone-Ashley, A. M. (1980). Mainstreaming children with visual impairments. *Journal of Research & Development in Education, 13*, 22–36.

Ayres, A. J. (1981). *Sensory integration and the child*. Los Angeles: Western Psychological Services.

Bagley, M. (1985). Service providers assessment of the career development needs of blind and visually impaired students and rehabilitation clients and resources available to meet those needs. *Journal of Visual Impairment and Blindness, 79*, 434–443.

Bailey, B. R., & Downing, J. (1994). Using visual accents to enhance attending to communication symbols for students with severe multiple disabilities. *RE:view, 26*, 101–118.

Bailey, B. R., & Head, D. N. (1993). Providing O & M services to children and youth with severe disabilities. *RE:view, 25*, 57–66.

Baird, S. M., Mayfield, P., & Baker, P. (1997). Mothers' interpretations of the behavior of their infants with visual and other impairments during interactions. *Journal of Visual Impairment and Blindness, 91*, 467–483.

Barraga, N. (1964). *Increased visual behavior in low vision children*. New York: American Foundation for the Blind.

Barraga, N. C. (Ed.). (1970). *Visual Efficiency Scale*. Louisville, KY: American Printing House for the Blind.

Barraga, N. C. (Ed.). (1980a). *Program to develop efficiency in visual functioning: Design for instruction*. Louisville, KY: American Printing House for the Blind.

Barraga, N. C. (Ed.). (1980b). *Program to develop efficiency in visual functioning: Diagnostic assessment procedure (DAP)*. Louisville, KY: American Printing House for the Blind.

Barraga, N. C. (Ed.). (1980c). *Source book on low vision*. Louisville, KY: American Printing House for the Blind.

Barraga, N. C. (1983). *Visual handicaps and learning* (2nd ed.). Austin, TX: PRO-ED.

Barraga, N. C. (1986). Sensory perceptual development. In G. T. Scholl (Ed.), *Foundations of education for blind and visually handicapped children and youth: Theory and practice* (pp. 83–98). New York: American Foundation for the Blind.

Barraga, N. C. (1989, June). Dreams of the future. In A. L. Corn (Chair), *Through the looking glass*. Symposium conducted at The University of Texas at Austin.

Barraga, N. C., & Collins, M. E. (1979). Development of efficiency in visual functioning: Rationale for a comprehensive program. *Journal of Visual Impairment and Blindness, 73*, 121–126.

Barraga, N. C., Collins, M., & Hollis, J. (1977). Development of efficiency in visual functioning: A literature analysis. *Journal of Visual Impairment and Blindness, 71*, 387–391.

Barraga, N. C., Dorward, B., & Ford, P. (1973). *Aids for teaching basic concepts of sensory development*. Louisville, KY: American Printing House for the Blind.

Barraga, N. C., & Morris, J. (1980). *Program to develop efficiency in visual functioning*. Louisville, KY: American Printing House for the Blind.

Barraga, N. C., & Morris, J. (1998). *Source book on low vision* (Rev. ed.). Louisville, KY: American Printing House for the Blind.

Barraga, N. C., Morris, J., & Stallings, J. (1998). *Program to develop efficiency in visual functioning: Vol. III. Design for instruction of learners with developmental delays*. Louisville, KY: American Printing House for the Blind.

Barth, J. (1982). The development and evaluation of a tactile graphics kit. *Journal of Visual Impairment and Blindness, 76*, 269–273.

Bateman, B. (1965). Psychological evaluation of blind children. *The New Outlook for the Blind, 59*, 193–197.

Bateman, B., & Weatherall, J. L. (1967). Some educational characteristics of partially seeing children. *International Journal for the Education of the Blind, 17*, 33–40.

Bayley, N. (1993). *Bayley Scales of Infant Development–Second Edition*. San Antonio, TX: Psychological Corporation.

Bell, J. (1986). An approach to the stimulation of vision in the profoundly handicapped, visually handicapped child. *British Journal of Visual Impairment, 4*, 46–48.

Bentzen, B. L., & Peck, A. F. (1979). Factors affecting traceability of lines for tactile graphics. *Journal of Visual Impairment and Blindness, 73*, 264–269.

Berla, E. P., Rankin, E. F., & Willis, D. H. (1980). Psychometric evaluation of the low vision diagnostic assessment procedure. *Journal of Visual Impairment and Blindness, 75*, 297–301.

Bina, M. (1982). Morale of teachers of the visually handicapped: Implications for administrators. *Journal of Visual Impairment and Blindness, 76*, 121–128.

Birch, J., Tisdall, W., Peabody, R., & Sterrett, R. (1966). *School achievement and effect of type size on reading in visually handicapped children*. (Cooperative research project No. 1766, U. S. Office of Education). Pittsburgh, PA: University of Pittsburgh.

Birns, S. L. (1986). Age at onset of blindness and development of space concepts: From topological to projective space. *Journal of Visual Impairment and Blindness, 80*, 577–82.

Bishop, V. E. (1986). Identifying the components of success in mainstreaming. *Journal of Visual Impairment and Blindness, 80*, 939–945.

Bishop, V. E. (1990). *Futures in low vision research project*. (Unpublished report). The University of Texas at Austin, Department of Special Education.

Boehm, A. E. (1971). *Boehm Test of Basic Concepts*. San Antonio, TX: Psychological Corporation.

Boldt, W. (1969). The development of scientific thinking in blind children and adolescents. *Education of the Visually Handicapped, 1*, 5–11.

Bower, T. G. (1977). Blind babies see with their ears. *New Scientist, 73*, 255–257.

Bradley-Johnson, S. (1986). *Psychological assessment of visually impaired and blind students: Infancy through high school*. Austin, TX: PRO-ED.

Brothers, R. J. (1972). Arithmetic computation by the blind: A look at current achievements. *Education of the Visually Handicapped, 4*, 1–8.

Brown, D., Simmons, V., & Methvin, J. (1978). *The Oregon project for visually impaired and blind preschool children* (Rev. ed.). Medford, OR: Jackson Education Service District.

Bruner, J. S. (1966). *Toward a theory of instruction*. New York: Norton.

Bullard, B., & Barraga, N. C. (1971). Subtests of evaluative instruments applicable for use with preschool visually handicapped children. *Education of the Visually Handicapped, 3*, 116–122.

Bush-LaFrance, B. (1988). Unseen expectations of blind youth: Educational and occupational ideas. *Journal of Visual Impairment and Blindness, 82*, 132–136.

Campbell, P. (1987). The integrated program team: An approach for coordinating professionals of various disciplines in programs for students with severe and multiple handicaps. *Journal of the Association for Persons with Severe Handicaps, 12*, 107–116.

Caton, H. (1977). The development and evaluation of a tactile analog to the Boehm Test of Basic Concepts. *Journal of Visual Impairment and Blindness, 71*, 382–386.

Caton, H. R. (1980). *The Tactile Test of Basic Concepts*. Louisville, KY: American Printing House for the Blind.

Caton, H., Bradley, E. J., & Pester, E. (Eds.). (1982). *Patterns: The primary braille reading program*. Louisville, KY: American Printing House for the Blind.

Chang, S., & Schaller, J. (2000). Perspectives of adolescents with visual impairments on social support from their parents. *Journal of Visual Impairment and Blindness, 94*, 69–84.

Chase, J. B. (1972). Evaluation of blind and severely visually impaired persons. In M. D. Graham (Ed.), *Science and blindness: Retrospective and prospective* (pp. 53–58). New York: American Foundation for the Blind.

Chase, J. B. (1975). Developmental assessment of handicapped infants and young children: With special attention to the visually impaired. *The New Outlook for the Blind, 69*, 341–349, 364.

Chase, J. B. (1986a). Application of assessment techniques to the totally blind. In P. J. Lazarus & S. S. Strichart (Eds.), *Psychological evaluation of children and adolescents with low-incidence handicaps* (pp. 75–102). New York: Grune & Stratton.

Chase, J. B. (1986b). Psychoeducational assessment of visually impaired learners. In P. J. Lazarus & S. S. Strichart (Eds.), *Psychoeducational evaluation of children and adolescents with low-incidence handicaps* (pp. 41–74). New York: Grune & Stratton.

Cobb, E. S. (1977). Learning through listening: A new approach. *Journal of Visual Impairment and Blindness, 71*, 302–308.

Cohen, S. E., & Beckwith, L. (1979). Preterm infant interaction with the caregiver in the first year of life and competence at age two. *Child Development, 50*, 767–776.

Coleman, C. L., & Weinstock, R. E. (1984). Physically handicapped blind people: Adaptive mobility techniques. *Journal of Visual Impairment and Blindness, 78*, 113–117.

Colenbrander, A. (1977). Dimensions of visual performance. *Archives of American Academy of Ophthalmology, 83*, 335.

Colenbrander, A. (1999). *Guide for the evaluation of visual impairment*. San Francisco: Pacific Vision Foundation.

Collins, M. E., & Barraga, N. C. (1980). Development of efficiency in visual functioning: An evaluation process. *Journal of Visual Impairment and Blindness, 74*, 93–96.

Corn, A. (1980). *Development and assessment of an in-service training program for teachers of the visually handicapped: Optical aids in the classroom*. Unpublished doctoral dissertation, Teachers College, Columbia University, New York.

Corn, A. (1983). Visual function: A theoretical model for individuals with low vision. *Journal of Visual Impairment and Blindness, 77*, 373–377.

Corn, A. (1989). Employing critical thinking strategies within a curriculum of critical things to think about for blind and visually impaired students. *Journal of Vision Rehabilitation, 3*, 17–36.

Corn, A., & Rosenblum, L. P. (2000). *Finding wheels: A curriculum for non-drivers with visual impairments for gaining control of transportation needs*. Austin, TX: PRO-ED.

Corn, A., & Ryser, G. (1989). Access to print by students with low vision. *Journal of Visual Impairment and Blindness, 83*, 340–349.

Corn, A. L. (1985). Strategies for the enhancement of visual function in individuals with fixed visual deficits: An interdisciplinary model. *Rehabilitation Literature, 46,* 8–11.

Corn, A. L. (1989). Instruction in the use of vision for children and adults with low vision: A proposed program model. *RE:view, 21,* 26–38.

Corn, A. L., & Bishop, V. E. (1984). Acquisition of practical knowledge by blind and visually impaired students in grades 9–12. *Journal of Visual Impairment and Blindness, 78,* 552–556.

Corn, A. L., & Bishop, V. E. (1985). Occupational interests of visually handicapped secondary students. *Journal of Visual Impairment and Blindness, 79,* 475–478.

Corn, A. L., & Huebner, M. H. (Eds.). (1998). *A report to the nation: The National Agenda for the education of children and youth with visual impairments, including those with multiple disabilities.* New York: American Foundation for the Blind.

Corn, A. L., & Koenig, A. J. (1996). Perspectives on low vision. In A. L. Corn & A. J. Koenig (Eds.), *Foundations of low vision: Clinical and functional perspectives* (pp. 3–25). New York: American Foundation for the Blind.

Craft, D. H. (1986). Physical education. In G. Scholl (Ed.), *Foundations of education for blind and visually handicapped children and youth: Theory and practice* (pp. 396–403). New York: American Foundation for the Blind.

Cratty, B. J. (1971). *Movement and spatial awareness in blind children and youth.* Springfield, IL: Charles C. Thomas.

Cratty, B. J., & Sams, T. (1968). *Body Image of Blind Children.* New York: American Foundation for the Blind.

Cress, P. J., Spellman, C. R., DeBriere, T. J., Sizemore, A. C., Northam, J. K., & Johnson, J. L. (1981). Vision screening for persons with severe handicaps. *TASH Journal, 6,* 41–50.

Curry, S. A., & Hatlen, P. H. (1988). Meeting the unique educational needs of visually impaired pupils through appropriate placement. *Journal of Visual Impairment and Blindness, 82,* 417–424.

D'Andrea, F. M. (1997). Teaching braille to students with special needs. In D. Wormsley & F. M. D'Andrea (Eds.), *Instructional strategies for braille literacy* (pp. 145–188). New York: American Foundation for the Blind.

Davidson, F. W. K., & Simmons, J. N. (1984). Mediating the environment for young blind children: A conceptualization. *Journal of Visual Impairment and Blindness, 78,* 251–255.

Davis, J. E., & Hawke, S. (Project directors). (1978). *Materials adaptation for visually impaired students in social studies* (MAVIS). Boulder, CO: Social Science Education Consortium.

Dekker, R., Drenth, P. J. D., Zaal, J. N., & Koole, F. D. (1991). An intelligence test for visually impaired children. *Journal of Visual Impairment and Blindness, 85,* 261–267.

Del Frari, P. (1978). Meeting the O & M needs of the multiply handicapped blind individual. *Journal of Visual Impairment and Blindness, 72,* 324–325.

DeLucchi, L., & Malone, L. (1982). SAVI (Science activities for the visually impaired). In S. Mangold (Ed.), *A teacher's guide to the educational needs of blind and visually handicapped children* (pp. 72–93). New York: American Foundation for the Blind.

DePauw, K. (1981). Physical education for the visually impaired: Review of the literature. *Journal of Visual Impairment and Blindness, 75,* 162–164.

DeWitt, J., Schreier, E., & Leventhal, J. (1988). A look at closed circuit television systems (CCTV) for persons with low vision. *Journal of Visual Impairment and Blindness, 82,* 151–160.

Dickman, I. (1975). *Sex education and family life for visually handicapped children and youth: A resource guide.* New York: American Foundation for the Blind.

Diderot, D. (1916). *Letter on the blind for the use of those who see* (Margaret Jourdain, Trans.). In *Diderot's early philosophical works.* Chicago: Open Court.

Dodds, A. G. (1983). Mental rotation and visual imagery. *Journal of Visual Impairment and Blindness, 77,* 16–18.

Dodds, A. G., & Davis, D. P. (1989). Assessment and training of low vision clients for mobility. *Journal of Visual Impairment and Blindness, 83,* 439–446.

Dodds, A. G., Howarth, C. E., & Carter, D. C. (1982). The mental maps of the blind: The role of previous visual experience. *Journal of Visual Impairment and Blindness, 77*, 5–12.

Dote-Kwan, J., Hughes, M., & Taylor, S. L. (1997). Impact of early experiences on the development of young children with visual impairments. *Journal of Visual Impairment and Blindness, 91*, 131–144.

Downing, J., & Bailey, B. (1990). Developing vision use within functional daily activities for students with visual and multiple disabilities. *RE:view, 21*, 209–220.

Duehl, A. N. (1979). The effect of creative dance movement on large muscle control and balance in congenitally blind children. *Journal of Visual Impairment and Blindness, 73*, 127–133.

Dunn, L. M. (1965). *Peabody Picture Vocabulary Test*. Circle Pines, MN: American Guidance Service.

Dunn, L. M., & Dunn, L. M. (1981). *Peabody Picture Vocabulary Test–Revised*. Circle Pine, MN: American Guidance Service.

Dunnett, J. (1999). Use of activity boxes with young children who are blind, deaf–blind, or who have severe learning disabilities and visual impairments. *Journal of Visual Impairment and Blindness, 93*, 225–232.

Eakin, W., Pratt, R., & McFarland, F. (1961). *Type-size research for the partially seeing child*. Pittsburgh, PA: Stanwix House.

Easton, R. D., & Bentzen, B. L. (1980). Perception of tactile route configurations by blind and sighted observers. *Journal of Visual Impairment and Blindness, 74*, 254–265.

Education for All Handicapped Children Act of 1975, 20 U.S.C. §1400 *et seq*.

Eichel, V. J. (1979). A taxonomy for mannerisms of blind children. *Journal of Visual Impairment and Blindness, 73*, 167–178.

Erhardt, R. P. (1987). Visual function in the student with multiple handicaps: An integrative transdisciplinary model for assessment and intervention. *Education of the Visually Handicapped, 19*, 87–98.

Erin, J. (1996). Functional vision assessment and instruction of children and youth with multiple disabilities. In A. Corn and A. Koenig (Eds.), *Foundations of low vision: Clinical and functional perspectives* (pp. 221–245). New York: American Foundation for the Blind.

Erin, J., Daughtery, W., Dignan, K., & Pearson, N. (1990). Teachers of visually handicapped students with multiple disabilities: Perceptions of adequacy. *Journal of Visual Impairment and Blindness, 84*, 16–20.

Erin, J., & Koenig, A. (1997). The student with a visual disability and a learning disability. *Journal of Learning Disabilities, 30*, 309–320.

Erin, J., & Paul, B. (1996). Functional vision assessment and instruction of children and youth in academic programs. In A. Corn & A. Koenig (Eds.), *Foundations of low vision: Clinical and functional perspectives*. New York: American Foundation for the Blind.

Erin, J. N. (1988). The teacher-consultant. *Education of the Visually Handicapped, 20*, 57–63.

Faye, E. E. (1970). *The low vision patient*. New York: Grune & Stratton.

Faye, E. E. (Ed.). (1984). *Clinical low vision* (2nd ed.). Boston: Little, Brown.

Felix, L., & Spungin, S. J. (1978). Preschool services for the visually handicapped: A national survey. *Journal of Visual Impairment and Blindness, 72*, 59–66.

Ferrell, K. (1985). *Reach out and teach: Meeting the needs of parents of visually and multiply handicapped young children*. New York: American Foundation for the Blind.

Ferrell, K. (1987). State of the art of infant and preschool services in 1986. *Yearbook of the Association for Education and Rehabilitation of the Blind and Visually Impaired, 4*, 22–32.

Ferrell, K. A. (1984). A second look at sensory aids in early childhood. *Education of the Visually Handicapped, 16*, 83–101.

Fewell, R. R., & Langley, M. B. (1984). *Developmental Activities Screening Inventory–Second Edition*. Austin, TX: PRO-ED.

Fieandt, K. (1966). *The world of perception*. Homewood, IL: Dorsey Press.

Fletcher, J. G. (1981). Spatial representation in blind children: Effect of task variations. *Journal of Visual Impairment and Blindness, 75,* 1–3.

Fonda, G. (1966). An evaluation of large type. *The New Outlook for the Blind, 60,* 296–298.

Foulke, E. (1968). Non-visual communication. *International Journal for the Education of the Blind, 18,* 77–78.

Foulke, E. (1981). Impact of science and technology on the early years. *Journal of Visual Impairment and Blindness, 75,* 101–108.

Fraiberg, S. (1977). *Insights from the blind: Comparative studies of blind and sighted infants.* New York: Basic Books.

Fraiberg, S., Smith, M., & Adelson, E. (1969). An educational program for blind infants. *Journal of Special Education, 3,* 121–39.

Furth, H. G. (1969). *Piaget and knowledge.* Englewood Cliffs, NJ: Prentice Hall.

Gallagher, W. (1988). Categorical services in the age of integration: Paradox or contradiction? *Journal of Visual Impairment and Blindness, 82,* 226–229.

Gardner, L. (1982). Understanding and helping parents of blind children. *Journal of Visual Impairment and Blindness, 76,* 81–85.

Gates, C. (1985). Survey of multiply handicapped, visually impaired children in the Rocky Mountain/Great Plains region. *Journal of Visual Impairment and Blindness, 79,* 385–391.

Gerhardt, J. B. (1982). The development of object play and classificatory skills in a blind child. *Journal of Visual Impairment and Blindness, 76,* 219–223.

Giangreco, M., Edelman, S., Luiselli, T., & MacFarland, S. (1997). Helping or hovering? Effects of instructional assistant proximity on students with disabilities. *Exceptional Children, 64,* 7–18.

Giangreco, M., Edelman, S., Nelson, C., Young, M., & Kiefer-O'Donnell, R. (1999). Changes in educational team membership for students who are deaf–blind in general education classrooms. *Journal of Visual Impairment and Blindness, 93,* 166–173.

Gipsman, S. C. (1981). Effect of visual condition on use of proprioceptive cues in performing a balancing task. *Journal of Visual Impairment and Blindness, 75,* 50–54.

Gleason, D. (1984). Auditory assessment of visually impaired preschoolers: A team effort. *Education of the Visually Handicapped, 16,* 102–113.

Glenshaft, J. L., Dare, N. L., & O'Malley, P. L. (1980). Assessing the visually impaired child: A school psychology view. *Journal of Visual Impairment and Blindness, 74,* 344–349.

Goetz, L., & Gee, S. (1987). Functional vision programming: A model for teaching visual behaviors in natural contexts. In G. Goetz, D. Guess, & K. Stremel-Campbell (Eds.), *Innovative program design for individuals with dual sensory impairments* (pp.77– 98). Baltimore: Brookes.

Goetz, L., Guess, D., & Stremel-Campbell, K. (1987). *Innovative program design for individuals with dual impairments.* Baltimore: Brookes.

Goldish, L. (1968). *Teaching aids for the visually handicapped.* Watertown, MA: Perkins School for the Blind.

Goodenough, F. L., & Harris, D. B. (1963). *Goodenough-Harris Drawing Test.* New York: Harcourt, Brace, Jovanovich.

Goodrich, G. (1984). Applications of microcomputers by visually impaired persons. *Journal of Visual Impairment and Blindness, 78,* 408–414.

Gottesman, M. (1976). Stage development in blind children: A Piagetian view. *The New Outlook for the Blind, 70,* 94–100.

Graves, W., & Lyon, S. (1985). Career development: Linking education and careers of blind and visually impaired ninth graders. *Journal of Visual Impairment and Blindness, 79,* 444–449.

Griffin, J. C., & Gerber, P. J. (1982). Tactual development and its implications for the education of blind children. *Education of the Visually Handicapped, 13,* 116–123.

Groenendaal, F., & Hof-Van Duin, J. (1992). Visual deficits and improvements in children after perinatal hypoxia. *Journal of Visual Impairment and Blindness, 86*, 215–218.

Hackney, P. W. (1986). Education of the visually handicapped gifted: A program description. *Education of the Visually Handicapped, 18*, 85–95.

Hadary, D. (1977). Science and art for visually handicapped children. *Journal of Visual Impairment and Blindness, 71*, 203–209.

Hall, A. (1981). Mental images and the cognitive development of the congenitally blind. *Journal of Visual Impairment and Blindness, 76*, 281–285.

Hall, A. (1983). Methods of equivalence grouping by congenitally blind children: Implications for education. *Journal of Visual Impairment and Blindness, 77*, 172–174.

Hall, A., & Bailey, I. L. (1989). A model of training vision functioning. *Journal of Visual Impairment and Blindness, 83*, 390–403.

Hall, A. P., Kekelis, L. K., & Bailey, I. L. (1986). *Development of an assessment program and intervention guidelines for visually impaired children* (Final report). Sacramento: California State Department of Education.

Hamilton, K. W. (1950). *Counseling the handicapped in the rehabilitation process*. New York: Ronald Publishing.

Hammill, D., & Crandell, J. N. (1969). Implications of tactile–kinesthetic ability in visually handicapped children. *Education of the Visually Handicapped, 1*, 65–69.

Harcourt Brace Educational Measurement. (1996). *Stanford Achievement Test–9th Edition*. San Antonio: Author.

Hardy, J. (1983). *Cerebral palsy*. Englewoods Cliffs, NJ: Prentice Hall.

Harley, R., Truan, M., & Sanford, L. (1987). *Communication skills for visually impaired learners*. Springfield, IL: Charles C. Thomas.

Harley, R. K., DuBose, R. F., & Bourgeault, S. E. (1980). *Peabody Model Vision Project Scales*. Chicago: Stoelting.

Harley, R. K., & English, W. H. (1989). Support services for visually impaired children in local day schools: Residential schools as a resource. *Journal of Visual Impairment and Blindness, 83*, 403–406.

Harley, R. K., Henderson, F. M., & Truan, M. B. (1979). *The teaching of braille reading*. Springfield, IL: Charles C. Thomas.

Harley, R. K., Wood, T. A., & Merbler, J. B. (1981). *Peabody Mobility Scales*. Chicago: Stoelting.

Harrell, L., & Akeson, N. (1987). *Preschool vision stimulation: It's more than a flashlight*. New York: American Foundation for the Blind.

Harrell, R., & Strauss, F. (1980). Approaches to increasing assertive behavior and communication skills in blind and visually impaired persons. *Journal of Visual Impairment and Blindness, 74*, 794–798.

Harrell, R. L., & Curry, S. A. (1987). Services to blind and visually impaired children and adults: Who is responsible? *Journal of Visual Impairment and Blindness, 81*, 368–376.

Harris, L., Humphrey, G. K., Muir, D. M., & Dodwell, P. C. (1985). Use of the Canterbury child's aid in infancy and early childhood: A case study. *Journal of Visual Impairment and Blindness, 79*, 4–11.

Hatlen, P. (1990). Meeting the unique needs of pupils with visual impairments. *RE:view, 22*, 79–82.

Hatlen, P. (1996). Comprehensive literacy. *Journal of Visual Impairment and Blindness*, 90, 174–175.

Hazekamp, J., & Huebner, K. M. (1989). *Program planning and evaluation for visually impaired students: National guidelines for educational excellence*. New York: American Foundation for the Blind.

Hebb, D. O. (1949). *The organization of behavior*. New York: John Wiley.

Heersema, D. J., & Hof-Van Duin, J. V. (1990). Age norms for visual acuity in toddlers using the acuity card procedure. *Clinical Vision Sciences, 5*, 167–173.

Heiden, J. (1989). A ten-year follow-up study of former students of the Wisconsin School for the Visually Handicapped. *RE:view, 21*, 81–87.

Heinze, T. (1986). Communication skills. In G. Scholl (Ed.), *Foundations of education for blind and visually handicapped children and youth: Theory and practice* (pp. 301–314). New York: American Foundation for the Blind.

Held, R., & Hein, A. (1963). Movement-produced stimulation in the development of visually guided behavior. *Journal of Comparative and Physiological Psychology, 56*, 872.

Heller, K. W., D'Andrea, F. M., & Forney, P. E. (1998). Determining reading and writing media for individuals with visual and physical impairments. *Journal of Visual Impairment and Blindness, 92*, 162–175.

Heller, M. A. (1985). Tactual perception of embossed Morse code and braille: The alliance of vision and touch. *Perception, 14*, 563– 570.

Heller, M. A. (1989). Picture and pattern perception in the sighted and the blind: The advantage of the late blind. *Perception, 18*, 379–389.

Henderson, F. (1973). Communication skills. In B. Lowenfeld (Ed.), *The visually handicapped child in school* (pp. 185–219). New York: John Day.

Higgins, L. C. (1973). *Classification in congenitally blind children*. New York: American Foundation for the Blind.

Hill, E., & Hill, H. M. (1980). *Hill Performance Test of Selected Positional Concepts*. Chicago: Stoelting.

Hill, E. W., Dodson-Burk, B., & Smith, B. A. (1989). Orientation and mobility for infants who are visually impaired. *RE:view, 21*, 47–60.

Hill, E. W., & Jacobson, W. H. (1985). Controversial issues in orientation and mobility: Then and now. *Education of the Visually Handicapped, 17*, 59–70.

Hill, E. W., Rosen, S., Correa, V. E., & Langley, M. B. (1984). Preschool orientation and mobility: An expanded definition. *Education of the Visually Handicapped, 16*, 58–72.

Hoben, M., & Lindstrom, V. (1980). Evidence of isolation in the mainstream. *Journal of Visual Impairment and Blindness, 74*, 289–292.

Houser, L., Moses, E., & Kay, J. (1987). A family orientation to transition. *Education of the Visually Handicapped, 19*, 109–119.

Howze, Y. (1987). The use of social skills training to improve interview skills of visually impaired young adults: A pilot study. *Journal of Visual Impairment and Blindness, 81*, 251–255.

Huebner, K. (1986). Social skills. In G. Scholl (Ed.), *Foundations of education for blind and visually handicapped children and youth: Theory and practice* (pp. 341–362). New York: American Foundation for the Blind.

Heubner, K. M. (1989). Shaping educational intervention for blind and visually impaired learners in response to social change. *RE:view, 21*, 137–144.

Huebner, K. M., & Strumwasser, K. P. (1987). State certification of teachers of blind and visually impaired students: Report of a national study. *Journal of Visual Impairment and Blindness, 81*, 244–250.

Hull, W. A., & McCarthy, C. G. (1973). Supplementary programs for preschool visually handicapped children. *Education of the Visually Handicapped, 5*, 97–104.

Hupp, S., & Rosen, S. (1985). The team approach to designing instruction for visually impaired multiply handicapped children: A decision-making paradigm. *Education of the Visually Handicapped, 17*, 85–96.

Individuals with Disabilities Education Act of 1990, 20 U.S.C. §1400 *et seq*.

Jan, J., Groenveld, M., Sykanda, A., & Hoyt, C. (1987). Behavioral characteristics of children with permanent cortical visual impairment. *Developmental Medicine and Child Neurology, 29*, 571–576.

Jan, J. E., & Groenveld, M. (1993). Visual behaviors and adaptations associated with cortical and ocular impairment in children. *Journal of Visual Impairment and Blindness, 87*, 101–105.

Jankowski, L., & Evans, J. (1981). The exercise capacity of blind children. *Journal of Visual Impairment and Blindness, 75*, 248–251.

Jastrzembska, Z. S. (1982). *Model for a workshop on assessment of blind and visually impaired students*. New York: American Foundation for the Blind.

Jones, J. (1961). *Blind children—Degree of vision, mode of reading*. Washington, DC: U. S. Government Printing Office.

Jones, J. W., & Collins, A. T. (1966). *Educational programs for visually handicapped children*. Washington, DC: U. S. Government Printing Office.

Jose, R. T. (1992). *Understanding low vision*. New York: American Foundation for the Blind.

Kates, L., & Schein, J. D. (1980). *A complete guide to communication with deaf–blind persons*. Silver Spring, MD: National Association for the Deaf.

Kaufman, A. S., & Kaufman, L. (1983). *Kaufman Assessment Battery for Children*. Circle Pines, MN: American Guidance Service.

Keeffe, J. (1994a). *Assessment of low vision in developing countries: The effects of low vision and assessment of functional vision*. Melbourne, Australia: Low Vision Project International, University of Melbourne.

Keeffe, J. (1994b). *Assessment of low vision in developing countries: Screening for impaired vision*. Melbourne, Australia: Low Vision Project International, University of Melbourne.

Kekelis, L. S., & Andersen, E. S. (1984). Family communication styles and language development. *Journal of Visual Impairment and Blindness*, *78*, 54–65.

Keogh, B. K. (1973). Perceptual and cognitive styles: Implication for special education. *First Review of Special Education*, 83–109.

Kershman, S. M. (1976). A hierarchy of tasks in the development of tactual discrimination. *Education of the Visually Handicapped*, *8*, 73–82.

Kim, Y., & Corn, A. (1998). The effect of teacher characteristics on placement recommendations for students with visual impairments. *Journal of Visual Impairment and Blindness*, *92*, 491–502.

Kirchner, C., & Peterson, R. (1980). Multiple impairments among non-institutionalized blind and visually impaired persons. *Journal of Visual Impairment and Blindness*, *74*, 42–44.

Kirchner, C., Peterson, R., & Suhr, C. (1979). Trends in school enrollment among legally blind school children, 1963–1978. *Journal of Visual Impairment and Blindness*, *73*, 373–379.

Kirchner, C., & Schmeidler, E. (1997). Prevalence and employment of people in the United States who are blind or visually impaired. *Journal of Visual Impairment and Blindness*, *91*, 508–511.

Klatzky, R. L., & Lederman, S. J. (1988). The intelligent hand. In G. H. Bower (Ed.), *The psychology of learning and motivation* (pp. 121–151). New York: Academic Press.

Klatzky, R. L., Lederman, S. J., & Metzger, V. A. (1985). Identifying objects by touch: An expert system. *Perception*, *37*, 299–302.

Klatzky, R. L., Lederman, S., & Reed, C. (1987). There's more to touch than meets the eye: The salience of object attributes for haptics with and without vision. *Journal of Experimental Psychology*, *116*, 336–369.

Klein, J. W. (1845). Guide to provide for blind children the necessary education in the schools of their home communities and in the circle of their families. In B. Lowenfeld (Ed. and Trans.), *Berthold Lowenfeld on blindness and blind people* (pp. 144–147). New York: American Foundation for the Blind.

Knappett, K., & Wagner, N. N. (1976). Sex education and the blind. *Education of the Visually Handicapped*, *8*, 1–5.

Knowlton, M. (1987). Directional sensitivity of the fingertip. *Education of the Visually Handicapped*, *18*, 157–164.

Koenig, A. J., & Holbrook, M. C. (1995). *Learning media assessment for students with visual impairment: A resource guide for teachers* (2nd ed.). Austin, TX: Texas School for the Blind and Visually Impaired.

Koestler, F. (1976). *The unseen minority: A social history of blindness in the United States*. New York: David McKay.

Kratz, L. E., Tutt, L. M., & Black, D. A. (1987). *Movement and fundamental motor skills for sensory deprived children*. Springfield, IL: Charles C. Thomas.

Langley, M. B. (1980). *Functional Vision Screening Inventory for the Severely and Multiply Handicapped*. Chicago: Stoelting.

Langley, M. B. (2000). *Individualized Systematic Assessment of Visual Efficiency*. Louisville, KY: American Printing House for the Blind.

Leong, S. (1996). Preschool orientation and mobility: A review of the literature. *Journal of Visual Impairment and Blindness, 90*, 145–153.

Lewis, M. (1979). Teaching arithmetic computation skills. *Education of the Visually Handicapped, 2*, 66–72.

Lewis, S., & Russo, R. (1998). Educational assessment for students who have visual impairments with other disabilities. In S. Sacks & R. Silberman (Eds.), *Educating students who have visual impairments with other disabilities* (pp. 39–71). Baltimore: Brookes.

Linville, J., & Bliss, J. (1966). *A direct translation reading aid for the blind*. (Report SEL-65-055, TR No. 4819-1). Stanford, CA: Stanford Electronic Laboratories.

Lowenfeld, B. (1969). Multihandicapped blind and deaf–blind children in California. *Research Bulletin, 19*, 1–72.

Lowenfeld, B. (1973). History of the education of visually handicapped children. In B. Lowenfeld (Ed.), *The visually handicapped child in school* (pp. 1–25). New York: John Day.

Lowenfeld, B. (1981). The preschool child and his needs. In B. Lowenfeld (Ed.), *Lowenfeld on blindness and blind people* (pp. 35–45). New York: American Foundation for the Blind.

Ludel, J. (1978). *Introduction to sensory processes*. San Francisco: W. H. Freeman.

Luxton, K. (1980–1981). A jigsaw puzzle: Constructing a sound bridge to adulthood for visually handicapped adolescents. *Blindness*, 97–105.

Lydon, W. T., & McGraw, M. L. (1973). *Concept development for visually handicapped children*. New York: American Foundation for the Blind.

MacCuspie, P. A. (1992). The social acceptance and interaction of visually impaired children in integrated settings. In S. Z. Sacks, L. S. Kekelis, & R. J. Gaylors-Ross (Eds.), *The development of social skills by blind and visually impaired students* (pp. 83–103). New York: American Foundation for the Blind.

Mamer, L. (1995). Tactile defensiveness. *Journal of Visual Impairment and Blindness News Service, 89*, 9–10.

Mamer, L. (1999). Visual development in students with visual and additional impairments. *Journal of Visual Impairment and Blindness, 93*, 360–369.

Mangold, S., & Mangold, P. (1989). Selecting the most appropriate primary learning medium for students with functional vision. *Journal of Visual Impairment and Blindness, 83*, 294–295.

Mangold, S. S. (1978). Tactile perception and braille letter recognition. *Journal of Visual Impairment and Blindness, 72*, 259–266.

Mangold, S. S., & Roessing, L. J. (1982). Instructional needs of students with low vision. In S. S. Mangold (Ed.), *A teacher's guide to the special educational needs of blind and visually handicapped children* (pp. 29–34). New York: American Foundation for the Blind.

Mar, H. H., & Cohen, E. J. (1998). Visually impaired students who exhibit emotional and behavior problems. In S. Z. Sacks & R. K. Silberman (Eds.), *Educating students who have visual impairments and other disabilities* (pp. 263–302). Baltimore: Brookes.

Maxfield, K. E., & Bucholz, S. (1957). *Maxfield-Bucholz Social Maturity Scale for Blind Pre-school Children*. New York: American Foundation for the Blind.

McCarron, L., & Hurst, J. (1985). Vocational readiness curriculum: Preparing visually multi-handicapped students for the world of work. *Journal of Visual Impairment and Blindness, 79*, 450–457.

McCarthy, K. (1972). *McCarthy Scales of Children's Abilities*. San Antonio, TX: Psychological Corporation.

McConnell, J. (1984). Integration of visually handicapped students in industrial arts classes: An overview. *Journal of Visual Impairment and Blindness, 78*, 319–323.

McGinnis, A. R. (1981). Functional linguistic strategies of blind children. *Journal of Visual Impairment and Blindness, 75*, 210–214.

McHugh, E., & Pyfer, J. (1999). The development of rocking among children who are blind. *Journal of Visual Impairment and Blindness, 93*, 82–95.

McLaughlin, W. J. (1974). Reading attainment of blind and partially sighted children: A comparative study. *Teacher of the Blind, 2*, 98–106.

McMahon, E. (2000). Council of Schools for the Blind learning outcomes project. *Journal of Visual Impairment and Blindness, 94*, 267–274.

Millar, S. (1985). The perception of complex patterns by touch. *Perception, 14*, 293–303.

Miller, C., & Levak, N. (1997). *A paraprofessional handbook for working with students who are visually impaired*. Austin, TX: Texas School for the Blind and Visually Impaired.

Miller, D. (1985). Reading comes naturally: A mother and her blind child's experiences. *Journal of Visual Impairment and Blindness, 79*, 1–4.

Miller, J. W. (1982). Development of an audio-tutorial system for teaching basic geographic concepts. *Education of the Visually Handicapped, 13*, 109–115.

Miller, S. E. (1982). Relationship between mobility level and development of positional concepts in visually impaired children. *Journal of Visual Impairment and Blindness, 76*, 149–153.

Moore, M. A., & McLaughlin, L. M. (1992). Assessment of the visually handicapped preschool child. In E. V. Nuttall (Ed.), *Assessing and screening preschoolers: Psychological, social, and educational dimensions*. New York: Allyn & Bacon.

Moore, S. (1984). The need for programs and services for visually handicapped infants. *Education of the Visually Handicapped, 16*, 48–57.

Mori, A., & Olive, J. (1978). The blind and visually mentally retarded: Suggestions for intervention in infancy. *Journal of Visual Impairment and Blindness, 72*, 273–279.

Morse, J. L. (1975). Answering the questions of the psychologist assessing the visually handicapped child. *The New Outlook for the Blind, 69*, 350–353.

Morse, M. (1991). Visual gaze behaviors: Considerations in working with visually impaired multiply handicapped children. *RE:view, 23*, 5–15.

Mundy, P., Kasan, C., & Sigman, M. (1992). Nonverbal communication, affective sharing, and intersubjectivity. *Infant Behavior and Development, 15*, 377–381.

Murphy, L. B. (1972). Infants' play and cognitive development. In M. W. Pier (Ed.), *Play and development* (pp. 119–126). New York: Norton.

Myerson, L. (1963). Somatopsychology of physical disability. In W. M. Cruickshank (Ed.), *Psychology of exceptional children and youth* (pp. 1–52). Englewood Cliffs, NJ: Prentice Hall.

Neff, J. (1982). Sexuality education methodology. In S. Mangold (Ed.), *A teachers' guide to the special educational needs of blind and visually handicapped children* (pp. 63–71). New York: American Foundation for the Blind.

Newborg, J., Stock, J. R., Wnek, L., Guidabaldi, C., & Svinicki, J. (1984). *Battelle Developmental Inventory*. Allen, TX: DLM/Teaching Resources.

Newland, T. E. (1961). *The Blind Learning Aptitude Test*. Paper presented at the Conference on Research in Braille, New York.

Newland, T. E. (1979). The Blind Learning Aptitude Test. *Journal of Visual Impairment and Blindness, 73*, 134–139.

Nielsen, L. (1991). Spatial relations in congenitally blind infants: A study. *Journal of Visual Impairment and Blindness, 85*, 20–22.

Nietupski, J. A., & Hamre-Nietupski, S. M. (1987). An ecological approach to curriculum development. In L. Goetz, D. Guess, & K. Stremel-Campbell (Eds.), *Innovative program design for individuals with dual sensory impairments* (pp. 225–250). Baltimore: Brookes.

Nolan, C. (1959). Readability of large types—A study of type sizes and type styles. *International Journal for the Education of the Blind, 9*, 41–44.

Nolan, C. (1966). *Reading and listening in learning by the blind: Progress report*. Louisville, KY: American Printing House for the Blind.

Nolan, C. Y., & Kederis, C. J. (1969). *Perceptual factors in braille word recognition*. New York: American Foundation for the Blind.

Nolan, C. Y., & Morris, J. E. (1965). Development and validation of the Roughness Discrimination Test. *International Journal for the Education of the Blind, 15*, 1–6.

Nolan, C. Y., & Morris, J. E. (1973). *Aural study systems for the visually handicapped*. Louisville, KY: American Printing House for the Blind.

Office of Special Education. (1981). *Program for education of the handicapped* (Federal Register, 5379). Washington, DC: U. S. Government Printing Office.

Olson, M. (1982). Play behavior of young preschoolers and its meaning for parents and teachers. *DVH Newsletter, 26*, 32–36.

Overbury, O., Goodrich, G. L., Quillman, R. D., & Faubert, J. (1989). Perceptual assessment in low vision: Evidence for a hierarchy of skills. *Journal of Visual Impairment and Blindness, 83*, 109–113.

Palazesi, M. A. (1986). The need for motor development programs for visually impaired preschoolers. *Journal of Visual Impairment and Blindness, 80*, 573–576.

Parker, R. (1983). *Occupational Aptitude Survey and Interest Schedule*. Austin, TX: PRO-ED.

Parsons, A. A. (1982). *An exploratory study of the patterns of emerging play behavior in young children with low vision*. Unpublished doctoral dissertation, The University of Texas at Austin.

Parsons, S. (1986). Function of play in low vision children: Emerging patterns of behavior. *Journal of Visual Impairment and Blindness, 80*, 777–784.

Pereira, L. M. (1990). Spatial concepts and balance performance: Motor learning in blind and visually impaired children. *Journal of Visual Impairment and Blindness, 84*, 109–110.

Piaget, J. (1966). *The psychology of intelligence*. Totawa, NJ: Littlefield, Adams.

Piaget, J. (1973). *The child and reality*. New York: Grossman.

Piers, E. V., & Harris, D. B. (1984). *The Piers-Harris Children's Self-Concept Scale*. Los Angeles: Western Psychological Services.

Pogrund, R. L., Fazzi, K. L., & Schreier, E. M. (1993). Development of a preschool "kiddy cane." *Journal of Visual Impairment and Blindness, 87*, 52–54.

Pogrund, R. L., & Rosen, S. J. (1989). The preschool blind child can be a long cane user. *Journal of Visual Impairment and Blindness, 83*, 431–39.

Ponchillia, P., & Ponchillia, S. (1997). *Foundations of rehabilitation teaching with persons who are blind or visually impaired*. New York: American Foundation for the Blind.

Pugh, G., & Erin, J. (Eds.). (1999). *Blind and visually impaired students: Educational service guidelines*. National Association of State Directors of Special Education and the Hilton-Perkins Program. Watertown, MA: Perkins School for the Blind.

Ramirez, S. (1986). *Children's Fear Survey Schedule–Revised*. Unpublished doctoral dissertation, University of Wisconsin–Madison.

Rasmussen, R. (1985, February). *Echolalia and the blind child*. Paper presented at a workshop at the Texas School for the Blind, Austin, TX.

Read, L. (1989). Social skills of blind kindergarten children. *RE:view, 20*, 142–155.

Rehabilitation Act of 1986, 20 U.S.C. § 701 *et seq*.

Reiser, J. J., Guth, A., & Hill, W. E. (1982). Mental processes mediating independent travel: Implications for orientation and mobility. *Journal of Visual Impairment and Blindness, 76*, 213–218.

Rettig, M. (1994). The play of young children with visual impairments: Characteristics and interventions. *Journal of Visual Impairment and Blindness, 88*, 410–420.

Rex, E. J. (1970). A study of basal readers and experimental supplementary instructional materials for teaching primary reading in braille. *Education of the Visually Handicapped, 2*, 97–107.

Rex, E. J. (1989). Issues related to literacy of legally blind learners. *Journal of Visual Impairment and Blindness, 83*, 306–313.

Reynell, J., & Zinkin, P. (1980). *Reynell–Zinkin Developmental Scales for Young Visually Handicapped Children*. Chicago: Stoelting.

Reynolds, C., & Richmond, B. (1985). *Revised Children's Manifest Anxiety Scale*. Los Angeles: Western Psychological Services.

Roberts, F. K. (1986). Education for the visually handicapped: A social and educational history. In G. T. Scholl (Ed.), *Foundations of education for blind and visually handicapped children and youth: Theory and practice* (pp. 1–18). New York: American Foundation for the Blind.

Robinson, L. (1982). *Growing up: A developmental curriculum*. Ogden, UT: Parent Consultants.

Rogers, S. J., & Puchalski, C. B. (1988). Development of object permanence in visually impaired infants. *Journal of Visual Impairment and Blindness, 82*, 137–142.

Rogow, S. (1988). *Helping the visually impaired child with developmental problems*. New York: Teachers College Press.

Rogow, S. (1992). Visual perceptual problems of visually impaired children with developmental disabilities. *RE:view, 24*, 57–64.

Rogow, S. M. (1978). Considerations in assessment of blind children who function as severely or profoundly retarded. *Child Care, Health and Development, 415*, 327–335.

Rosenblum, L. P. (1997). Adolescents with visual impairments who have best friends: A pilot study. *Journal of Visual Impairment and Blindness, 91*, 224–235.

Rosenblum, L. P., & Erin, J. N. (1998). Perceptions of terms used to describe individuals with visual impairments. *RE:view, 30*, 15–26.

Rossi, P. (1986). Mathematics. In G. Scholl (Ed.), *Foundations of education for blind and visually handicapped children and youth: Theory and practice* (pp. 367–374). New York: American Foundation for the Blind.

Rubin, J. A. (1975). The exploration of a "tactile aesthetic." *The New Outlook for the Blind, 70*, 369–375.

Sacks, S. (1998). Educating students who have visual impairments with other disabilities. In S. Z. Sacks & R. K. Silberman (Eds.), *Educating students who have visual impairments with other disabilities* (pp. 3–37). Baltimore: Brookes.

Sameroff, A. J. (1993). Models of development and developmental risk. In C. H. Zeanah, Jr. (Ed.), *Handbook of infant mental health* (pp. 3–13). New York: Guilford Press.

Sanctin, S., & Simmons, J. N. (1977). Problems in the construction of reality in congenitally blind children. *Journal of Visual Impairment and Blindness, 71*, 425–429.

Scadden, L. (1984). Blindness in the information age: Equality or irony? *Journal of Visual Impairment and Blindness, 78*, 394–400.

Scadden, L. (2000). Technology and society. In B. Silverstone, M. Lang, B. Rosenthal, & E. Faye (Eds.), *The Lighthouse handbook on vision impairment and vision rehabilitation*. New York: Oxford University Press.

Scholl, G. T. (1981). *Self-study and evaluation guide for day programs for visually handicapped pupils: A guide for program improvement*. Reston, VA: Council for Exceptional Children.

Scholl, G. T. (Ed.). (1986). *Foundations of education of blind and visually handicapped children and youth: Theory and practice*. New York: American Foundation for the Blind.

Scott, E. (1982). *Your visually impaired student: A guide for teachers*. Baltimore: University Park Press.

Scott, R. (1969). *The making of blind men*. New York: Russell Sage.

Seidenberg, B. H. (1975). Pediatric low vision. In E. G. Faye & C. M. Hood (Eds.), *Low vision* (pp. 117–129). Springfield, IL: Charles C. Thomas.

Shurrager, H. (1961). *Haptic Intelligence Scale for Adult Blind*. Chicago: Illinois Institute of Technology.

Sicilian, S. P. (1988). Development of counting strategies in congenitally blind children. *Journal of Visual Impairment and Blindness, 82*, 331–335.

Sigelman, C. K., Vengroff, L. P., & Spanhel, C. L. (1984). Disability and the concept of life functions. In R. P Marinelli & A. E. Dell Orto (Eds.), *The psychology and social impact of physical disability* (2nd ed., pp. 3–13) New York: Springer.

Silberman, R. (1986). Severe multiple handicaps. In G. Scholl (Ed.), *Foundations of education for blind and visually handicapped children and youth: Theory and practice* (pp. 145–164). New York: American Foundation for the Blind.

Silberman, R., & Sowell, V. (1998). Educating students who have visual impairments and learning disabilities In S. Z. Sacks & R. K. Silberman (Eds.), *Educating students who have visual impairments and other disabilities* Baltimore: Brookes.

Silberman, R. K. (1981). Assessment and evaluation of visually handicapped students. *Journal of Visual Impairment and Blindness, 75*, 109–114.

Silberman, R. K., & Brown, F. (1998). Alternative approaches to assessing in classroom and environments. In S. Z. Sacks & R. K. Silberman (Eds.), *Educating students who have visual impairments and other disabilities* Baltimore: Brookes.

Silverstein, R. (1985). The legal necessity for residential schools serving deaf, blind, and multiply impaired children. *Journal of Visual Impairment and Blindness, 79*, 145–149.

Simon, J. D. (1974). A course in spoken communications for high school students who are visually handicapped *Education of the Visually Handicapped, 6*, 41–44.

Simpkins, K. A. (1979a). Tactual discrimination of household objects. *Journal of Visual Impairment and Blindness 73*, 86–92.

Simpkins, K. A. (1979b). Tactual discrimination of shapes. *Journal of Visual Impairment and Blindness, 73* 93–101.

Simpson, F. (1986). Transition to adulthood. In G. Scholl (Ed.), *Foundations of education for blind and visually handicapped children and youth: Theory and practice* (pp. 405–422). New York: American Foundation for the Blind

Skellenger, A., & Hill, E. (1997). The preschool learner. In B. Blasch, W. Weiner, & R. Welsh (Eds.), *Foundations of orientation and mobility* (2nd ed.). New York: American Foundation for the Blind.

Skellenger, A. C., & Hill, E. (1991). Current practices and considerations regarding cane instruction with preschool children. *Journal of Visual Impairment and Blindness, 85*, 101–104.

Smith, A., & Cote, K. (1982). *Look at me: A resource manual for the development of residual vision in multiply impaired children*. Philadelphia: Pennsylvania College of Optometry.

Smith, A., & Geruschat, D. (1996). Orientation and mobility for children and adults with low vision. I A. Corn & A. Koenig (Eds.), *Foundations of low vision: Clinical and functional perspectives* (pp. 306–321 New York: American Foundation for the Blind.

Smith, M., & Levak, N. (1996). *Teaching students with visual and multiple impairments: A resource guide*. Austin TX: Texas School for the Blind and Visually Impaired.

Sonksen, P. M. (1983). Vision and early development. In K. Wybar & D. Taylor (Eds.), *Pediatric ophthalmology Current aspects* (pp. 85–94). New York: Marcel Dekker.

Sparrow, S. S., Balla, D. A., & Cicchetti, D. V. (1984). *Vineland Adaptive Behavior Scales–Expanded Form*. Circle Pines, MN: American Guidance Service.

Spungin, S. (1984). The role and function of the teacher of the visually handicapped. In *Quality services for blind and visually handicapped learners: Statements of position* (pp. 31– 34). Reston, VA: Division for Visual Handicapped, Council for Exceptional Children.

Spungin, S. J. (1980). *Guidelines for public school programs serving visually handicapped children*. New York: American Foundation for the Blind.

Spungin, S. J. (1982). The future role of residential schools for visually handicapped children. *Journal of Visual Impairment and Blindness, 76*, 229–233.

Stager, J. D. (1978). Assessing public school programs for visually handicapped students. *Journal of Visual Impairment and Blindness, 72*, 170–172.

Stephens, B. (1972). Cognitive processes in the visually impaired. *Education of the Visually Handicapped, 4*, 106–111.

Stephens, B., & Grube, C. (1982). Development of Piagetian reasoning in congenitally blind children. *Journal of Visual Impairment and Blindness, 76*, 133–143.

Stephens, B., Simpkins, K., & Wexler, M. (1976). A comparison of the performance of blind and sighted subjects, age 6–10 years on the rotation of squares test. *Education of the Visually Handicapped, 8*, 66–70.

Stewart, I., Van Hasselt, V., Simon, J., & Thompson, W. (1985). The community adjustment program (CAP) for visually impaired adolescents. *Journal of Visual Impairment and Blindness, 78*, 49–54.

Stillman, R. (Ed.). (1979). *The Callier–Azusa Scale*. Dallas: The Callier Center for Communication Disorders of The University of Texas.

Sussman, M. B. (1969). Dependent disabled and dependent poor: Similarity of conceptual issues and research needs. *Social Service Review, 42*, 383–395.

Suvak, P. (1999). What do they really do? Activities of teachers of students with visual impairments. *RE:view, 30*, 181–190.

Swallow, R., & Huebner, K. (1987). *How to thrive, not just survive: A guide to developing independent life skills in blind and visually impaired children and youth*. New York: American Foundation for the Blind.

Swallow, R. M., & Conner, A. (1982). Aural reading. In S. S. Mangold (Ed.), *A teacher's guide to the special educational needs of blind and visually handicapped children* (pp. 63–71). New York: American Foundation for the Blind.

Swenson, A. (1987). Art experiences for young children with severe visual impairments. *Education of the Visually Handicapped, 19*, 120–124.

Sykes, K. C. (1971). A comparison of the effects of standard print and large print in facilitating the reading skills of visually impaired students. *Education of the Visually Handicapped, 3*, 97–105.

Sykes, K. C. (1972). Print reading for visually handicapped children. *Education of the Visually Handicapped, 4*, 71–75.

Tait, P., & Kessler, C. (1976). The way we get babies: A tactual sex education program. *The New Outlook for the Blind, 70*, 116–120.

Tavernier, G. F. (1993). The improvement of vision by vision stimulation and training: A review of the literature. *Journal of Visual Impairment and Blindness, 87*, 143–148.

Texas School for the Blind. (1870). Annual Report 1869–1870, By-Laws. Austin, TX: Author.

Todd, J. (1986). Resources, media, and technology. In G. Scholl (Ed.), *Foundations of education for blind and visually handicapped children and youth: Theory and practice* (pp. 285–296). New York: American Foundation for the Blind.

Tronick, E., Als, H., & Brazelton, T. B. (1980). Monacid phases: A structural descriptive analysis of infant–mother face to face interaction. *Merrill-Palmer Quarterly, 26*, 3–24.

Troster, H., & Brambring, M. (1994). The play behavior and play materials of blind and sighted infants and preschoolers. *Journal of Visual Impairment and Blindness, 88*, 421–432.

Tuttle, D. (1984). *Self-esteem and adjusting with blindness*. Springfield, IL: Charles C. Thomas.

Urwin, C. (1983). Dialogue and cognitive functioning in the early language development of three blind children. In A. E. Mills (Ed.), *Language acquisition in the blind child* (pp. 142–161). San Diego, CA: College-Hill Press.

Uslan, M., Hill, E., & Peck, A. (1989). *The profession of orientation and mobility in the 1980s: The AFB competency study*. New York: American Foundation for the Blind.

Uslan, M., Malone, S., & De l'Aune, W. (1983). Teaching travel to multiply handicapped blind adults: An auditory approach. *Journal of Visual Impairment and Blindness, 77*, 18–20.

Utley, B., Duncan, D., Strain, P., & Scanlon, K. (1983). Effects of contingent and noncontingent vision stimu lation on visual fixation in multiply handicapped children. *Journal of the Association for Persons with Sever Handicaps, 8,* 29–42.

Uzgiris, I. C., & Hunt, J. M. (1975). *Assessment in infancy: Ordinal scales of psychological development.* Urban University of Illinois Press.

Valvo, A. (1971). *Sight restoration after long-term blindness: The problems and behavior patterns of visual rehabilita tion.* New York: American Foundation for the Blind.

VanderKolk, C. J. (1981). *Assessment and planning with the visually impaired.* Baltimore: University Park Press.

Van Dijk, J. (1965). The first steps of the deaf/blind child towards language. *Proceedings of the Conference on th Deaf/Blind.* Boston: Perkins School for the Blind.

Van Weelden, J. (1967). *On being blind.* Amsterdam: Netherlands Society for the Blind.

Venn, J., & Wadler, F. (1988). Deaf–blind independent living project: A status report. *Education of the Visuall Handicapped, 20,* 23–28.

Wan-Lin, M. M., & Tait, P. E. (1987). The attainment of conservation by visually impaired children in Taiwa *Journal of Visual Impairment and Blindness, 81,* 423–428.

Warren, D. H. (1974). Early vs. late vision: The role of early vision in spatial reference systems. *The New Ou look for the Blind, 68,* 157–162.

Warren, D. H. (1984). *Blindness and early childhood development* (2nd ed.). New York: American Foundation fo the Blind.

Wechsler, D. (1981). *Wechsler Adult Intelligence Scale–Revised.* San Antonio, TX: Psychological Corporation.

Wechsler, D. H. (1989). *Wechsler Preschool and Primary Scale of Intelligence–Revised.* San Antonio, TX: Psycho logical Corporation.

Wechsler, D. H. (1991). *Wechsler Intelligence Scale for Children–Third Edition.* San Antonio, TX: Psychologic Corporation.

Wehrum, M. (1977). *Techniques of daily living: A curriculum guide.* Pittsburgh, PA: Greater Pittsburgh Guild f the Blind.

Weiner, B. B. (1967). A new outlook on assessment. *The New Outlook for the Blind, 61,* 73–78.

Whitmore, J. R., & Maker, C. J. (1985). *Intellectual giftedness in disabled persons.* Rockville, MD: Aspen Syster Corporation.

Wiederholt, L., & Larsen, S. (1983). *Test of Practical Knowledge.* Austin, TX: PRO-ED.

Wilhelm, J. G. (1989). Fear and anxiety in low vision and totally blind children. *Education of the Visually Han icapped, 20,* 163–172.

Willoughby, D., & Duffy, S. (1989). *Handbook for itinerant and resource teachers of blind and visually impaired st dents.* Baltimore: National Federation of the Blind.

Witkin, H. A., Oltman, C. K., Chase, J. B., & Friedman, F. (1971). Cognitive patterning in the blind. In J. He muth (Ed.), *Cognitive studies: Deficits in cognition* (pp. 16–46). New York: Brunner/Mazel.

Wolffe, K. (1998). Preparing people with visual impairments for work. *Journal of Visual Impairment and Blindne 92,* 110–113.

Wolffe, K. (Ed.). (1999). *Skills for success: A career education handbook for children and adolescents with visual i pairments.* New York: American Foundation for the Blind.

Wolffe, K., & Sacks, S. (1997). The lifestyles of blind, low vision, and sighted youths: A quantitative compa son. *Journal of Visual Impairment and Blindness, 91,* 245–257.

Wormsley, D. (1981). Hand movement training in braille reading. *Journal of Visual Impairment and Blindness, 7* 327–331.

Wormsley, D., & D'Andrea, F. M. (1997). *Instructional strategies for braille literacy.* New York: American Found tion for the Blind.

Wright, B. A. (1960). *Physical disability: A psychological approach*. New York: Harper, Row.

Zambone, A., Ciner, E., Appel, S., & Grayboyes, M. (2000). Children with multiple impairments. In B. Silverstone, M. Lan, B. Rosenthal, & E. Faye (Eds.), *The Lighthouse handbook on vision impairment and vision rehabilitation*. New York: Oxford University Press.

Zanandrea, M. (1998). Play, social interaction, and motor development: Practical activities for preschoolers with visual impairments. *Journal of Visual Impairment and Blindness*, *92*, 176–188.

Zimmerman, G. (1985). *An exploratory study of preferred textures of objects for visually handicapped infants and young children*. Unpublished doctoral dissertation, University of Texas at Austin.

Index

About the Authors

Natalie C. Barraga, EdD, is professor emerita of the Program for Visually Impaired, Department of Special Education, The University of Texas at Austin. She is author of *Increased Visual Behavior in Low Vision Children,* previous editions of *Visual Handicaps and Learning,* several monographs and book chapters, numerous journal articles, and assessment instruments and instructional programs. She is active in state, national, and international professional organizations and programs, having conducted courses and seminars in many countries around the world. She continues to be available for consultations and presentations on a variety of topics.

Jane N. Erin, PhD, is an associate professor in the Department of Special Education, University of Arizona at Tucson, where she is coordinator of the program to prepare mobility specialists and teachers of students with visual impairments. She is an experienced classroom teacher and supervisor of programs related to children with visual and multiple impairments. She is editor of the *Journal of Visual Impairment and Blindness* and the author of several books, monographs, and articles. She is active in state and national professional organizations concerned with the visually impaired and multiply disabled, in which she holds numerous leadership positions.